ANWAR SADAT
Visionary Who Dared

President Sadat and his wife, Jihan

ANWAR SADAT
Visionary Who Dared

Joseph Finklestone

FRANK CASS
LONDON • PORTLAND, OR.

First published in 1996 in Great Britain by
FRANK CASS PUBLISHERS
Crown House, 47 Chase Side
Southgate, London N14 5BP

and in the United States of America by
FRANK CASS PUBLISHERS
c/o ISBS, 5824 N.E. Hassalo Street
Portland, Oregon 97213-3644

Website: www.frankcass.com

Copyright © 1996 Joseph Finklestone

Reprinted 2003

Transferred to Digital Printing 2004

British Library Cataloguing in Publication Data

Finklestone, Joseph
     Anwar Sadat: Visionary Who Dared
     I. Title
     962.054092

     ISBN 0-7146-3487-5 (cloth)
     ISBN 0-7146-4165-0 (paper)

Library of Congress Cataloging-in-Publication Data

Finkelstone
     Anwar Sadat : visionary who dared / Joseph Finklestone.
        p. cm.
     Includes index.
     ISBN 0-7146-3487-5 (cloth) -- ISBN 0-7146-4165-0 (paper).
     1. Sadat, Anwar, 1918–   . 2. Presidents-Egypt-Biography.
     I. Title.
     DT 107.828.S23F56   1996
     962.05'4'092-dc20
     [B]   95-6980
                                                              CIP

Typset by Vitaset, Paddock Wood

To Hadassah,
Ilana and Daphna

Contents

List of Illustrations

Acknowledgements and Select Bibliography

I am very grateful to many people in Israel, Egypt and other Arab countries, in Britain and the United States for aid and encouragement in undertaking the task of writing about one of the most complex as well as one of the most charismatic figures in modern world history. Many participants in the events described spoke to me frankly off the record during several visits to the area. I learned to admire the Egyptian people and their fortitude. I also wish to thank Frank Cass, who so quickly and enthusiastically accepted the idea for this book, and Norma Marson, who edited it with such intelligence, understanding and devotion.

Though the views expressed, and any shortcomings, are entirely my own, I wish particularly to thank, for their advice and recollections given over a number of years: Madame Jihan Sadat: Dr Osama al-Baz (chief political aide to President Hosni Mubarak of Egypt); Mr David Kimche; the late Jon Kimche; Mr Martin Fuller (British Foreign and Commonwealth Office Research Department); and Mr Alexander Golytsin (Minister-Counsellor, Russian Embassy, London).

All writers about Anwar Sadat will always feel grateful to Professor Raphael Israeli for his finely researched *Man of Defiance: A Political Biography of Anwar Sadat* (London: Weidenfeld & Nicolson, 1985). Although Mohamed Heikal's books are very controversial and I accept few of his opinions, I cannot deny the power and value of his writings on the Nasser–Sadat period. Other books which I found very helpful or stimulating were:

Jimmy Carter, *Keeping Faith: Memoirs* (London: Collins, 1982)
Moshe Dayan, *Story of My Life* (London: Weidenfeld & Nicolson, 1976)
—— *Breakthrough* (London: Weidenfeld & Nicolson, 1981)

Abba Eban, *An Autobiography* (London: Weidenfeld & Nicolson, 1978)

—— *Personal Witness* (London: Jonathan Cape, 1993)

Felipe Fernandez-Armesto, *Sadat and his Statecraft* (Oxford: Kensal Press, 1982)

Mohamed Heikal, *The Road to Ramadan* (London: Collins, 1975)

—— *Autumn to Fury* (London: André Deutsch, 1983)

—— *Illusions of Triumph* (London: Harper Collins, 1992)

Major-General Chaim Herzog, *The War of Atonement* (London: Weidenfeld & Nicolson, 1975)

David Hirst and Irene Beeson, *Sadat* (London: Faber & Faber, 1981)

Mohamed Ibrahim Kamel, *The Camp David Accords* (London: Routledge & Kegan Paul, 1986)

Doreen Kays, *Frogs and Scorpions* (London: Frederick Muller, 1984)

Elie Kedourie, *Politics in the Middle East* (Oxford: Oxford University Press, 1992)

David Kimche, *The Last Option* (London: Weidenfeld & Nicolson, 1991)

Henry Kissinger, *Years of Upheaval* (London: Weidenfeld & Nicolson/ Michael Joseph, 1982)

Joseph P. Lorenz, *Egypt and the Arabs* (Boulder, CO: Westview Press, 1990)

Golda Meir, *My Life* (London: Weidenfeld & Nicolson, 1975)

Conor Cruise O'Brien, *The Siege* (London: Weidenfeld & Nicolson, 1986)

David Pryce Jones, *The Closed Circle* (London: Weidenfeld & Nicolson, 1989)

Yitzhak Rabin, *The Rabin Memoirs* (London: Weidenfeld & Nicolson, 1979)

.Gideon Raphael, *Destination Peace* (London: Weidenfeld & Nicolson, 1981)

Anwar el-Sadat, *In Search of Identity* (London: Collins Fontana, 1978)

—— *Those I Have Known* (London: Jonathan Cape, 1985)

Jihan Sadat, *A Woman of Egypt* (London: Bloomsbury, 1987)

Sa'ad Shazli, *The Crossing of Suez* (San Francisco: American Mid-East Research, 1980)

—— *Negotiating for Peace in the Middle East* (New York: Johns Hopkins, 1983)

P.J. Vatikiotis, *History of Modern Egypt* (London: Weidenfeld & Nicolson, 1991)

Ezer Weizman, *The Battle For Peace* (London: Bantam Books, 1981)

Introduction

When I first met Jihan Sadat I was struck by her dignity and beauty as she moved around the room with an unhurried calm. As the wife of President Anwar Sadat, she was invariably stylishly dressed – some Egyptians used to envy her smartly-cut dresses, assuming them to be expensive European imports, although this was by no means always the case. They failed to understand that Jihan was merely determined to look her best as befitted the wife of the President of Egypt. She was, in fact, far less vain than her husband, whom she used to chide gently for his love of elaborate uniforms.

After centuries of living under the shadow of great powers, often humiliated and derided, Egypt, under Sadat, was grappling with tremendous, almost insoluble problems – inadequate resources, insufficient fertile land and a burgeoning population which was increasing at the rate of over one million every year. In dealing with these enormous problems, President Sadat realized that he had to find a way of breaking an age-old taboo in order to make peace with the Jewish State of Israel. For Sadat, unlike others, saw a link between solving problems at home and making peace with Israel. Jihan Sadat understood better than anyone the huge difficulties he faced. She also understood that she had to be strong, and aspects of that strength remain today.

Jihan, who now lectures at the University of Maryland in the US, was happy when I told her that I was writing a biography of Anwar Sadat, and she was touched to learn of the friendship that had developed between the leader of the largest Arab state and a journalist working at the time for two Jewish newspapers – the Tel Aviv daily *Maariv* and the *Jewish Chronicle* in London.

I had written to Sadat, two years before his historic trip to Jerusalem in 1977, saying that while others saw him as a man of war I saw him as a man of peace. I believed that he would be the man to bring peace between the Jewish and Arab peoples. My words must have struck a chord. He showed an interest in my writing and wished to speak to me in order to explain his ideas for a new relationship between Jews and Arabs, between Israelis and Egyptians. I felt that he saw me as a potential bridge, through my journalism, between warring peoples. I also had the impression that he wanted to make amends for previous harsh words spoken about the Jewish people. This book has been written as a direct outcome of this relationship. Jihan Sadat understood the basis for my friendship with her husband. She herself bridged two cultures. Her mother, Gladys Correll, was born in Sheffield in England. Jihan speaks her measured English without a trace of an accent, while her Arabic has remained pure.

I particularly wanted to ask her about the last days of Anwar Sadat. He had arrested a considerable number of intellectuals and professional people. Critics were later to claim that he had lost all hope of achieving his aims in Egypt and was bitter at the failure of his negotiations with the Israelis regarding Palestine self-rule. Jihan rejected the notion of a disheartened, bitter Sadat and she insisted that the arrests were absolutely essential. 'If these people had not been arrested in time the situation would have become very bad', she said. 'Egypt would have had to face terrible problems.' Although Sadat's assassins were Islamic extremists, Jihan totally rejects the widespread belief that he was killed because he refused to establish an Islamic republic. 'I am one hundred per cent certain that my husband was killed because he made peace with Israel.'

Who, however, was really responsible for his death? Who conceived it, planned it, carried it out? Was it only the work of a small group of Islamic extremists who had managed to penetrate the army? Were none of Sadat's foreign detractors involved? Libya's leader, Muammar al-Quaddafi, hated Sadat and Israel's intelligence agency Mossad had warned Sadat that Quaddafi was involved in a plot to assassinate him. Sadat took the warning seriously and for once adopted protective measures. Quaddafi saw Sadat's desire to make peace with Israel as a 'betrayal'. Would it not have been logical for the Egyptian extremists to turn to the Libyan leader for support in their assassination plans? Is it not possible that Quaddafi had himself suggested, through his agents in Egypt, that the time had come to liquidate Anwar Sadat?

Jihan Sadat looked thoughtful when I put these questions to her, but they did not appear to surprise her. 'No, I do not rule out the possibility that Quaddafi was behind the assassination plot against my husband', she said slowly. Then there was a pause and she added, 'but I have no definite proof.'

Historians and commentators have repeatedly asked why the plotters found it relatively easy to assassinate Sadat. Jihan Sadat has complained, with some justification, about the poor security at that fatal commemorative parade for the Armed Forces on 6 October 1981. However, Anwar Sadat did appear to adopt an attitude which some later saw as fatalistic. There was even a suggestion by a respected historian that he deliberately sought his own death. This notion can be instantly quashed for one very good reason. He had taken to the parade not only Jihan but also his beloved grandson, dressed in an imitation of his own uniform. It is inconceivable that he would have wished to die in their presence. It is true that he amazed and disturbed his ministers, officials and security chiefs and, above all, Jihan, by his reluctance to take precautions against the would-be assassins. But he did not underestimate them and he told Jihan that he was aware that the fanatics had the determination to kill him. Jihan told me that she had pleaded with the President to be more careful about his safety.

> There were actually intelligence reports about a plot to kill Anwar ... The then Interior Minister sent a tape in which a man was heard speaking about assassinating the President. But my husband refused to take extra precautions. He would not cease riding in an open car to meet the people. He insisted that he would not allow a few extremists to keep him from his Egyptian fellow citizens.

Jihan talked about how the Palestinians and many of Anwar Sadat's former critics have now come to the conclusion that he was right and that they were wrong. They have realized that it is time to put away the gun and to embrace peace. But without Anwar Sadat's bold initiative there would have been no Oslo Agreement between

Israel and Yasser Arafat's Palestine Liberation Organization. Jihan Sadat had this to say about the Accord:

> Without President Sadat's policy nothing would have happened in the Middle East. Yasser Arafat once declared, 'I salute the hand that killed Sadat', and the Palestinians accused him of being a traitor. All these things I have forgotten and I forgive them. I am happy because the Israeli–PLO Accord is a continuation of what my husband started. It proves that my husband was right.

I was sitting only a few feet away from the signing of the Oslo Accord at the White House in Washington in 1993 and I saw Yasser Arafat shaking hands with Yitzhak Rabin. I wanted so much to ask Arafat: 'Why did you wait all these years? Why did you not seize the opportunity before? Why did you accuse President Sadat of betraying you?'

When President Sadat stunned the world by travelling to Jerusalem in 1977 he created the perfect opportunity, in that euphoric atmosphere, for the Palestinians to join in the peace effort, but they stayed away. Now, at long last, as Jihan Sadat acknowledges, they are seizing the opportunity to tread the path of peace set out by President Sadat.

J. Finklestone
1995

Prologue: meeting the President

After Anwar Sadat succeeded Nasser as President of Egypt in 1970 I wrote a personal letter to him. I have asked myself several times what prompted me to do so, whether I intended to ingratiate myself with him in the hope of obtaining a valuable interview with him or whether, as I hope and as I have claimed, I saw a unique aspect in his character which would make it possible for Israel to have a dialogue with him.

As Foreign Editor of the London *Jewish Chronicle*, a respected weekly newspaper with a strong foreign news service, with special emphasis on Israel and the Middle East, I did indeed ask for an interview. I pointed out that 'although naturally we support legitimate Jewish causes we try to be as impartial as possible and to give both sides of any issue'. I added that a year previously I had surprised the newly appointed representative of the Palestine Liberation Organisation, Said Hammami, by offering to publish an interview with him in the *Jewish Chronicle*. At the time, the PLO, led by Yasser Arafat, was still fully committed to the destruction of Israel. For the leading Jewish newspaper in the the Jewish diaspora to give publicity to the PLO seemed a heinous act to most Jews and a suspicious, though acceptable, move to any PLO official. However, Said Hammami had attracted my attention for the same reason as had President Sadat of Egypt; a willingness to talk about peace without accusing the Israelis of being war criminals and usurpers of Arab land. Hammami had met a number of well-meaning Israelis and had incurred the wrath of Arab terrorist groups, such as that of Abu Nidal, for whom prospects of peace would never divert him from attempting to extinguish Israel by murder. Although he had met Israelis, Hammami was still surprised by my action which I had not discussed with the editor of the *Jewish Chronicle*, William Frankel. Israelis who met him did so secretly, whereas I was offering Hammami the columns of a prestigious Jewish newspaper to express his views. He was eager to meet me but half suspected a trap.

When I, accompanied by a photographer carrying heavy photographic equipment which might have made him appear to any nervous person as a missile-carrying gangster, entered Hammami's room in the Arab League office in London, he rose slowly, his face displaying utter horror. He seemed to push his elbows into his sides and to be signalling to me that he was surrendering and, therefore, I should not shoot. 'You are not a journalist, you are an Israeli soldier come to shoot me', he croaked. It took me several minutes to calm him down and convince him that I was indeed a journalist whose knowlege of firearms was very limited. Outside his rather cramped, dirty room, men with guns were roaming about and I had a momentary fear that, were he to shout for help, I and my photographer would be quickly riddled with bullets. However, after accepting my credentials, Hammami showed himself to be a man not merely of passion but also of wisdom. He complained vehemently that, though born in Haifa, he would not be allowed by the Israeli government to visit the city, whereas Jews from Tashkent or Brooklyn could not only visit the city but become citizens almost immediately under the Israeli Law of Return. I pointed out to him that had the Arabs not invaded Israel when it was first established in 1948 and continued to harass Israel, refusing to accept it as a nation, there would have been no Arab refugees and no humiliation and suffering. Yet even while he was expressing this traditional Arab view which made him shake with genuine and understandable emotion, Hammami used words and expressions which I had not previously heard from any Arab personality, and certainly not from one representing the PLO. This impression was confirmed when he began to deplore the sterile past and to speak of the fruitful future, as he saw it. He spoke of living together with the Israelis, of the Palestinian Arabs accepting a small state on the West Bank and Gaza.

It was the first time that I had heard what later became known as the two-State solution and many, many years before Yasser Arafat, seeking American approval, was painfully made to say that he recognised the existence of the State of Israel.

When the interview appeared in the *Jewish Chronicle*, occupying more than half a page, there were angry reactions in Israel, in the PLO leaders' camp in Beirut and at the Israeli Embassy in London. The PLO headquarters told inquiring pressmen that the whole interview was an invention. A PLO representative could not possibly have said the things attributed to him. This was clearly one more Zionist plot to discredit the Palestinian people in their struggle. The Israeli Embassy in London reacted somewhat more diplomatically. There was no public statement but I was made quickly aware of the displeasure I had caused. The editor was asked to receive a three-man delegation from the Embassy who protested volubly at the heinousness of the crime I had committed – giving publicity to an enemy of the Jewish people and of Israel. The editor, who had actually in the past been critical himself of the attitudes adopted by Embassy officials, nevertheless felt he had to ask me for an assurance that in future I would discuss with him such sensitive interviews intended for the newspaper. I promised I would.

The response of Said Hammami to the statement issued by his leaders in Beirut was one that made an immense impact on me and helped to shape for ever my attitude to people in opposing camps. Any skilled politician knows how to get out of such a dilemma. Though well aware that the text accurately represented his views, he would say that his words had been taken out of context, as if any interview since the beginning of time ever carried every word uttered. He could even have claimed that I had deliberately fabricated the interview. What Said Hammami actually did was more interesting and significant. He said that he had given the interview to the Foreign Editor of the *Jewish Chronicle* and what had appeared was an accurate account of his views.

This statement by Said Hammami cost him his life. A few months later a man speaking Arabic telephoned and asked for an interview. The man walked into Hammami's room at the Arab League and shot him dead. It was thought that the gunman was an agent of Abu Nidal, the most deadly of the Arab terrorists who had found even the most radical of Yasser Arafat's followers too soft on Israel. They were suspected of wishing to make peace with Israel. Hammami had gone further; he had said he wanted to make peace. In Abu Nidal's eyes that deserved death and Hammami was duly executed. Had Yasser Arafat had Said Hammami's courage and vision the peace talks with Israel would have started in the early 1970s and not in 1993.

My invitation to meet Sadat was totally unexpected. I was at a Romanian holiday resort, Brashov, near Bucharest. At the hotel were several Chief Rabbis, assembled in Romania at the suggestion of Chief Rabbi Moses Rosen, a truly remarkable personality who had managed to outmanoeuvre the Communist government of Nicolai Ceauçescu, devoted to bleak Leninism and bleaker secularism. Prayers could be heard daily in Romanian synagogues and Hebrew songs in Jewish schools. The great exodus of Romanian Jews to Israel was taking place and even accelerating. We were commemorating one of the many tragedies that had befallen Romanian Jewry, which had lost half its strength, about 400,000, as a result of the Holocaust and through killings by Romanian, Russian and Ukrainian fascists and Nazis. After the commemoration we were to take a short holiday in the luscious surroundings of Brashov, blissfully unaware of the privations of the ordinary Romanian citizen. It was only later that I was to see children on Bucharest streets who reminded me of pictures of starving Jewish children in Auschwitz.

To my astonishment I was informed on the Saturday that the Egyptian Embassy in London had telephoned the *Jewish Chronicle* with a surprising message: President Anwar Sadat was visiting Vienna for a meeting with Chancellor Kreisky. He had a tight schedule but President Sadat would like to see me. Could I come immediately to Vienna?

I did not hesitate for a moment. An invitation from any Arab leader to a Jewish journalist at a time when Israel was still formally in a state of belligerency, despite the armistice agreements, was a remarkable event. That it came from the leader of the most prestigious and largest Arab country was of significance to the whole Israeli–Arab conflict. Realising the importance of the message, my deputy as foreign editor and close friend, Sidney Lightman, broke the Sabbath injunction against using the telephone and spent several hours in trying to locate me. He appeared to be as excited as I was, and more tired from his exertions. When in my excitement I rushed in to inform the Chief Rabbis, including the Chief Rabbi of Israel, Rabbi Shlomo Goren, forgetting that I, too, had infringed the Sabbath law by responding to a telephone call, I caused a small sensation. The rabbis were ready to give me their blessing for the journey to Vienna.

My consternation and amazement can be imagined when half an hour later the telephone rang and the editor of the *Jewish Chronicle*, Geoffrey Paul, told me that I must on no account travel to Vienna and see President Sadat. 'Why?', I asked in utter stupefaction. I pointed out that an interview with the Egyptian President would provide a world scoop for our newspaper. Secret negotiations were taking place between the Egyptians and the Israelis, involving Moshe Dayan, the charismatic Israeli general and diplomat, and King Hassan of Morocco. So secret were these contacts that Dayan had to travel to Morocco to meet an Egyptian envoy. We did not then know the details of these conversations but there were rumours, sufficient to arouse intense newspaper interest. Here, I told Geoffrey Paul, we had a chance to scoop the world and find out what the leading Arab leader was planning. Other newspapers would be green with envy.

Geoffrey Paul was not impressed. He argued that if the *Jewish Chronicle* printed an interview with Sadat at this time the paper would be perceived as being pro-Arab. I would do it a great dis-service if I went to see Sadat. If, despite this admonition I saw and interviewed Sadat, not a word would be printed in the *Jewish Chronicle*; it would dissociate itself from the interview and, of course, there was no question of the paper paying my expenses.

I put down the receiver with a heavy heart. I had not made any commitment to cancel the interview but I knew that my position was untenable. For a moment I thought of offering the interview to the Israeli daily newspaper *Maariv*, of Tel Aviv, whose London correspondent I had been for many years. The *Maariv* editor and senior members of the staff were personal friends of mine, including such outstanding journalists as Arye Dissentchik, Shalom Rosenfeld, Shmuel Schnitzer and Moshe Zak. Undoubtedly they would have accepted an interview with Sadat enthusiastically. But I felt a sense of loyalty to the *Jewish Chronicle* and could not humiliate it in such a brazen manner. The journalistic world would have found Geoffrey Paul's action almost incredible, though I must mention that it was backed by the *Jewish Chronicle* board of directors.

On reflection today I believe I should, perhaps, have gone ahead with the interview and offered it either to *Maariv* or to one of the major world newspapers. Geoffrey Paul is an excellent journalist with wide experience yet perhaps even he would agree that he made a mistake. But fate can be strange. The interview which I eventually obtained from President Sadat caused such a sensation that it changed my life. Would the Vienna interview have done the same?

With reluctance and a feeling of shame I informed the Egyptian Embassy that I would be unable to travel to Vienna in the time specified by the President. I thought I would now never have an opportunity of meeting him and certainly not of receiving a personal invitation. Surely, I thought, the Egyptians had seen through my lame excuse.

Almost exactly a year later, in May 1979, I was sitting in my office at the *Jewish Chronicle* in Furnival Street, London, when a telephone call was put through to me from the Egyptian Embassy. President Anwar Sadat would like to see me immediately in Cairo. When could I travel? I replied that I would drop all the work I was doing and leave within a day for Egypt. I was informed I would be quickly granted a visa.

By then the situation had been transformed by President Sadat's dramatic flight to Jerusalem and address in Israel's parliament, the Knesset. He had offered peace to Israel, provided Israel withdrew from the Arab territories occupied in the Six-Day War. Sadat insisted that he had not come to sign a separate peace treaty with Israel. The Palestinian Arabs had to be given their land and their rights. It was a tough speech which drew a tough response from the Israeli Premier, Menachem Begin.

Euphoria was to give way to disappointment and the Egyptian delegation was to be recalled by an aggrieved Sadat. The call to me came at a crucial time before the signing of the Camp David Accords with the vigorous help of President Jimmy Carter but the road to Egyptian–Israeli peace appeared to have been marked out. What was needed was an imaginative leap, a ringing proclamation by the

Egyptian President that he was emotionally committed to a full peace settlement with Israel. Was I being used for this purpose? After the extraordinary interview which the President granted me I felt persuaded that such, indeed, was his intention, carried out by a superb actor. This time there was no opposition by the *Jewish Chronicle* to my travelling to Egypt but Geoffrey Paul stipulated that I should spend only three days there. In the event of President Sadat not seeing me during these three days, I was to return to London.

When I arrived in Cairo I did not sense any feeling of urgency among the President's officials. They had received no instructions about the interview. I should come the next day. On the second day I was concerned to learn that the President was not in Cairo. He had gone to his summer residence in Alexandria. The officials were surprised that I was staying only three days in Egypt. They had expected that the visit would last a fortnight, as the President was a very busy man and a time had to be found for the interview. Could I come the next day and perhaps there would be some information?

When I returned to my hotel I felt depressed. Also considerably angry – with the Egyptians for showing such a lack of interest in the interview and for displaying such lethargy. After all, their President had invited me to Egypt and nothing seemed to have been prepared. I naturally felt somewhat resentful, too, that I had been given only three days in Egypt. It seemed to me an unnecessary handicap.

Convinced that I would never meet the President if I kept waiting at the hotel for a telephone call, I decided on the evening of the second day to visit the Abden palace used by the presidential staff and speak directly to President Sadat's secretary or director-general. I was spurred on by a sense of outrage that, although I had been personally invited by the President, none of his officials seemed to be making any effort to arrange the meeting. It was anger that propelled me past the guard at the gate of the palace, past further guards on the staircase despite their startled looks and protests in Arabic which, of course, I did not understand. 'I have been invited by President Sadat to see him and nothing is going to stop me', I repeatedly announced to the guards. My voice was so passionate and apparently so convincing that they made no attempt to stop me. Had they done so I could not even have shown them any identification papers. In my nervous anger and frustration, I had left my passport in the hotel. I certainly would have been arrested.

'Where is the President's Secretary-General?' I demanded in a peremptory voice. Two guards stared at me uncomprehendingly but an official, who happened to be passing, pointed a finger at a door. I walked in without knocking and encountered a startled middle-aged man. 'Who are you and how did you get in?' he asked in surprise. I immediately launched into a passionate description of my problem, ending up by saying that I would personally protest to the President about the treatment I had received. 'You have insulted the President by treating me in such a manner', I said. I demanded that he should communicate immediately with the President. 'He is not here, he is in Alexandria at his summer house', he replied. I told him that there was no reason why he should not telephone him there. The official looked at me hard once again and noted both my determination and indignation. 'Please wait in the next room while I telephone the President', he said.

The door was left partly open and I heard him speak to someone in a deferential tone. I understood he was speaking to President Sadat. The conversation must have lasted ten minutes. At the end, the official called me into his room and said: 'The President will see you tomorrow morning in Alexandria. He will provide a car to take you there. Be ready at six o'clock in the morning.'

I could hardly sleep that night and was up and about long before the designated time. Waiting in the hotel lobby, I heard my name called and rushed out. I saw a large black car with the Egyptian national flag flying on its bonnet. A smartly dressed chauffeur asked me: 'Are you Joseph Finklestone?' I said I was. He opened the car door for me. 'I have been asked to take you to see the President in Alexandria', he said in good English.

The thought immediately occurred to me how little attention had been paid to even elementary security. The man did not ask for any identification papers before taking me to the President. I could have been an impostor set up by plotters who had heard that I was to see the President. This lack of security was eventually to lead to the President's assassination.

During the long journey to Alexandria I was frequently surprised to note that people on the road looked curiously at the car and some even appeared to be saluting it. After an hour's travelling I could

xxiv

not contain my curiosity and asked the driver for the reason. He laughed: 'They think you may be the President or someone very high up. You are in one of the President's own cars!' I could not help reflecting what a strange situation it was; a Jewish journalist in the Egyptian President's car being saluted by Egyptian citizens!

As we approached the lovely city of Alexandria, with its distinctly French atmosphere, the car had to stop at a road block set up by armed soldiers. The car door was opened and a soldier asked politely who I was and what I was carrying. I told him I had been invited to see the President and had a camera and a notebook. He noted my name and gave a cursory look at the case with the small Olympus Trip camera which I had bought for about £30. Curiously, he assumed that my surname was my first name for I heard him telephone the next checkpoint about 'Yussef'. My driver explained to me: 'He is saying "Joseph is coming".' I could not help smiling, remembering the Bible story of Joseph being welcomed by Pharaoh. Arriving at the presidential summer house, I was met by an official, taken to a room and asked to wait. But I had hardly sat down when a vivid figure in blue rushed into the room, shook me warmly by the hand and said 'Welcome, Joseph, welcome!' At this precise moment, several photographers appeared, the flashlights of their cameras making the room bright, and then disappeared just as suddenly.

The President, still exuding goodwill and friendship, although this was our very first meeting, propelled me to a large room where a young official was waiting. The President told him to leave, saying in English: 'Your presence is not necessary.' The official showed surprise, as it was normal for a member of the presidential staff to be present when the President gave an interview to a foreign journalist and for that matter any journalist or any visiting personality. However, after looking questioningly at the President and being given the same instruction, he left. Clearly the President saw our meeting as more than a mere journalistic occasion.

As he invited me to sit down on the stairs next to a low table and then sat near me, I was intrigued by what he was wearing. It looked at first like silk pyjamas but I quickly realised it was a kind of thin suit, very bright and fine. I recalled the siren suit that Winston Churchill liked to wear. I was startled to notice how dark his complexion was. Then I remembered that Sadat's mother was born in the Sudan, where the majority of the people are almost black.

The President invited me to have tea with him. The tea came in very small silver-plated pots and proved to be green mint tea which I quite liked. The President insisted on pouring the tea for both of us. As I took out my tape-recorder from the case I was carrying I suffered a humiliating experience. I had bought the recorder just before my hurried journey to Egypt. I did not use a recorder for interviews, relying on my somewhat inadequate shorthand – inadequate in the sense that I often found it impossible to decipher some complicated outlines. I felt that for such an important interview with an Arab leader it would be advisable to have a tape recording in case the report was challenged.

My embarrassment was acute when I realised that the tape recorder was not working. The President, noticing my consternation and realising the cause, said with a smile: 'Let me see if I can make it work.' He fiddled with the tape recorder for what seemed an eternity and then said benignly: 'I think it will work now.' I thanked him profusely but inwardly I was castigating myself: 'What an idiot! You obtain an interview with the President of Egypt and have to spend precious minutes having your machine fixed by him!' It was a very chastened journalist who began the interview with the President, with the tape recorder now working satisfactorily.

As I wrote at the time, I was struck by President Sadat's warm smile, his friendliness and his total lack of pomposity. He knew of my admiration of his courage and foresight but his reception went beyond anything that could have been imagined. President Sadat was clearly anxious that our meeting should be totally informal. I had been told by an official that the President was so busy with affairs of state and with scheduled appointments with television interviewers and visiting statesmen that although he had personally invited me to visit him, he could grant me only half an hour. When the thirty minutes had passed, an official entered the room to escort me out but the President told him that the interview had not finished yet and he wanted more time. When an hour had elapsed the same official returned to the room but was again told that the interview had not yet been concluded. A bewildered and obviously worried official left the room, shaking his head in disbelief. A quarter of an hour later he returned once again and again was told to leave without me. The President told me with a smile that a European television group was waiting to see him and could not understand the delay.

It was only after two full hours had elapsed that the President finally decided to end our interview. Officials had twice more entered the room, without result. I saw them making signals to the President, pointing out that visitors were urgently waiting for him. One of the officials later told me he had never known the President prolong an interview so long and disorganise his entire schedule for the day. It was clear to me from the President's voice and words that I was being used as a messenger to tell the world, and the Jewish and Israeli publics in particular, that he was deeply sincere in his wish to make peace and abandon war for ever.

President Sadat succeeded in convincing me at this long interview that he was not a devious politician trying to trick a possibly naive foreign journalist but a practical visionary, an Arab prophet who, having tasted partial victory and then a bitter defeat in the Yom Kippur War, was now determined to see an end to the bloodshed between Israelis and Arabs. He looked with contempt upon all Arabs who still deceived themselves with dreams of wiping out Israel. Courage and vision were qualities which appealed to him above all. It was these qualities that took him to Jerusalem to proclaim an era of peace – but a peace with honour, a peace which saw every inch of Egyptian territory free of Israeli occupation. Nothing disgusted him more than lack of courage and the abandonment of friends in their direst need. I can still feel his anger and hear the sharp derision in his voice as he castigated the Americans and the British for refusing to offer asylum to the Shah of Iran, forced to give up his throne and flee abroad. Only a few months earlier the Americans had been lauding him as a bulwark of peace and stability in the area, and their closest friend. Sadat spoke of the American abandonment of a sick man, their refusal to welcome him officially to the United States and grant him full asylum. He saw it as a particularly horrible piece of cowardice and treachery because the Americans feared offending Iran's new ruler, Ayatollah Khomeini. It was the only time in our interview that the President was not fully in control of his emotions.

Vivid in my memory is the intense derision with which he filled his deep voice as he castigated the British and American leaders, especially the Americans who had advised the Shah to give up the throne. There was such passion in President Sadat's voice that it inspired the most surprising statement in the whole interview. 'Very, very tragic', he had described the situation in Iran. 'A Muslim revolution never used blood as a means of reigning. It is against Islam. The whole thing is in chaos. They have severed their relations with me and I shall be asking my new Parliament, whenever it convenes, to give the Shah asylum in my country – officially I shall be giving him asylum because this is the morality of Egypt. I am very deeply sad about those who are scared to give the man asylum.'

For the head of a Muslim country to announce to a Jewish journalist that he was about to grant political asylum to the rejected ruler of another Muslim State, before informing his own Parliament, must be a unique occurrence in the Middle East – or anywhere in the world. Once again President Sadat was breaking with tradition, insisting that he could use a Jewish writer to proclaim a courageous act of mercy. His gesture moved me deeply.

Reflecting on these passionate declarations, I became convinced that Anwar Sadat saw our meeting as a means of achieving a reconciliation between the Egyptian and Jewish peoples. Probably he recalled the virtual expulsion of thousands of stateless Jews from Egypt as a result of Nasser's edicts against foreign businesses, which hit the Jewish community particularly hard. Probably, too, he remembered the less than complimentary remarks he had made in his younger days about Jews. Now he spoke of the golden age of Arab–Jewish collaboration and hoped it could flourish again.

Angrily he dismissed notions that his policy of friendship with Israel was based on the whims of one person or that the Egyptian people were merely affected by dreams of great possessions which, if disappointed, would lead to convulsions and the overthrow of his designs. As he repeated later to Greville Janner MP, then President of the Board of Deputies of British Jews, peace with Israel was the wish of the whole of the Egyptian people. They would insist that the peace should continue even when the chief architect was no longer on the scene. In this, at least, he was to be proved right. Sadat's enthusiasm at the prospect of peace with Israel is shown in many of the exchanges between us, reproduced below.

I: The people of Israel are quite happy about the peace agreement but they are still worried whether they have done the right thing, for, after all, they are to give up a great deal of land. Could not Egypt do more to reassure them, to open the border to two-way traffic of tourists and of scholars?

Sadat: They should not worry. We have agreed we shall fulfil the words 'good neighbour' to the maximum. And how could they think this when in every way we are going to normalise the relations after the first phase of withdrawal by Israel from Sinai? Whenever Begin takes one step I shall move two. I have fulfilled the promise I made to the Israeli people during my visit to Jerusalem in 1977. My promise has two points. First, there will be no more war after the October (Yom Kippur) War and I have fulfilled the promise. Secondly, Israel has a security issue which should be met and I have done all my best, even more than anyone can imagine, and fulfilled the security issue and so they should not be nervous.

I: Should there not be immediate tourism between Israel and Egypt?

Sadat: But why was not the first phase of withdrawal from Sinai completed in three or six months? This could have happened. Now you are asking something unimaginable. The first phase will be completed in nine months but despite the fact that some part of our land will continue to be occupied for the next two or three years, we are going to normalise relations. Now you are asking me to normalise relations before the nine months are out.

I: Were you surprised by Saudi Arabia's rejection of your peace initiative with Israel?

Sadat: Let us be fair. Any new ideas or moves need some time to be absorbed. The Arab world has been mobilised in the last 31 years vehemently against Israel, and in Israel the same thing took place against the Arabs. So it is not easy for some of my colleagues to absorb the spirit behind them.

I: And what do you make of King Hussein?

Sadat: Hussein is really different. It has been reported and known all over the Arab world that his grandfather King Abdullah and he have since 1948 been in constant contact with Israel when contact was a crime. I was not surprised, really, by the position that has been adopted by King Hussein, for the very simple reason that it does not fulfil his dream of a united Arab kingdom giving him the West Bank. It is not in my power, or in Begin's power or anyone's, to decide the fate of the Palestinians behind their backs.

I: What about the rest of the Arab world? It seems that apart from one or two countries, like the Sudan, they are all against the peace initiative?

Sadat: Not at all. After Saudi Arabia severed relations with us I received messages from lots of colleagues in the Arab world. The majority of them have taken this position (against the peace initiative) as a compliment to Saudi Arabia. This is our Arab way – giving compliments even if it is against the biggest cause in the Arab world.

I: Do you believe that in the end the Arab world will accept your peace initiative?

Sadat: It is a challenge. I accepted the challenge. Egypt is either right or wrong. This will be proved in the near future. I am accustomed to this. After the first and second disengagement agreements in Sinai, after my peace initiative, after Camp David the same thing took place. It never stopped the clock or made the clock go back.

I: The Saudis are not an unreasonable people. Why should they so strongly have rejected the peace initiative?

Sadat: They were scared because the Palestinians, Syrians and Iraqis threatened to assassinate every member of the royal family. Also the Saudis want to prove to the Americans that they are the leaders of the Arab and Muslim world.

I: Are you not concerned that Egypt was suspended from membership at the meeting of Muslim Foreign Ministers in Morocco?

Sadat: Not at all. I consider this a side issue. I do not waste my time with side issues. When I succeed in the main problem, the side issues are automatically solved.

I: Are you not, nevertheless, worried that Saudi Arabia and other rich rejectionist Arab states have threatened to cut off aid to Egypt or even boycott her?

Sadat: They will never scare me. Before we started the October War my economy was below zero. Now our economy is not below zero and we shall survive. Money cannot build leadership or principles. Hussein will always be influenced by Saudi Arabia.

The man receives money from Saudi Arabia, personally and for the State.

I: Israeli Defence Minister Ezer Weizman protested against his own Prime Minister opening presentation of the Israeli autonomy plan for the West Bank and Gaza. What is your view of this?

Sadat: I like Ezer and we shall miss him if he does not attend the negotiations. In El Arish and Beersheba we shall be conducting difficult and very complicated talks. We have to work and persevere. By nature I am optimistic, even in the darkest hour. But let us not talk about Ezer. I don't want to create difficulties for him among his colleagues. Statements can really do a lot of damage. I have always told Begin 'Let us refrain at this precise moment from statements because in the Arab world they take statements by Begin as facts'.

I: What statements do you have in mind?

Sadat: Settlements [in occupied Arab territories]. Our view Begin knows. They are illegal and should be removed by Israel. The American position is the same. But every day whenever they [the Israelis] declare the start of a new settlement or Sharon [the general and former Defence Minister, then Agriculture Minister] starts to antagonise – well am I going to make a statement? This is a side issue which we should not be tackling now.

I: What about the Palestinians? What was the meaning of the secret talks one of your Ministers held with them?

Sadat: In this phase of the negotiations for full autonomy I do not see any need for representatives for the Palestinian side because we are not going to decide the fate of the Palestinians. No one has the right to decide. They should decide for themselves. During the phase of the negotiations which will take place in one year we will decide on full autonomy on the West Bank and Gaza Strip. We want to end the suffering of those who are occupied on the West Bank and Gaza and put them on the correct approach to decide their fate after the transition period. But we must have the Palestinians with us two years before the expiration of the five-year transition period. In this we even give the Palestinians the veto. They are shouting and saying that Sadat is taking the responsibility to decide the fate of the Palestinians. But I shall never speak for the Palestinians. I advise no one to speak for them.

I: What role do you envisage for the Americans in the Middle East in
the future?

Sadat: The victory for Egypt and Israel is really that the United
States has joined as a full partner. This is a victory for both of us,
a victory for peace. So I see the role of the United States as more
important in the future. No one believed me when I said that 99
per cent of the cards of the game were in the hands of the
Americans. That does not mean at all that Israel and Egypt have
been deprived of their responsibilities but we needed someone in
whom both of us could have confidence to overcome the rift of 30
years of bloodshed, hate, violence and four wars. And it worked.

I: As a military man as well as a statesman can you foresee the possibility of the Arab world without Egypt going to war with Israel?

Sadat: There will be no war after the October War for the very
simple reason that Egypt is the key to war or peace in this area.
Without Egypt there will be no war but Israel should learn the
facts of the area because we shall be living together.

I: France seems to be much colder towards you and is there not a
danger that now that Britain is more strongly in Europe the
French might try to turn the Common Market into an anti-Sadat
and anti-Israel force?

Sadat: No. If they went against my peace initiative they would go
against my people. Forty million of them voted for my peace
initiative and only 5,000 were against. Also Mrs Thatcher has
a very productive attitude to the Arab–Israeli conflict. And she
is very independent. And Chancellor Schmidt [of Germany].
I don't think anyone can drag this man. This is one of the real
statesmen that I admire as a man and as a friend. President
Giscard d'Estaing [of France] is a friend but let us hope he can
overcome the difficulties in the economy which may influence
some of his positions, because France since de Gaulle has played
a very pioneering role. I think Chancellor Schmidt, Thatcher and
all the others will never go against peace or against the aspirations
of other peoples.

I: Can you see a solution for the problems of Jerusalem?

Sadat: Yes, yes, yes! In the first place, let us recognise the fact that,
much as Jerusalem is a very sensitive question for you, so it is also
for 800 million Arabs and Muslims. The approach to the problem

xxxii

is not difficult any more. We can solve it on the basis that the city should not be divided and there should be free access to the holy shrines for the three religions. But 800 million Arabs and Muslims will refuse to accept Israeli sovereignty over the Arab part of Jerusalem. These are facts and if we can sit together in the spirit of my initiative, it will not be a problem to reach a solution.

I: The Russians are known to be angry with you. Do you believe they are scheming against you?

Sadat: Yes, they are not only behind what is happening in the Arab world, and Moscow Radio was the most happy when the Arabs severed relations with me, but they even instigated it openly. I am not against the Russians, if only they would drop their policy of interference. They are behind the Palestinians, the Syrians, the Iraqis and, unfortunately, the Saudis and are stirring up the moderate Arabs. That does not concern me. What really concerns me is the movement of the Soviet Union in Africa and in the Gulf. They are now hand in hand with Gadaffi on my western border. They are hand in hand with the Ethiopians against Somalia and Sudan. They are hand in hand with South Yemen against North Yemen and automatically against Saudi Arabia but the Saudis are now fighting the Soviet Union's battle.

I: What do you think is the Soviet plan in Africa?

Sadat: They were uprooted from this area when I sent 17,000 Russian advisers out of this country in a week. Despite the fact that the Soviet Union is in Syria and Iraq they are uprooted in this area. They are planning against three countries – Egypt, Sudan and Saudi Arabia. In the first place they want to get rid of me, who started all this and uprooted them from this area.

I: When was the moment when you actually decided that you wanted to go to Jerusalem?

Sadat: You may not believe it. I have never told this to anyone. I was on my way from Romania to Iran after meeting my friend Ceauşescu. He is a friend of both Begin and me. I asked him two questions about Begin. First, is the man strong enough and, secondly, is the man genuinely for peace? Ceauşescu confirmed to me that the man is genuine and the man is strong. From that moment I was thinking and while flying over Turkey the first idea came to me.

I: Suppose Yitzhak Rabin [Prime Minister now for the second time]
   had been Prime Minister and not Menachem Begin, would you
   still have gone to Jerusalem?

Sadat: I would have hesitated because I dealt with him [Rabin] in
   the second disengagement agreement. For that reason I asked
   Ceauşescu is the man strong enough and Rabin was not strong. It
   was the only cause that could have prevented me but in the main
   idea I did not waver at all.

I: If Golda Meir had been Premier would you have gone?

Sadat: I would have gone. Two men in Israel could have done it
   with me – the old lady and Begin!

These words, published in their entirety for the first time, give an
idea of Sadat's way of talking in English and the intensity of his
feelings.

His revelation about giving asylum to the dying Shah astonished
the Arab and Western worlds. His ministers must have voiced
consternation at this impulsive action before even telling them and
his Parliament but it was typical of the man. He could become very
indignant and excited and this certainly happened during our
interview when the subject of the Shah came up.

Sadat was very careful not to annoy the Israelis at this point.
When I asked whether Begin was stopping the early evacuation by
Israel of Egyptian land, Sadat laughed loudly. 'Please don't ask me
that!', he pleaded mockingly.

When I raised with him the question of Arab–Jewish relations, as
distinct from Egyptian–Israeli relations, and pointed to the golden
Jewish age under Muslim rule, Sadat reacted warmly.

> Yes, Maimonides and the philosophers, doctors, writers. Muslim–Jewish
> relationship has always been like that. Let me hope that the future will
> see this repeated but that will depend a lot upon the attitude and
> atmosphere created by Israel and the Jewish people because we have
> been living with each other all through the ages and let me tell you this
> – in this part of the area we know of no discrimination. For instance in
> my family you can see the dark, the blond and the brunette. One family.
> We have a very small Jewish community here. Last summer I ordered
> my officials to ensure that whoever from the Egyptian Jews wants to go
> back to Egypt should be welcomed here.

Brief historical background

The picture presented by Sadat of a sunny, harmonious Muslim–Jewish relationship through the ages is, of course, much exaggerated. The tone was set for ever by Mohammed, the founder of Islam, who believed that there was no contradiction between Judaism and Islam but when the Jews refused to recognise him he became deeply embittered and attacked several Jewish tribes whom he either annihilated or expelled. However, Mohammed legislated that Jews, like other 'Peoples of the Book', should not be compelled to embrace Islam but should be permitted to observe Judaism, although subjected to certain ignominies.

Egypt itself ('Mitzrayim' in Hebrew and in the Bible) has had a special relationship with the people of Israel. Abraham visited Egypt and Jacob spent the last years of his life there. Jacob and his sons joined his son Joseph, the man of dreams, after the young man had been sold into captivity and later became Pharoah's chief lieutenant. Jacob's descendants were harshly treated by Pharoah and left Egypt under the leadership of Moses. There were constant relations between the state of Israel and Egypt. King Solomon married an Egyptian princess and subsequently Egypt invaded both Judah and Israel.

The sharp rivalry between Egypt and Assyria-Babylonia deeply influenced Israeli history. Egypt and Babylonia were the scenes of the first Jewish Diaspora dispersion and the prophet Jeremiah fled to Egypt after the murder of Gedaliah, the Jewish governor of Judah.

After the conquests of Alexander the Great, many Jews settled in Egypt and Alexandria became the outstanding Jewish settlement outside Israel, with a strong Jewish communal and cultural life. It has been estimated that no fewer than a million Jews lived in Egypt in the first century AD. However, their situation deteriorated following anti-Jewish riots and the Christianisation of the Roman Empire.

For several centuries the Jewish community in Egypt was under a shadow but it sharply revived in the later Middle Ages. The great philosopher and scholar, Maimonides, settled in Fostat-Cairo and he and his descendants served as the leaders of Egyptian Jews.

Under the Ottoman Empire the history of Egyptian Jews was not particularly notable but there was a major change when Western influences penetrated Egypt in the nineteenth century. Many foreign

Jews began to settle in Egypt, mainly in Cairo and Alexandria and built up prosperous businesses. By 1947 about 90,000 Jews were living in Egypt and playing a distinguished role in Egyptian cultural and economic life.

The establishment of the State of Israel in May 1948 created severe tensions between Jews and Egyptians. These were exacerbated when a poorly equipped and poorly led Egyptian Army was humiliated by Israeli troops after it joined other Arab troops in an attempt to destroy the newly founded Jewish State. Further Egyptian defeats at the hands of the Israelis fuelled the anti-Jewish feelings among the ruling groups in Cairo. Sadat's predecessor, Abdel Nasser, destroyed the Jewish community by making it impossible for foreign-born or stateless Jews to retain their businesses. Jews became subject to imprisonment and other discrimination, particularly after the humiliating Six-Day War of 1967, when Israel destroyed the Egyptian Army and Air Force, and Nasser resigned in despair, returning only after a huge popular demonstration in his favour. Jews left in great numbers and by the time of Sadat's historic visit to Jerusalem in 1977 there were only 100 Jews, mostly elderly, living in Cairo. So depleted did the Cairo Jewish community become that there were not, on occasions, enough male members to hold a service in the huge synagogue in Adli Pasha Street. (Jewish religious laws require a minimum of ten males, a 'minyan', for a service and even on a Sabbath day it was not always possible to obtain such a number. Synagogue elders had to rely on members of the Israeli Embassy in Cairo to make up a 'minyan', not always successfully as the majority of the Embassy staff were secular Jews and came to the synagogue merely out of a sense of duty.)

Before the second exodus from Egypt in the 1950s and 1960s, a considerable number of the Jews, particularly the younger ones, were Zionists. A small number of them became involved in 1954 in a tragic and ill-conceived terrorist action which became known as 'the Lavon Affair' in Israel, after the then Israeli Defence Minister, who denied ordering the operation which led to the execution and suicide of a number of young Egyptian Jews. This case further inflamed anti-Jewish feelings in Egypt and was used for attacks on Jews. Egyptian Radio and newspapers conducted virulent anti-Jewish and anti-Israeli campaigns but, surprisingly, they did not have a lasting effect on the feelings of the ordinary people.

1 · *The peasant*

Throughout his life Anwar Sadat referred repeatedly to his origins as a peasant boy, as a man of the earth, a man of his beloved birthplace, the village of Mit Abul-Kum, in the fertile Nile Delta. His critics and opponents ridiculed his claims. They pointed derisively at his beautiful uniforms, his expensive shirts and ties, the smart dresses and jewellery of his pretty wife, Jihan. As in so many other things, they totally misunderstood his character or the values he cherished. One has only to read his autobiography, *In Search of Identity*, to become convinced that his pride in being a man of the earth, a man who shared the beliefs and joys of the peasant was of immense and fundamental importance to him. He attributed to the peasant qualities of steadfastness, honesty, loyalty, dependability and common sense which may have been somewhat exaggerated but there is no doubt that he sincerely believed that the peasant possessed virtues absent from the town-dweller. He believed that the quiet skills of the peasant were factors in overcoming his enemies at home and abroad. He used tricks he had learned in the village, dissimulation being the foremost. He deliberately played on his friends' and opponents' assumption that he was not particularly bright and, therefore, not a dangerous rival. Gamel Abdel Nasser may well have chosen him as his Vice-President precisely because he thought that Sadat would never be a threat to him. And his fellow-officers in the Egyptian government may have calmly acquiesced in this choice because they believed that Sadat was such a weak and indecisive man, so dull and so unintelligent, that he could never be a credible rival in any contest for the presidency, should it arise. He was to prove how wrong they were to underestimate him.

1

In his speeches throughout his life, Sadat referred to himself as a man of the land. The memories of the village never grew dim in his mind. It was his grandmother rather than his mother, apparently lacking in character, who fascinated and dominated him. Anwar was proud to be in the company of this remarkable grandmother, whom men stood up to greet as she passed. Though illiterate she was perceived to have unusual wisdom, and families with problems turned to her for advice. Moreover, she was accepted as a gifted healer. Her medicinal concoctions were credited with almost magical properties.

When the treacle arrived in the village, its arrival proclaimed by the local crier, it was the grandmother who rushed outside, dragging Anwar along towards the canal where a ship had just arrived from nearby Kafr Zirqan. Sadat delighted to describe how he, a small, dark boy, barefooted and wearing a long Arab dress over a white calico shirt, used to trot along with his grandmother, his eyes never leaving the jar of treacle. The delicious taste of the treacle mixed with curdled milk never left him. He spoke of it with a smile many times in the years to come. His years in the village took on a special hue of contentment and happiness which could not possibly have been as unclouded as he described them. They contrasted so sharply with his later years of disappointment and bitterness that seemed to him a haven, a lost fairyland in which everything was beautiful and just, with his beloved grandmother as the revered heroine. He never, he insisted, forgot her words to him: 'Nothing is as significant as your being a child of this land.' Such words from this remarkable woman are conceivable, but could she have added: 'Land is immortal, for it harbours the mysteries of creation'? He certainly believed she did, for Anwar Sadat dressed her in a cloak of wisdom and vision. It was all part of the creation in his mind of this eternally happy village, with lovely food, beautiful trees, in which the spirit of God resided, splendid young companions, and, above all, the spirit of a wonderful grandmother. Too soon he was to be expelled from this Eden.

His father played a lesser role. Anwar's grandfather, who had the rare distinction of being literate in the village, and read secular as well as religious books, made a fateful decision that his son should not join al-Azhar Islamic University and become a sheikh of

2

a mosque but should receive a secular education, and helped him to obtain the General Certificate of Primary Education. As all the subjects were taught in English, this certificate was to prove vital for the father in obtaining employment with the British occupation army. Service in the Sudan kept the father away from the village for long periods. It meant that little Anwar fell under the spell of his grandmother. She believed that he should eventually follow in his father's footsteps. She sent him to the village Koranic Teaching School where he was taught to read and write and learn passages from the Koran by heart. (In a typical bit of exaggeration Sadat implied that he had learned the whole of the Koran by heart.) Then he went to a Christian Coptic school in nearby Toukh but it is the Koranic school which appears to have made the deeper impression on him. He recalled particularly the 'kind teacher', Sheikh Abdul-Hamid, who instilled in him the love of learning and 'the spirit of the true faith'. He recalled sitting among the other children, holding a writing tablet and a reed pen. His Arab dress had a large, deep pocket which he used to fill in the morning with dry cheese and bread crusts. He would snatch mouthfuls during the lessons and during the intervals.

Sadat loved to emphasise that he was a true boy of the village and that work was part of his pleasure – not merely colourful weddings and tasty food. He took part in the cotton harvesting. He picked enough cotton to fill the front part of his Arab dress and then dash to a woman who sold dates, and barter it for the fruit. He was thrilled when he took the cattle to drink from the canal, or worked the ox-drawn threshing machines or joined the other boys in picking the cotton crop.

Sadat did mention his mother in one important activity which may well have influenced his whole life. He recalled how she and his grandmother told him unusual bedtime stories – not the old traditional stories of ancient war exploits and adventures but of near contemporary heroes in the fight for national independence. There was even the unlikely tale of the poisoning of Mustafa Kamil, an Egyptian political leader, by the British 'who wanted to put an end to his struggle against their occupation of Egypt'. Little Anwar had no idea who Kamil really was but he learned repeatedly that the British were evil forces and poisoned people.

3

A less bizarre story – Sadat claimed it was based on facts – concerned the ballad of Adham al-Sharqawi. It spoke of his heroism and resourcefulness in fighting the British and the subservient Egyptian authorities of the day. But the ballad which affected him most deeply was probably Zahran, the hero from Denshway, a place only three miles away from the village. Again Sadat insists that the ballad was based on a true incident. British soldiers, the story went, were shooting pigeons in Denshway when a stray bullet set fire to a wheat silo. Farmers gathered to put out the fire but a British soldier fired at them and ran away. The farmer pursued him and in the ensuing fight, the soldier was killed. Many people were arrested and court-martialled on the spot. Scaffolds were erected before the sentences were even passed. Some farmers were whipped, others were hanged. Zahran, the hero of the struggle against the British, was the first to be hanged. The ballad went on to speak of Zahran's courage and how he walked with head held high to the scaffold and even managed to kill one of the 'aggressors' on the way. Sadat claimed to have listened to this ballad night after night, half-awake and half-asleep: he lived his heroism in dream and reverie. He wished he was Zahran.

Again one notices a taste for exaggeration in Sadat, a wish to dramatise even childish memories. Undoubtedly he was a boy of unusual imagination. The actor in him which was to play such a large role in his later behaviour, so much so that even his beloved wife, Jihan, was amused, was already evident.

The village is also given as the unlikely setting for his discovery of Mahatma Gandhi, according to a *New York Times* report of 18 June 1971. His sister Sekina recalled that 'as a boy of ten in his village of Mit Abul-Kum in the Nile Delta he had discovered the works of Mahatma Gandhi; soon he could recite chapter and verse of British despotism not only in Egypt but eastwards across the Euphrates to beyond the Hindu Kush. When he was still in primary school, Anwar began dressing up in a white sheet like Gandhi and he would walk through the village leading a goat on a string. Then he would go and sit under a tree and pretend he did not want to eat.'

If this charming event really took place, his age at the time could not have been ten, or his discovery of Gandhi did not occur in the village. By the time he was ten, Anwar had long since departed

4

from his cherished village. However, the story, even if somewhat flawed, does indicate that Anwar Sadat was indeed an unusual child, with an imagination far beyond any of his friends in the village, and outside.

Anwar Sadat's own version of the Gandhi saga is different but still beguiling. Claiming that by the time he left school he had a deep hatred of all aggressors and admiration for all those striving to liberate their land, Sadat recalled how vividly the charismatic Indian leader affected him. In 1932 Gandhi passed through Egypt on his way to Britain. The Egyptian newspapers were full of descriptions of his unique personality. Anwar said that he fell in love with his image. He began to imitate him, taking off his clothes, and covering himself with an apron. He made himself a spindle and withdrew to a solitary spot on the roof of the house. He stayed there for a few days until persuaded by his father to come down. He told Anwar that what he was doing would not help Egypt but would certainly make him catch pneumonia, since it was a bitterly cold winter.

Significantly, Anwar Sadat did not mention aspects in his early life which might not reflect so brightly on him, particularly in the West. It was in Mit Abul-Kum that Eqbal Afifi, the woman who was his wife for ten years and whom he left, was also born. Her family was of higher social standing than Anwar's, being of Turkish origin and distantly related to the Khedive Abbas, one of the successors of the renowned Mohammed Ali. Her family owned some land in the village, of which her father was the headman. Eqbal Afifi recalled later that when as children they used to play together in the village square, her parents cautioned her against associating with 'that black one'. Not only did Anwar belong to a poor, landless family but he had a black Sudanese mother. When Anwar asked Eqbal to marry him, her family objected because of the great social gap between them. Being a dutiful daughter she rejected Anwar's offer and it was only after Anwar completed his course at the military academy in 1938 that her family accepted him as a husband for their daughter. Even then Anwar had to wait two more years for the wedding.

Flamboyant courage, which was to distinguish him so much as a plotter and leader, was already evident in the village. Anwar had to pass a swimming test. He was desperate because he did not know how to swim and eagerly accepted an offer from two of his friends

5

to teach him. In his enthusiasm he jumped into the waters of a tributary of the Nile and very nearly drowned. Only quick action by one of the friends saved his life. This incident made a profound impression on Sadat. According to his daughter, Rawiya, he frequently sat and meditated on this spot.

The village and its ways retained an intense influence on Sadat throughout his life. Those among his critics who scoffed at his emotional attachment to the village and ridiculed his claim to having been a man of the land, a peasant, a *fellah*, the poorest of the land workers, were cruelly undiscerning.

Anwar Sadat may have been wrong and hypocritical in several of his claims during his life, especially during his presidency, but his devotion to the village and its virtues was intense and genuine. He began building a house for himself in Mit Abul-Kum, hoping to live there after retirement from high office. Only his assassination prevented the house from being completed. He presented the royalties of his autobiography and the proceeds from his Nobel Peace Prize to the village. He wanted the village to bloom, to be distinct. In several respects he succeeded in his aim. Mit Abul-Kum does look different. The brown grey of the mud-brick houses has been replaced by the light colours of the new village. He wanted to see the whole village renovated, though retaining the traditional dwellings of the *fellahin*.

Being so proud of his village and of belonging to the simple people of the land, Anwar Sadat might have been expected to refer with sympathy and even compassion to his mother, Sitt-al-Barrein, the daughter of a freed African slave. But clearly he shied away from mentioning her in his autobiography. Sitt-al-Barrein lived with his father, Mohammed Sadati (the 'i' was later dropped from the name) in Sudan when he obtained employment with a British medical team. But her four children were not born in the Sudan. When her pregnancies were advanced, her husband sent her to Mit Abul-Kum, where she was looked after by the grandmother. When the babies were weaned their mother would return to the Sudan, leaving the children in their grandmother's care. Sitt-al-Barrein was very dark-skinned and Sadat inherited her complexion.

It is possible that Anwar Sadat's reluctance to mention his mother arose partly from his embarrassment at the way she was treated by

6

his father, who took other wives in accordance with Muslim custom. Sitt-al-Barrein appears to have lost her primacy among the wives. Sadat, a man of fierce pride, would have found this treatment of his mother deeply wounding.

The end of the village paradise for Sadat came with the return from Sudan of his father who lost his job following the assassination in 1924 of the British head of the Egyptian Army, Sir Lee Stack, and the consequent withdrawal of Egyptian troops from the area. The family moved to a small house in Kubri al-Qubbah, near Cairo, when Sadat was only six. He remembered the move vividly. No longer could he enjoy the pleasures of the village. Some people sneered at his village accent. Life in the overcrowded house, with his father with three wives and their children, and the grandmother, could not have been at all comfortable, especially as the father's income was small – £16 sterling a month. Sadat claimed that he lived below the poverty line. Not surprisingly then, when Anwar was sent to school, he encountered difficulties and failed at first to obtain the General Certificate of Education, the gateway to a high school. The shock of failure, Sadat later recalled, had a profound effect on him. God, he felt, was not satisfied with him. He had become negligent and over-confident. Showing the determination which was to become the hallmark of his later life, he took the examination again, in a different school, and passed.

With his keen sense of justice and fairness, Anwar Sadat noted the privileges of the pampered sons of high officials. The sons of the Minister of War and the Under-Secretary to the Education Minister, arrived at school by car. Other students were better dressed. He claims that he did not resent these differences but they were, in fact, to influence his later outlook on social justice. It was by sheer chance that poverty did not sink him, as it did so many other bright Egyptian children, into the morass of near-illiteracy. His father would not have been able to pay school fees for both Anwar and his elder brother Talat: £32 was twice his father's monthly salary. But Talat ran away with the money meant for the school and when he came back he declared that he was not interested in further education. Had this not happened, the father would have been forced to educate only one of his sons, and he would almost certainly have chosen his elder son.

As a teenager and young man Sadat revealed a love for the theatre. He responded to an advertisement in the newspapers for a stage role but without success. His was a serious ambition and, despite his poverty, he took lessons in acting. One of his teachers was a Jewish woman in Cairo who remembers his keenness to do well. But the Cairo theatre did not welcome him. It was said that his dark skin did not aid his ambition. However, theatrical and dramatic gestures were to become part of his life. He loved to shock and surprise his opponents and catch the attention of a world audience. If acting is a kind of deception, the invention of the real and the imaginary, then Anwar Sadat was not merely an actor but a dramatist of distinction.

Failing in his ambition to be a professional actor, he turned his mind to joining the army. With much difficulty he managed to obtain a place in the military academy in 1937, graduating as a second lieutenant nine months later. He greatly enjoyed wearing the dashing officer's uniform and brandishing his swagger cane. Now that he had won for himself a privileged status, Sadat was no longer barred from marrying Eqbal Afifi, though he had to wait until 1940 to achieve it.

On graduation, he was posted to a signal unit in a fashionable Cairo suburb, Ma'adi. But enjoyment was far from Anwar Sadat's mind. He was a very serious young man deeply concerned by Egypt's humiliating position as a vassal state of Britain. It was then that he contacted other young men eager to oppose the British occupation and to target those Egyptians who were aiding it. This was eventually to propel him into politics, conspiracy, power, fame and death.

2 · *Search for an identity*

It is significant that Sadat gave the title *In Search of Identity* to his autobiography. He was always, almost to the last day of his life, trying to comprehend what precisely was his ultimate role in transforming Egypt and why the country had fallen so far behind his ideals. With his strong sense of justice, fairness, and pride, which he learned from his grandmother, Anwar Sadat felt a sense of disgust with the state of the country.

Around him he recognised that there was corruption and mismanagement. Privilege affected promotion in the higher and lower levels of society and the armed forces. Even entering the army was a struggle for an underprivileged boy like Anwar. While the Royal Military Academy permitted the entry of middle-class and even lower middle-class boys, the application forms required details of the father's property and of the highly placed 'reference'. It was sheer good luck that Anwar's father had a friend who arranged to meet the all-important pasha who could act as the reference. Without that friend, Anwar's life might have been totally insignificant.

Although he admired Gandhi, it was not the Indian statesman but the Turkish warrior-politician who became Anwar's ideal and model. Anwar already felt that only by force could the British be driven from Egypt and the country's corrupt system changed. As leader of the new Turkish state, who had driven out the feeble previous rulers, Ataturk provided Anwar with the example for dealing with corrupt politicians and proud, insensitive conquerors. He became obsessed with the British occupation in 1882 which, he believed, was achieved by deception. He felt intense disgust that Egypt was being ruled by a royal family which was not Egyptian.

He was outraged that Egyptian politicians had helped to legitimise the British occupation.

Anwar Sadat was preoccupied also with a question which has absorbed many sensitive Egyptians. He was very proud of the unique history of the Egyptian people and of the rich legacies bequeathed by the ancient Pharaonic regimes. But these were neither Islamic nor Arab. How could the ancient and modern achievements of the country be coalesced? And did not this rich tapestry of history give the Egyptians an advantage over the Arab nomads of the desert? Was wealth, achieved by chance in the discovery of oil, as important as an ancient heritage? These questions were never entirely resolved. They were to come to the fore when Anwar Sadat was considering breaking the ring of hatred around Israel and then facing the outcry of the Arab leaders whom he had ignored.

Displaying the impatience which was to characterise his whole life, Anwar Sadat wished to organise a revolutionary organisation in the army which would drive Britain from Egypt and start the inner revolution. Meetings took place in his room in the officers' mess in Manqabad, a small town in Upper Egypt. He and his fellow officers drank tea and talked. He managed, Sadat later recalled, to inculcate into the officers, who lacked any political education, a feeling that something was basically wrong with Egypt. Yet, surprisingly, the long discussions were interspersed with jokes and stories. The discussion was even dubbed 'The National Assembly'. Although Sadat suggested that he fell in with the wishes of his comrades in having a lighter side to the discussions it is probable that he himself set the tone. Throughout his life, Anwar Sadat would laugh heartily at even a mild joke.

When still a second lieutenant, Anwar Sadat showed qualities which were to distinguish him from his friends. He felt a hunger for more knowledge, more culture. He tried to join the British Institute in Egypt and obtain a BA degree from the University of London. He failed – it was really an impossible attempt.

Discovering in himself a need to read books, he wrote to publishers and bookstores for booklists. He bought second-hand books. When he and his fellow officers were taken on trips, he was happy to sit in a café reading while they went to see films or seek other entertainment.

Sadat saw a rich irony in that it was a representative of the privileged classes, Pasha Ibraim Khayiri, who enabled him to join the army. Sadat was glad to be able to show his gratitude to Khayiri when, later, he came to him as a supplicant. An even more delicious irony in his eyes was the fact that it was a British decision which set him on his career. With British approval, the size of the Egyptian Army was notably increased and more officers were required, including some from the lower classes. 'The British helped me to join the Military Academy when the reason I wanted to join in the first place was to kick them out of Egypt,' he remarked.

It was in Manqabad that Anwar Sadat first met Khalid Muhiaddin with whom he forged a lasting friendship. Khalid developed left-wing views and he often clashed with Sadat but their friendship never ceased entirely. For most of Sadat's presidency, Khalid led the left-wing opposition and his party was excluded from power-sharing. One of the most poignant tributes paid to the assassinated leader came from Khalid.

It was in the debating room in Manquabad that Anwar Sadat first saw Abdel Nasser who was so greatly to affect his life and the history of Egypt. 'My impression was that he was a serious-minded youth who did not share his fellows' interest in jesting, nor would he allow anyone to be frivolous with him as this, he felt, would be an affront to his dignity. Most of my colleagues therefore kept their distance and even refrained from talking to him for fear of being misunderstood.' This is a devastating summing up of Nasser whom Anwar Sadat was to serve so loyally – apparently Sadat was intrigued by Nasser and wanted to know him better but was rebuffed. Nasser created a barrier that prevented any friendship at this point with Sadat. There was mutual respect, Sadat believed, though perhaps mutual suspicion would be a better description of their early relationship. Although Nasser is usually credited with forming the Free Officers' Association which was to overthrow the feeble Farouk kingdom and usher in the republican revolution in 1952, Anwar Sadat did not acccept this version of events. To him the Free Officers, which Nasser undeniably led, were merely the successors to the original group of army revolutionaries which, he, Sadat, had moulded by scheming and talking. Nevertheless, Sadat felt, almost unwillingly, a strong admiration for Nasser's charismatic leadership and single-mindedness. Nasser, who was to become a symbol of pan-Arabism, might never have been able to lead successfully a revolutionary group of officers if Sadat had not prepared the ground.

While Nasser was alive, Sadat was willing to allow him all the glory of the revolution. After Nasser's death, Sadat felt free to remove the myths. These myths not only affected Nasser's personality; they also disfigured his professed social and economic achievements. The startling vehemence with which Sadat attempted to dismantle Nasser's state structure reflected his strongly felt but suppressed indignation at the leader's failures.

What held the young officers together was not a common social ideology but a burning desire to expel the British. For Anwar Sadat, proud of the imperial glories of the Pharaonic regimes of the past, Egypt's sad subservience to an arrogant European power was particularly humiliating.

Disgust with the monarchy of King Farouk did not at the time play a prominent role in the officers' thinking. It is difficult now, when we know what a bloated, cowardly figure King Farouk became, to learn without incredulity that Sadat saw him as synonymous with the patriotic idea. As the king began to deteriorate morally and physically, following the humiliation inflicted on him in 1942 when British tanks surrounded his palace, forcing him to accept Britain's choice for Prime Minister, Sadat's views drastically changed.

Later Sadat was to enumerate six principles which influenced the young officers – the elimination of imperialism, the destruction of feudalism, the establishment of social justice, the formation of a strong Egyptian Army, the creation of sound democratic life and the liberation of the government from the control of capitalists.

This attack on capitalists was most likely promoted by Nasser, who was to establish his own version of a socialist government. Arab socialism in Nasser's Egypt was to include large-scale confiscation of properties of foreign nationals, particularly Jews, a move which contributed to the country's further impoverishment.

Ironically, the principles, Sadat claimed, were dedicated to Sheikh Hassan al-Banna, founder of the Muslim Brotherhood in 1928. It advocated an orthodox Islamic view of society and politics, in contrast to the rule of the secular politicians, and totally rejected the

12

imported European model of government. Towards the end of the Second World War, the Brotherhood became increasingly militant, prepared to use assassination to promote their aims (it was a fanatical offshoot of the Brotherhood that murdered Anwar Sadat in 1981). When he met the sheikh and listened to his sermons, Sadat thought him too cautious. With his frankness and daredevil approach, which was to frighten his associates later and already gave the impression to his young friends that he was somewhat wild, Anwar Sadat told the sheikh: 'Listen, Sheikh Hassan, you are obviously being too wary, too cautious and I dare say, unnecessarily so! Frankly, I am trying to set up a military organisation to overthrow the existing regime.' The amazed sheikh remained silent, apparently believing that Sadat was working for the intelligence services and might even be an *agent provocateur*. Only after asking several questions was the sheikh reassured. Sadat told him: 'It is true. I seek to carry out an armed revolution, and a considerable number of army officers from all services are already working for me.'

It is notable that Sadat insisted that he was already the leader of an organisation and that the members worked for him. The sheikh rmained cautious and refused to co-ordinate their activities. 'Co-operation will be sufficient,' he remarked. However, Sheikh al-Banna successfully recruited Abdul-Rauf, second to Sadat in the Free Officers' Association, to work for the Muslim Brotherhood.

Nazi Germany's successes in the war with Britain and France and later with the Soviet Union, encouraged many young Egyptians to believe that they were being given an opportunity to get rid of the British troops. Sadat's and other revolutionary groups striving, however ineffectually for the removal of the British, were inspired by a remarkable military figure, General Azis al-Masri, the former Egyptian Chief-of-Staff. His hatred of the British became so well known that the British Ambassador, Sir Miles Lampson, asked the Prime Minister, Ali Maher, to remove the general from the post. The Premier felt he could not do so but effectively removed him from power by sending him on an 'indefinite vacation'. Sadat met him on a number of occasions, displaying his usual frankness, which at first startled the general. But he was clearly impressed by the 22-year-old Anwar Sadat. The general had, he said, met tricksters whose brave patriotic declarations led only to mischief and fiascos but he was ready to accept that Sadat and his group were serious as well as practical. The fact that Sadat had got to know him through Sheikh al-Banna proved decisive. Sadat's meetings with al-Masry were to have a profound effect on his life.

As Britain's position in the war against Nazi Germany became increasingly perilous, Egyptians openly displayed their opposition to the war into which, they felt, they had been dragged without being asked for their consent. The sheikh of Al-Azhar, al-Maraghi, a prominent figure in the country, preached a sermon in which he stated: 'We have nothing to do with the war', a sentiment, said Sadat, which every Egyptian echoed. The Prime Minister Ali Maher even proposed to Parliament a policy of saving Egypt from the scourge of war, and this was unanimously adopted. The subsequent Egyptian withdrawal from Mersah Matruh, an area of vital import-ance for the defence of the country from the expected German assault, naturally angered the British authorities who demanded that Egyptian soldiers hand in their arms. Sadat claimed that he instigated protests at this humiliation and the British finally allowed him and his comrades to withdraw with their arms.

It was in the summer of 1941 that Anwar Sadat made his first attempt at a revolution in Egypt. The sheer naïveté of the plan is breathtaking. The plan was that all the troops withdrawing from Mersah Matruh would meet at the Mena House Hotel on the out-skirts of Cairo, close to the pyramids. His own unit duly arrived at the hotel and waited for the others to join them. They were all to march on Cairo, expel the British and their Egyptian supporters and take over the government. The British, Sadat thought, were so weak and so demoralised because of German successes that they would offer no resistance.

Alas, Sadat's unit waited in vain. No other unit joined them. Sadat, nevertheless, saw a consolation in the fiasco. Had the coup been attempted and failed, the authorities would have been on the alert, the army dissidents would have been more closely watched and the revolution in July 1952 might never have taken place.

Sadat was involved in another fiasco soon afterwards. He was approached by al-Masri with a request that the Free Officers should help him flee to Iraq. Al-Masri had been asked by the Germans to

14

escape to Iraq and provide aid to Rashid Ali al-Kilani who had mounted a revolt against the British occupying troops. Although Sadat was warned to keep away from al-Masri, who had been dismissed from the army and whose contacts with the Free Officers were known to British intelligence, Sadat decided, characteristically, to help him. Sadat told him that they could offer him transport, perhaps to Beirut, which was then under Vichy French control, and he might be able to make his own way to Baghdad. However, al-Masri was then told by the Germans that they would provide an aircraft. But the truck which was to take him to it was apparently seized by the British. The two pilots assigned to fly the general were forced to capture a military plane but a few minutes after take-off they discovered they had no oil. They had apparently turned off the oil pump, instead of turning it on! They were forced to make an emergency landing and ended up on top of a tree.

Farcical as the whole incident might appear to the observer, it was no laughing matter for the participants. Although al-Masri and his two pilots managed to extricate themselves from the plane with the help of a friendly police officer and escape to Cairo, the identity of the plotters was soon known to the police and the intelligence agencies. As Sadat's connection with al-Masri had been discovered, he was suspected of being involved in the plot. He was arrested and questioned but, as there was no evidence against him and he denied any knowledge of the escape plan, he was freed and allowed to return to his unit. But his position was badly compromised.

At the time and later, when he was already President of Egypt, Sadat made no secret of his wish to help the German force led by Rommel defeat the British in the desert, at the gate of Egypt, and for Rashid Ali to succeed in his revolt in Iraq. He stated that 'anything that weakened the British position in the Middle East was of prime importance to me' because it created better opportunities for the Free Officers to strike at the enemy. Nor did Sadat hide his admiration for Hitler. He recalled that when, as a twelve-year-old, he was visiting his village and heard that 'Hitler had marched from Munich to Berlin to wipe out the consequences of Germany's defeat in World War I and rebuild his country, I gathered my friends and told them to follow Hitler's example by marching forth from Mit Abul-Kum to Cairo. They laughed and went away.'

Sadat was fascinated by Rommel's strategy and ingenuity in the desert battles with the British. So great was his admiration that he established a museum in El-Alamein in honour of the German commander. This museum was later expanded into a general war museum but Rommel remains a central figure.

Sadat's admiration for Hitler is much more difficult to understand. Even as late as 1953, Sadat publicly said he admired Hitler 'from the bottom of my heart'. Undoubtedly his attitude to Nazi Germany stemmed from his hatred of the British occupation. As soon as the British left Egypt, Sadat's attitude began to change. After he gained power in 1970, all Sadat's public references to Hitler implied some criticism and he spoke favourably of Winston Churchill. When condemning Israel for occupying Arab land, he compared its conduct with that of Nazi Germany. His admiration for the German Army may also have been soured by his perception that Israel, with its tiny population compared with the huge masses in the Arab world, yet succeeded in adopting Teutonic qualities to become a powerful state and a 'fierce enemy'.

It is likely that in his youth Sadat's admiration for Nazi Germany was linked to his dislike of Jews. Inevitably the Koran's derogatory references to the Jews and the subordinate place accorded to Jews in Islamic political theory must have affected his attitude. Even after becoming President, Sadat often used expressions made familiar by Nazi anti-Semitic propagandists. He spoke of Jews taking part in an international conspiracy, of world economic domination by Jews, and accused Zionism of aligning itself with world imperialism. He condemned some American presidents, particularly Lyndon Johnson, for allegedly succumbing to Zionist-Jewish pressure. His anti-Jewish feelings reached such depths that he attacked German reparations 'unjustifiably paid to the Jews' who had suffered under the Nazis. Only after the 1973 Yom Kippur War was Sadat to undergo a change of heart about Israel and the Jewish people.

Fiascos appeared to dominate Sadat's early life. As the German offensive in May 1942 brought them to the very gates of Egypt, the young officers intensified their efforts to aid the Germans or at least to negotiate with them. Having heard rumours that Rommel intended, after conquering Egypt, to give it to the Italians, the officers sought to assure Rommel that they would form an army to help him fight the British if he granted Egypt's independence. One of the Egyptian pilots was told to fly with this message to Rommel near El-Alamein. Alas for the plotters, the message never reached Rommel. The pilot was flying a British-made aircraft and, although on arrival over the German lines he gave a friendly salute, the Germans shot down the plane, killing the pilot.

Another drama also ended farcically. Told that two German officers wished to contact him, Sadat responded enthusiastically. Two more unsuitable agents could hardly be imagined. One, Eppler, had a German mother and an Egyptian father – a judge – and spoke Arabic fluently. But the other, known only as Sandy, spoke not a word of Arabic. They spent their evenings at the Kit-Kat nightclub, spending huge amounts of sterling. This naturally attracted the attention of both staff and customers, and the police began to watch them.

When they were arrested, Eppler and Sandy quickly mentioned Sadat's name. He had visited them on their houseboat and found they had two transmitters, one lacking a switch. He took it home with him. Warned of the agents' arrest, he managed to hide it so that when the security police arrived they could not find it. Under interrogation Sadat again displayed the skill which had enabled him to escape imprisonment. Though circumstantial evidence and the testimonies of the two Germans pointed to his guilt, he outwitted his prosecutors and avoided jail. However, he was taken back in custody to the officers' mess. An Egyptian general told Anwar's father that he would be executed if he did not confess, but Anwar convinced his father that it was a trick.

However, Sadat's days of freedom were numbered. With the appointment of Montgomery as commander-in-chief of the Eighth Army, following the visit by Winston Churchill, the British tightened their grip on Egypt. Sadat was dismissed from the army, arrested and taken to the Aliens' Jail.

3 · *Traumatic years in prison*

In the two years that he spent in various prisons until he escaped from a military hospital in October 1944, Anwar Sadat attempted to understand himself better and seek deeper meanings for his life. His thoughts veered to the future and to the kind of life he would lead when he regained his freedom. Though existence in the prisons was not always solitary and there was a certain amount of socialising, Sadat fell back on his village for reflection and consolation.

As he lay in his cell, his thoughts took him to Mit Abul-Kum, earthly paradise, as he saw it. It was the peasant in him, he believed, that gave him the fortitude and resolve to survive the prison regimes without being harmed either physically or mentally. He learned to be more cunning, more secretive, as he attempted to outwit the various prison guards and governors. Later he was to use cunning to get the better of men who, like the governors, thought themselves cleverer, more cultured, better educated. Being at heart an actor, taking pleasure in dissembling, he could easily play the simpleton. The two years of imprisonment and escape when he lived in extreme poverty and considerable hardship were to prove vital for surviving even greater prison tests later.

Though isolated from his army colleagues, Sadat always felt himself part of the group and of the coming revolution in Egyptian history. He was emotionally stirred when he learned that his colleagues had decided to grant his family £10 a month, a considerable sum in those days. That his colleagues should remember him and make sacrifices on his behalf when he was hundreds of miles away was an immense boost to his morale. Sadat had a profound sense of loyalty and gratitude and equally a deep hatred of crude

selfishness. His opponents paid a heavy price for failing to understand him and heed his peasant cunning. When Anwar Sadat's
opponents doubted his resolve and ability to survive they should
first have considered his behaviour during his years in prison and
detention centres and his desperate days on the run. He delighted
in humiliating the authorities, escaping from prisons and openly
announcing his escape, before returning. He engineered his final
escape from prison by staging a hunger strike which led to his being
taken to a hospital. From there, with the aid of his devoted friend,
Hassan Izzat, who had shared prison days with him, he had little
problem in escaping.

Living as a fugitive for a year from October 1944 was made much
more difficult for Sadat by the need to support his wife and children.
He could not call upon his father for aid. Though ever willing to
help his son, the father hardly possessed the means to look after
Anwar's mother and her children, as well as his other wives and
children.

Emerging from his hideout, Sadat disguised himself by growing
a beard and calling himself Hadji Mohammad. He worked as a
porter for a time, loading and unloading a truck belonging to Izzat.
Together with a driver, Sadat took vegetables and fruit to British
Army camps, working for a rich man – 'almost a millionaire' – called
Ghuwaybah. Sadat noted that the first consignment consisted of
poor-quality oranges and later found that Ghuwaybah had struck a
deal with the British quartermaster. Soon afterwards the British
began obtaining their supplies from the Palestine Jews instead,
prompting Sadat to remark that perhaps the Jews proved better
swindlers and bribers, although he admitted he had no proof. In
any event, his work for the rich man ended.

Sadat's curious morality at this time, and even later when he
became President, is revealed by his story that when President
Nasser proclaimed his 'socialist' laws in 1961, confiscating much
of the funds of the so-called 'war-rich', who had allegedly made
their fortunes by bribery and corruption, Ghuwaybah hid his
ill-gotten riches under the floorboards and went about in rags.
According to Sadat, many rich people behaved similarly. Instead
of censuring such conduct, Sadat praised it, saying that in their
long history the Egyptian people had always found ways to

deceive oppressive rulers whose orders went against their interests.

Sadat had several jobs involving heavy manual work for little pay. So dire was his poverty that it has even been suggested that one of his daughters died of malnutrition. Yet Sadat could recall with amusement that it was his truck that transported the marble to build a resthouse for King Farouk. And he wrote with nostalgia of the day he decided to pawn his beloved jacket, but walked away from the pawnshop for fear that the owner, seeing his rags, might accuse him of stealing the jacket. Significantly, Sadat used highly emotive terms in describing the jacket as his pride and his love, and admitted his near-obsession with smart uniforms.

With the end of the war and the lifting of martial law in 1945, Anwar Sadat could stop running from the authorities and resume a normal way of life. He returned to his house and family, having suffered three years of homelessness and deprivation. But he did not feel like a free man enjoying his liberty after years in jail. For Sadat his country was still in a dark prison, with the jailers, the British, showing no sign of wishing to leave.

Sadat had no moral qualms about shooting British soldiers or Egyptian politicians who, in his eyes, had betrayed the Egyptian people. Particularly offensive to him was the group led by Mustafa el-Nahas, head of the Wafd Party, who had agreed to be imposed as Prime Minister on King Farouk by British tanks in 1942. The Wafd Party was at one time seen as the great Egyptian freedom party and el-Nahas was revered as a national hero. Sadat recalled that as a schoolboy he used to go twice a day to see el-Nahas ride to and from his office. By succumbing to British pressure and flattery, he had lost the nationalists' respect and was even seen as a traitor, wrote Sadat, adding laconically, 'We therefore decided to get rid of him'.

Chance saved el-Nahas. Sadat had trained his small team in the use of hand grenades. A young man, Hussein Tewfik, who had shot British soldiers, was given the task of throwing a grenade at el-Nahas's car. As it speeded up suddenly, the grenade missed and its splinters hit a bus carrying British servicewomen.

The conspirators, led by Sadat, then determined to shoot Amin Osman Pasha. His crime was not that he was in el-Nahas's Cabinet as Finance Minister, but that he was too friendly to the British.

This time the murder plot succeeded. On 6 January 1946 Tewfik shot Pasha in the party building, first shouting out 'Pasha, Pasha!' so that Osman would turn to face him and thus not be shot in the back, which was against the conspirators' code.

Sadat had given Tewfik two grenades for emergency use only. Cornered in the street, Tewfik used one to create a diversion and enable him to escape. Unluckily for him, the shooting had been seen by an air force officer. He was able to give an accurate description of Tewfik, who was duly arrested and interrogated. It was not long before he made a full confession. According to Sadat, Tewfik confessed not because he was tortured or saw no possibility of outwitting the police, but because the prosecuting attorney suggested to the press that they should hint that this was a *crime passionnel*. To 'defend his reputation', Tewfik confessed.

Within a few days there was a knock at Sadat's door and he was once again unceremoniously taken to the Aliens' Jail.

Had Nasser accepted all Sadat's ideas for removing the British, the officers' movement could have been seriously disrupted. One plan Sadat put forward was to blow up the British Embassy in Cairo with all its occupants. Nasser rejected the plan, pointing out that after Sir Lee Stack, Governor-General of the Sudan, was murdered in 1924, the British had carried out effective reprisals. It was not surprising that Sadat gained the reputation among Nasser's more cautious followers of being impetuous, even wild.

Sadat's contacts with the Muslim Brotherhood during his period as a fugitive and when he resumed his own identity were not strong or continuous but they were sufficient to keep alive his wish for immediate, violent actions to overthrow the existing system of government and drive out the British. Sadat was encouraged by the attitude of students and intellectuals. He remarked: 'Now the intellectual and politically conscious man in the street felt alike. Things must change. What had seemed impossible now seemed within our grasp. The battle was half-way to being won.'

Sadat was not frank about his attitude to terrorism in removing those he considered traitors. When the officers led by Nasser took over power, Sadat claimed that the terrorism section organised by Nasser for his revolutionary system was largely theoretical. 'Political assassinations,' wrote Sadat, 'were contrary to the principles of the revolutionaries. Glorification of violence was fatal for the hot-blooded people of the East because it unleashed their most animal instincts. In Egypt they witnessed in the Muslim Brotherhood the depth of degeneration to which such an approach could lead.' However, when he came to write his autobiography Sadat dropped his pretence, adopted a much more understanding attitude towards the Muslim Brotherhood, though he felt that they had no consistent policy, and fully admitted his role in the murder of Osman.

If his previous term in prison and his subsequent life on the run and acute poverty toughened and, possibly, coarsened Anwar Sadat, his experience in Cell 54 of Cairo's Central Prison was to have an overwhelming effect on his personality. By surviving the hardship and degradation of the prison, the dehumanising conditions of squalor and lack of hygiene, he felt that no human obstacle could break him and prevent him from getting to his set goal. Survival taught him patience and an even greater degree of dissimulation. He noted that others succumbed to the horror of the place, becoming hapless and demoralised. His own response was to feel increasing loathing for the corrupt regime that could inflict such suffering on its citizens, and determination, which never left him, to carry out a revolution.

His cell 54 in the prison had no bed, no small table, no chair and no lamp. It was completely bare, except for a palm fibre mat, hardly big enough for a man to sleep on, and a filthy blanket. Water oozed from the cell walls in the winter, while bugs appeared in the summer to torment Sadat. In order to demoralise the prisoners, the authorities forced them to use collectively the dirty unhygienic lavatories, so unhygienic that Sadat believed that they inevitably caused disease. In fact, a scabies ward was attached to the prison – and to most Egyptian prisons at the time – but in the Central Prison conditions were much worse. Large numbers of prisoners contracted diseases and had little chance of regaining their health. It was a hell which destroyed the will-power and the personalities of the victims.

For 18 months Anwar Sadat lived in this hellish hole, unable to read or write or listen to the radio. Yet unlike many of his fellow-prisoners involved in the murder case, he survived with his spirit unbroken. Again he attributed his survival to the hardiness he had gained in his beloved village. Yet he had brought this harsh regime on himself. The authorities rightly suspected that Sadat was cleverly sabotaging their attempt to prepare a convincing case against the suspected murderers of Amin Osman. Sadat advised those being interrogated how to avoid implicating themselves. He had no compunction at telling outrageous lies or making false accusations of torture against officials because he felt they were serving an evil regime.

For Sadat a welcome development was the reappearance of Sheikh al-Banna, Supreme Guide of the Muslim Brotherhood. He contacted Sadat's brother Talat to tell him that the Brotherhood had decided to send £10 a month to Sadat's family. Sadat's army colleagues had stopped their payments when he first escaped from prison. Perhaps, he wrote later, they had forgotten him, adding: 'God forgive them!'

This money was to prove of the highest importance for Sadat and his family. So poor was Talat that he was unable even to buy a bottle of Eno's fruit salts for his imprisoned brother. Sadat had started taking fruit salts early in the morning in the belief that the practice helped him to avoid infections. So powerful was this belief that he continued the custom for the rest of his life, to the surprise of his wife and officials.

Sadat was also enabled to rent a bed, a table and a chair for his cell. It was odd, he remarked later, that the inmates of the Aliens' Jail, 'the lowest of the low', enjoyed better conditions than 'ordinary Egyptians' in 'public' prisons. While the latter had to rent their pitiful furniture for their cells, the former were provided with comfortable beds, electricity and good food.

So great was Anwar Sadat's disgust at the conditions in 'public' prisons like the Cairo Central that when in 1975 he had a chance to use an axe to strike a first symbolic blow in the demolition of the Tulah Prison, he imagined that he was destroying a wall in his former jail. As he struck a blow, innumerable cockroaches emerged. Sadat almost believed that he was demolishing his former hellish home and started hitting the wall with fury. He was asked by the amazed officials to desist but he continued to hit the sodden, rotten bricks. He was dominated, he wrote, by the intense feeling that such prisons should be demolished and replaced by ones fit for human beings. As President, he did start to build prisons with proper sanitary conditions and equipment compatible with at least a minimal degree of human dignity, though those men he himself imprisoned were hardly thankful for his consideration.

When the other conspirators were transferred to the Central Prison, Sadat again became their skilful adviser on how to out-manoeuvre the prosecuting attorneys. The defence lawyers were delighted, advising the men to withdraw confessions they had made. Rebuking the prisoners for giving in so quickly to the authorities, the defence lawyers exclaimed 'If only you had listened to Anwar Sadat. He is a man and you are boys!' At this time Sadat was 27, while the oldest of the accused was 22 and the youngest only 14.

Not only did Sadat survive the ordeals of Cell 54 at the Cairo Central Prison but, through intensive suffering, he built up a new philosophy of living and religious faith. Sitting alone in the squalid cell, day and night, he thought about his personal life and his beliefs – political and religious. He had married young, as was usual in the village, but he now had nothing in common with his long-suffering wife. She was not interested in politics, nor did she dream of revolutions. Her entire life was concentrated on her children and how to feed them. She was obviously proud that her husband was an officer in the Egyptian Army but bewildered and distressed by his dangerous activities and long imprisonment.

Sadat became convinced that he would have to divorce her but he agonised over the break. He recognised that she was a good, loyal wife and that it was not her fault that her interests were not those of her unusual husband. He lashed himself mentally when, during his cadet days, he met a young well-brought-up girl who was learning French. He thought that she would make a more suitable wife than his own wife – and felt ashamed of disloyalty. However, these thoughts repeatedly returned to him – and he found it even difficult to sleep. Finally, he made up his mind. He sent a message to his wife not to visit him in prison. Strangely, for one claiming to have mastered Western ideas, Sadat seemed unaware how cruel such a step would seem to a Western reader. Curiously and significantly, Sadat in describing his dilemma, does not even mention the name of his wife, Eqbal Madi Afifi. Equally curious is his claim that his and her families were related. This was not true. It is possible that, subconsciously, Sadat was linking

24

himself to his wife's family because socially it was on a higher plane.

Cell 54 was also a place where he devoted many hours to thinking about his relationship with Abdel Nasser. When he wrote about it in his autobiography he was already President and Nasser was dead. He could consider their entire strange friendship, while in prison he could merely recall their nervous, abrupt encounters. But, significantly, he chose his early recollections with Nasser to discuss their total relationship.

Clearly, Sadat was stung by the suggestions by diplomats and by the media that the reason for his eventual emergence as Nasser's successor was his insignificance or that, unlike his colleagues, he never stood up against Nasser. There was also the suggestion that his colleagues did not object to his being vice-president, and nominally Nasser's successor, because he was perceived as a light-weight politician, given to outbursts of enthusiasm. Demolishing such concepts, Sadat emphasised that only when he was in prison did Nasser take over from him the leadership of the Free Officers. Sadat explained his retention of high posts in Nasser's administration, with short breaks, by saying that he was always loyal to the coup leader. Yet Sadat openly and by implication criticised Nasser's policies and style. Sadat claimed that he was happy when his 'colleague and friend' became President of Egypt, leader of the Arab world and 'surrounded himself with an aura of glory', a remark, which unwittingly, reveals Sadat's real feelings.

While claiming that it was 'genuine love' which made him stick to Nasser in triumph and defeat and prevented him from quarrelling with the leader, Sadat revealed that pity also played a part in his attitude. In his eyes, Nasser was an unhappy man, unable to enjoy either the excitement of a conspiracy or the fruits of power when it came. He died without ever experiencing *joie de vivre*. Worse still, Nasser was blinkered about some national problems and priorities. Suspicion about his colleagues' intentions and perpetual anxieties gnawed at Nasser's heart, which eventually collapsed. These suspicions and unresolved problems left a dangerous legacy for Anwar Sadat.

Sadat's criticism of Nasser went very deep. He accused Nasser of lacking a clear vision about the future of their country – an astonishing charge in view of the revolutionaries' claims about bringing about a new life for the Egyptians. Nasser, he claimed, failed to pay sufficient attention to the well-being of his citizens as human beings. Far from enlarging the horizons of his citizens, he narrowed them and their chances of self-fulfilment were diminished. Sadat confessed that his years as a member of Nasser's Revolutionary Council were agonising and destroyed the peace of mind which he had gained in the Cairo Central Prison. Even there, though, there were times when he was severely disturbed, as when he heard about Egypt's humiliating defeat in the 1948 war with Israel. However, Anwar Sadat was happy enough when the long drawn-out trial of the defendants of the Osman case ended in virtual victory for the defence. Early in July 1948 the trial finally concluded, with the main defendant being sentenced, *in absentia* – he had managed to escape from prison – to only ten years' jail. When Sadat heard the verdict, he felt certain that he himself would be acquitted. And so it was that Sadat was set free. But he did not rush to his Cairo home to see his wife and children but left for Hilwan where he rented a room in a cheap *pension* to consider his future. It was not long before he was thrown into the fever of revolutionary activities which led to the toppling of the corrupt Farouk regime.

Severe suffering in prison steeled Sadat's character rather than broke it, as happened to others. He built up a number of friendships in prison. He became convinced that loyalty by friends was a supreme factor in one's life, just as betrayal by friends brought human existence to its lowest level. He established an almost mystical link with God, whom he saw as a deity of love rather than vengeance. God, he claimed, had never let him down, far less betrayed him, as humans had done. It was this concept of God which was to lead him many years later to universalise the deity, in contrast to his Islamic co-religionists. God was not merely the God of Islam but of Christians and Jews, and in equal measure. His God was one of joy and laughter, not the morose, angry, vengeful entity of many of his colleagues. Rather unconvincingly, Sadat claimed that because of his new relationship with God, 'the last eight months in prison were the happiest of my life'. He, Sadat, wanted to make people smile and enjoy their lives. He sought a new world of harmony. If he failed in the end, as he undoubtedly did, it was not because he tired of trying to achieve his aims but because he

26

underestimated the sheer enormous size of the problems facing such a backward country – economically and educationally – as Egypt. Nor did he appreciate fully the rancour and the depths of fanaticism which closed the minds of millions of his citizens, propelling some of them to shoot him dead as he was enjoying the moments of his greatest triumph.

Anwar Sadat discovered in prison the need of another, carnal, love – the love of a woman. He had married young because it was expected of him. But although his wife gave him four children – one of whom died in infancy, possibly as a result of an insufficient diet, caused by poverty – he never felt a deep physical love for her. He claimed later that a woman's love was the greatest possible blessing and enabled him to achieve the pinnacle of his ambitions. Without such love a man might grow old without feeling that he had lived at all.

It is certain that these remarks were meant to explain his abandonment of his wife and his later marriage to the beautiful and sophisticated Jihan. It is probably true, too, that without the stability which she provided for him, without the sense of achievement which this marriage gave him, he might have lacked the confidence to stand up to Nasser and challenge and outwit his opponents in the dramatically tense struggle for power and survival.

4 · Crucial meeting with Jihan

Anwar Sadat adopted a distinctly defensive attitude towards his early role in the 1952 revolution which overthrew the Farouk regime with all its corruption and venality. Clearly he was aware of his less than heroic accomplishments in the critical night of the revolution. Release from prison did not bring happiness or contentment to Sadat. He had been in prison continuously for 31 months and he felt as if he had been reborn into a new world. The peace of mind of the prison cell had paradoxically deserted him as he sat reading in the Japanese gardens of Hilwan, a small town famous for its mineral waters which he was glad to use to repair his damaged digestion. He shunned human company and was even unwilling to hold conversations, unable to make the effort. On many future occasions, Sadat was to seek isolation and solitude when confronted with an intractable or major problem. He even found it difficult to drive a car in heavy traffic, as he discovered when he visited Cairo, though once he was proud of his driving. He sought a new direction in his life but what exactly was his role to be? At what goals were his efforts to be directed? How was he to gain satisfaction as an Egyptian patriot?

His life was soon to be crucially affected by two meetings. His old friend, Hassan Izzat, had not forgotten him and appeared unexpectedly in Sadat's room as he was praying. Sadat was beginning to feel uneasy about the lack of money and was becoming bored with his inactive life. Hassan quickly persuaded him to leave with him for his home in Suez. Noticing the old, threadbare clothes that Sadat was wearing, Hassan bought him suits and shirts.

Hassan's efforts for his friend were not entirely altruistic. He had problems with his business partners and believed that Sadat, whom many considered a hero of the Osman case, would provide him with a prestigious counterweight. Sadat noticed that after he had helped to set up a number of deals with the Saudis, Hassan gave him less than half of the profits due to him. Yet the sum was substantial and when Sadat returned to Hilwan to continue the mineral water treatment, he deposited the money in the hotel safe and he was able to pay for the 'good living' he subsequently enjoyed.

Far more important for Sadat than the money earned was his meeting with the 16-year-old Jihan Raouf when she called on her cousin, Hassan's wife. Jihan's father was a Muslim but her mother was English. Proud of her origins, the mother insisted on speaking English and brought English values into the household. Sadat was fascinated by Jihan, who was pretty, lively and sophisticated beyond anything he had ever seen in a woman or girl. Clearly, Jihan was precisely the woman who fulfilled his ideals. Most probably he doubted whether she would ever consent to marry him or even befriend him.

The impression he gives in his autobiography that their marriage was a straightforward event is obviously wrong. Even if we did not have Jihan's own impressive and at times moving account of her life with Anwar Sadat, it must have been obvious that Jihan's parents would not be pleased to have him seek the hand of their beautiful young daughter.

Anwar had spent years in prison, he had been destitute and even now he held no post nor had any profession. The money he had saved from his business transaction was not of an amount that could be used to win them over. Most of all, Anwar was still a married man with children. He could hardly be regarded as a suitable son-in-law. In Sadat's favour was his acting ability which enabled him to present himself as a man who could one day provide a comfortable life for the beautiful Jihan. He promised her parents that he would seek a respectable post. They and she were eager that he should regain his prestigious position in the Army. This was something that he himself sought and could, therefore, promise with a clear conscience. Above all, there was Jihan's enthusiastically romantic attachment to Anwar. She had seen his photograph daily in the newspapers while the Osman trial was taking place. To her, as to many other young people, he was a hero, prepared to give his life for the good of the Egyptian people. But before agreeing to marry him, she insisted that he divorce his wife. This was something that he had planned to do and so presented no problem. Yet he never abandoned his first wife, or his three daughters. He regularly sent them funds and eventually took two of his daughters into his new wife's household.

There are at least two conflicting accounts of how Sadat managed to be reinstated into the Army, a crucial event in his life. Had he not succeeded, he could never have taken part in the revolution and reached the presidency. In his own account, which sounds convincing, Sadat wrote that he had got in touch with an army doctor, Yusuf Rashad, whom he had befriended during his service and begged him to help him rejoin the forces, now that he had been finally acquitted of involvement in the Osman murder. Rashad, now a Royal Guard physician, contacted the Commander-in-Chief of the armed forces, Haidar Pasha, who agreed to see Sadat. The moment Sadat approached him, Haidar Pasha began to upbraid him. 'You are a trouble-maker. You have got a black record.' Sadat tried to speak but was stopped peremptorily by Haidar Pasha. 'You need not say anything. Keep quiet. Don't say a word.' Turning to his private secretary, the general commanded: 'This boy is to be reinstated immediately – from today!'

A military decree reinstated Anwar Sadat in the armed forces from 15 January 1950 with the rank of captain, the same rank he had on his dismissal. His colleagues, Sadat remarked, had already been promoted twice – to major and lieutenant-colonel, obviously a sore point with him, even in this gratifying moment. Rank was, indeed, to play some part in his later struggles with his colleagues in the Revolutionary Council.

In his hostile account of Sadat's life, his one-time collaborator, the journalist and author Mohammed Heikal adds a highly colourful and dramatic incident to the story. Dr Rashad, he wrote, advised Sadat to make a direct appeal to King Farouk when the king went to Friday prayers at the Hussein mosque in Cairo. This Sadat did, kissing the king's hand and asking forgiveness for anything he had done wrong. Farouk gave a nod of acknowledgement and this led to the reinstatement. This alleged incident was later used against

30

Sadat in the struggles within the Revolutionary Council. Heikal also alleges that Sadat had been in contact with the Palace during his time in prison and owed major privileges to the royal links.

As King Farouk and his Palace officials used shady characters and criminals to assassinate persons whom they feared or disliked, these links are clearly meant to tarnish Sadat's character. Sadat made no secret of his willingness to participate in the assassination of men whom he considered traitors to the Egyptian people. If Sadat thought that contacts with the king would help him and the national cause, there is no intrinsic reason why he would not want to co-operate. In his younger days he saw Farouk as a patriot who stood up against British domination. Yet one should consider Heikal's claims with caution. They make Sadat out to be venial and somewhat of a clown, charges which were widely echoed during the bitter internal struggles within the leadership. Sadat had some notable weaknesses but he was far more a master of himself than Heikal suggests. If Sadat ever used clowning, it was to deceive rather than be deceived. Heikal makes an even more distasteful charge against Sadat – that he was sensitive about his black complexion inherited from his mother, Sitt el-Barrein, the daughter of a former Negro slave. In the mid-1930s when replying to an advertisement from a film producer, Amina Mohammed, asking for young boys who could act, Anwar Sadat had stated: 'I am a young man, with a slender figure, well-built thighs, and good features. Yes, I am not white but not exactly black either. My blackness is tending to reddish.' There has also been a suggestion that Sadat found Jihan so immediately attractive because she was fair-haired as well as pretty.

The submissive nature of the young Sadat, which Jihan was to change, and his compulsion to act, which remained with him to the end of his days, are well illustrated in an article that Sadat wrote in *Ghomhouriyeh*, of which he became editor after the revolution:

> All my life I have felt attracted to acting. Even in the 1930s, before going to military college, I was always trying to meet anyone who would give me a part in a play. I saw an advertisement by Amina Mohammed asking for new faces for a film with a Chinese setting she was going to produce, called *Tita Wong*, so I went along to the offices of the film company in Sharia Ibrahim Pasha and stood in row with some other candidates. Amina came in and looked at us – we were about twenty

31

young men – but unfortunately she only picked out two, and I was not one of them. She told the rest of us to send her two more photographs, one in profile and one full face but I later found this was simply a way of getting rid of us.

Heikal, who mentions this article, stated that it also included a confession by Sadat that at one time he called himself Haji Mohammed, although he had never been on the Haj to Mecca, 'as part of an act'. Nobody challenged him, Sadat wrote, 'so I went on with it. I only feel myself really at home in the company of actors'.

One indirect result of Sadat's love of acting and ability to fantasise was his obsession with smart uniforms, even when he became President. Jihan wrote affectionately but amusingly of her husband's uniforms, which he ordered with meticulous care. Some appeared to strike a new note in military and presidential attire. Heikal, who had every reason to hate Sadat, who put him in prison but who disclaims personal hostility in his book *Autumn of Fury*, about the circumstances of the October 1981 assassination, reveals his true feelings when he captions a photograph of Sadat with the words 'military uniform by Cardin'.

According to Sadat, Nasser and his virtual deputy, and close friend, Abdel Hakim Amer, rushed to congratulate him and urged him to take exams to gain quick promotion, which he achieved, becoming a lieutenant-colonel. More important, Nasser informed him of the rapid growth of the Free Officers' movement. Although he advised Sadat not to take a conspicuous role in the work of the group, because of his prison record and the possibility that he was still being watched by the police security forces, Nasser, surprisingly, gave him a map showing the distribution of the Free Officers in the various army units. Such conduct by Nasser appears paradoxical but he may have thought that the authorities would be reluctant to arrest Sadat, now an army officer.

Sadat's enemies were later to claim that he was given a minor role because he was not seen as suitable to join the leadership group. Heikal even suggested that there was strong opposition among the leading Free Officers around Nasser who argued that Sadat was a lightweight trouble-maker. Nevertheless Nasser accepted Sadat as a possible valuable ally, though it can be inferred that, in view of the criticism, he decided to handle Sadat carefully.

Characteristically, Sadat later claimed that it was he who had recruited Nasser into the Free Officers' Association. Sadat explained that his second-in-command in 1942 was Abdul Munim Abdul-Rauf, who maintained contacts with the Muslim Brotherhood leader, Sheikh Al-Banna. When Nasser returned with his battalion from Sudan towards the end of 1942, Abdul-Rauf contacted him and suggested that he should join the Free Officers. Nasser agreed and later had no problem in taking Abdul-Rauf's place at the top, states Sadat.

The vacillation in Sadat's descriptions of the charismatic Nasser is remarkable. Sadat implies that had it not been for his policy of recruiting only outstanding officers for the revolutionary group, Nasser might never have joined the Free Officers. In one account written while Nasser was still alive, Sadat stated that it was around him that 'a group of young men collected. Nasser used to talk to us, educating us. We all had the greatest admiration for him. We would watch his silences, wondering what he was thinking. Then Gamal would start talking to us, explaining to us that the British were the source of all our troubles. Gamal made us all prematurely old because he made us feel that we had the whole burden of our country's future on our shoulders'. This version hardly suggests that Nasser was the lesser figure who owes his admission to the Free Officers to Sadat's vision.

Clearly Sadat was not altogether certain of Nasser's support. When referring to Nasser's decision to include him in the ruling body of the coming revolution, Sadat remarked that this might indicate a sense of loyalty by Nasser

for although I had originally created the Free Officers' Organisation I stayed away from it for eight years – from 1942 (when I was dismissed) to 1950 (when I was reinstated). However, Nasser was not the kind of man to be motivated by such loyalty to others – unless, of course, as the result of firm and long-established friendship, as was the case with Abdel Hakim Amer. Although Nasser and I had come to know each other at the tender age of nineteen, I cannot claim that our relationship ever exceeded mutual trust and respect; it was hardly what you would call a friendship. It was not easy for Nasser to have anybody for his friend because of his tendency to be wary, suspicious, extremely bitter and highly strung.

33

But Sadat suggested that Nasser realised that he would make a loyal and trustworthy colleague. Nasser had gathered that he, Sadat was a man of high principles and lofty values. Sadat did, indeed, prove a loyal colleague and was richly rewarded for it. Whether Nasser held this very high opinion of Sadat and his lofty principles is not known but he certainly appreciated his ability as a publicist, speaker and journalist.

Sadat's role in the revolution began on a farcical note. It had originally been planned that the Free Officers should take over power in 1955 to give themselves time for thorough preparation.

But the outbreak in January 1952 of rioting and looting in Cairo by mobs, who set fire to several buildings, changed their plan. As the army was called in to keep order in the city, the Free Officers decided to start the revolution in November 1952. Even this date had to be brought forward because King Farouk was about to appoint a new War Minister, Major-General Hussein Sirry Amer, who knew personally several members of the Free Officers and would quickly arrest them.

Sadat claimed later that Nasser had held long discussions with him about the coming revolution and had even suggested a major assassination as a prelude. Sadat stated that he dissuaded Nasser from taking such a harmful step. Sadat also recalled advising Nasser to dismiss some of his squabbling colleagues but, for some unexplained reason, the leader flew into a fierce rage against him.

Told by Nasser that the revolution would break out between 22 July and 5 August, Sadat left his unit and arrived in Cairo on 22 July. He expected Nasser to meet him at the railway station, as was customary, but Nasser did not come. Thinking that it was too early for the revolution, Sadat went home and took Jihan to the cinema. There was a long programme of feature films, one of them apparently being a drama starring Ronald Reagan, the future US President. (When President Sadat told President Reagan about the film on that fateful night of 22 July 1952, Reagan exclaimed: 'So I did take part in the Egyptian Revolution!') When Sadat returned home, near or after midnight, he saw a written message from Nasser asking him to go immediately to Abdel Amer's home as the revolution had broken out but when he arrived at the house the guards refused him entry. Distraught, Sadat realised what a ridiculous figure he would cut if, because of a visit to the cinema, he was not able to participate in the revolution. One guard, noticing that he was a lieutenant-colonel, told Sadat that Nasser had said that all officers should go home. A desperate Sadat persisted and spotted Amer directing army traffic. Although Amer could not see him, he recognised Sadat's voice. He told him that Farouk's army headquarters had already been stormed. Sadat then drove his car to the army command headquarters where he saw Nasser who instructed him to telephone all the unit commanders to ensure that everything was going well. Sadat proved useful because of his signals experience. Thus when the War Minister, Haidar Pasha, rang and asked to speak to the night duty officer, not knowing the true situation, Sadat put him through to Nasser.

Though originally his part in the revolution was virtually nil, Sadat quickly assumed a prominent role, certainly from the publicity aspect. Aware of his speaking ability Nasser told Sadat to go to the radio station and announce the revolution. Heikal told a typically wounding story about this incident. Nasser and his colleagues waited a long time for the expected announcement. When they asked Sadat the reason for the delay, he explained that a sheikh was reading the Koran and he did not want to interrupt him.

Yet undoubtedly Sadat was very useful to Nasser at this crucial time. His journalistic skills (before returning to the army he had been able to obtain an editorial post for a time), and his oratorical gifts proved important. Nasser sent him to see the experienced former Prime Minister Ali Maher to form an interim government. 'You have always been in politics. Go and find Ali Maher', Nasser told him. Sadat did not even know where he lived but a journalist told him and they went together to Ali Maher who accepted the post with much hesitation. Then Sadat was involved in the negotiations with King Farouk who was still in Alexandria for his summer holidays. Sadat had been told by one of the king's trusted advisers that he had decided to abdicate and leave the country. Sadat and Nasser were thus able to negotiate from a position of strength. At first Sadat gave the king the impression that his position was not being challenged. Nasser was waiting for his troops to advance on Alexandria. As soon as this was accomplished the ultimatum to the king was to be presented. It was Sadat who personally wrote out the ultimatum and presented it to Ali Maher. There was a short exchange of shots between the king's guards and Nasser's troops. Farouk took fright and called in his guards. He also called on the British and American representatives to come to his aid, fearing that he would be killed.

When Sadat saw an American official, who asked why the Nasser forces had besieged the Ras al-Tin Royal Palace and why there had been an exchange of fire, Sadat told him to mind his own business. Sadat had, what was to him, a particularly satisfactory clash with the British Chargé d'Affaires and the Military Attaché, dressed in full imperial uniform 'used to frighten their colonies' leaders'. They wanted to know the revolution's attitude to the Mohammed Ali (Farouk) royal family and stressed its historical rights. The British also demanded the imposition of a curfew to safeguard the lives of foreigners. Turning on them, Sadat claimed he said: 'Item one – surely it has nothing to do with you! It is not a British royal family. As for the protection of foreigners, you should remember this is our country. As from today, nobody should ever claim responsibility for it except us, and us alone. Is that clear? Besides we would like to know whether your note is official.'

According to Sadat, the British officials beat a hasty retreat, agreeing that their approach was unofficial, and that they were acting merely as personal friends. The approach should be forgotten as if it had not taken place, the Chargé d'Affaires pleaded. This, at any rate, is the Sadat version.

King Farouk hardly presented a heroic image when confronted with the ultimatum on the morning of 26 July 1952. Fearing that he would be murdered, he quickly succumbed. At six o'clock that evening he was taken to his yacht. Watched by members of Nasser's Revolutionary Command Council, the yacht took the king and a few loyal staff out of Egypt for ever to an ignominious exile. Sadat wrote that he watched the scene from the warship *Ibrahim* while aircraft flew above. It was the proudest moment of his life.

Surprisingly, for someone so astute, Sadat did not appear to understand why his prominent role in the announcement of the revolution and the departure of King Farouk, caused so much jealousy among his colleagues. It would have been unnatural if they had not asked themselves what Sadat had done to deserve such prominence. But they were to get temporary revenge, of a kind. When in 1953 Nasser decided that members of the Revolutionary Command Council, the new name given to the ruling body by the leader, should each be given a ministry, Sadat was the only one not allotted an official post but had to be satisfied with becoming editor of the council's newly created newspaper, *Gomhoriyeh*. What they did not realise was that Sadat, a born journalist and publicist, was delighted with his new duties. It was not the first time – and it would not be the last – that his opponents totally misunderstood him and then found themselves outwitted by him.

5 · *Sadat and Nasser in conflict*

For Sadat, as for Nasser, the triumph of the revolution brought with it frustration, sadness and even despair. Members of the revolutionary group, including Nasser, had not prepared themselves for the assumption of power. They were young and totally inexperienced. Apart from General Naguib, who was intended from the first to be merely a respected figure-head, a fact which was not appreciated for a long time in the West, the young officers did not even occupy very senior posts in the Egyptian Army. They believed that all that was needed was to seize power, remove the weak and corrupt king and then give orders. Sadat rightly pointed out that none of them had felt the stings of poverty and deprivation, as was customary among revolutionaries, none of them had suffered in prison cells as he had, none of them had been humiliated and degraded by the authorities as he had. For him the revolution itself was a fulfilment of a dream created as he sat for years in prison cells. For them the seizure of power from a corrupt administration was the beginning of a further struggle for position.

Yet his bitter account of the in-fighting of the revolutionary group, which culminated in the catastrophe of the Six-Day War of 1967, is not entirely convincing. One does not need to accept the acid version of the conflict given by Mohammed Heikal to realise that there are discrepancies in Sadat's self-justifying story of what went on within the ruling group. Yet with all its faults, his account sounds more convincing than Heikal's.

Gamal Abdel Nasser does not emerge as the colossus with mystical powers as seen in the Arab world and in the West. Sadat describes him as a flawed figure, indecisive, apart from a few dramatic acts that shook the Middle East. Nasser's life as leader and president is seen as a tragedy, ending in an early death. Sadat found Nasser's behaviour, when he appeared to seize power, incomprehensible. Nasser's first step was to start a sharp debate within the ruling group on whether they were to have a democracy or a dictatorship. For Sadat there could be only one answer: a dictatorship. The democratic parties had shown themselves to be corrupt, as well as ineffective. They had failed the patient, good Egyptian people. Now was the time for swift decisive action to help the people. And the officers, with their training in taking quick decisions were precisely the people to be in charge. But Nasser argued vigorously against this concept, insisting that it would be dangerous to abandon democracy. When he noticed that he was winning the argument, he dramatically resigned and left. Of course, his bewildered colleagues begged him to return on his own terms. Nasser had won but Sadat was greatly puzzled by Nasser's behaviour and did not quite see him as the pure democrat. Later he was to accuse Nasser of having dictatorial tendencies in contrast to his own belief in democracy. Nasser did, in fact, gain dictatorial powers and was able to make decisions alone on war or peace. Yet, if Sadat is to be believed, Nasser allowed his close friend, Amer to share that power to such an extent that he became afraid of him, preparing the ground for the 1967 catastrophe.

Contrary to what Heikal implies, Sadat claimed that he rejected formal office, saying: 'I don't think I want a portfolio; I know very little outside politics'. When a prominent member of the group, Salah Salem, sarcastically asked: 'And what is the politics you say you know?', Sadat replied: 'By politics I mean how to realise Egypt's hopes as quickly as possible. We want to usher in a new era in Egyptian history.'

As Sadat pointed out, it was impossible to understand why Salah Salem and even Nasser and the others turned on him, ridiculing his inoffensive remark. Clearly there were other factors. Nasser had already become angry with Sadat for apparently behaving as if he had ambitions for leadership. And now Nasser might have become irritated by Sadat's claim to higher principles. Sadat suspected that Nasser and the others, particularly the crude Salah Salem, were jealous of his fame, gained during the Osman trial. Sadat felt later that Nasser was so suspicious that he distrusted everybody until he had evidence to the contrary, while he, Sadat, trusted anyone until facts proved him wrong. And Sadat was one of those whom Nasser did not yet trust.

For a time, feeling deeply hurt, Sadat adopted the attitude of detached observer. Yet this did not prevent him from becoming the target of Mohammad Naguib's animosity, again out of jealousy and the belief that Sadat was after his job. Sadat wrote that he became so disillusioned, made greater presumably by Nasser's lack of support, that he wrote a letter to the Revolutionary Command Council offering his resignation and asking for passports for himself and Jihan so that they could settle in Lebanon, then not only beautiful but peaceful. Fortunately for Sadat, the resignation was not accepted.

From Sadat's own words it is clear that Nasser alone, with the probable help of a few colleagues, particularly Amer, made the vital decisions. By March 1953, Nasser realised that he had to abandon caution. Egypt became a republic, Abdul Hakim Amer was promoted from Major to Major-General and made Commander-in-Chief of the armed forces. Naguib, already at odds with several members of the ruling junta, was given the then purely ceremonial office of president.

These were not earth-shaking decisions yet the one affecting Amer was to prove catastrophic. But at least, Nasser was beginning to use the power at his disposal. A watchful and detached Sadat approved. It appears that he tried to befriend Amer who was becoming powerful. This is Heikal's claim. But Sadat, writing long after Amer was dead, saw him as a corrupt, inefficient politician, who tragically misled his close friend Nasser. If his own picture of himself had any truth, Sadat would not have wanted to befriend such a man. However, Sadat's critics, such as Heikal, would, no doubt, see such an analysis as somewhat naive.

Within a few months of declaring his faith in democracy Nasser, with the full approval of his colleagues decided on disbanding all political parties. They were accused of scheming with certain army officers to regain power. Their reaction to the ban was meek but that of the Muslim Brotherhood was violent. The Brotherhood disregarded any bans on them and made a serious attempt to assassinate Nasser in Alexandria. Nasser tried to fill the political vacuum by creating artificial organisations with high-sounding names but all failed miserably to obtain support. Nasser tried to use Tito's Yugoslavia as his model socialist state. It was not a good model, even when Nasser modified it to meet Egyptian needs and called it the Socialist Union. Sadat implied that there was only one major reformist act which proved of lasting benefit – the agrarian law which limited the amount of land any one person could possess.

On international issues, Nasser had the enthusiastic support of Sadat. Nasser finally stirred himself, forced Naguib's resignation and took over the premiership as well as the chairmanship of the revolutionary council, gaining virtual dictatorial powers. The negotiations for the withdrawal of British troops from the canal zone went ahead and were successfully concluded when Nasser won the approval of his council. Again, characteristically, Sadat turned on the opponents of the draft agreement, who sought further discussions: 'I accept the draft. We need not go into further discussions. What is there to be discussed? The British want 1,200 non-military experts who would thus be guarded by us, the Egyptians. Will such experts frighten us? Only a stupid politician could reject such a solution to a problem that is 75 years old!'. If one wished to find reasons why Sadat aroused such fury among his colleagues this outburst provides many clues.

In view of his later adoption of a pro-American policy, Sadat's overtures to Nasser are intriguing. They were undoubtedly hostile. After a year as an outsider, Sadat became a State Minister and, presumably, took a greater part in discussions about internal and external policy. He made clear that he seized the chance. As editor of *Al-Gumrihiyah* he had opposed a proposal by the United States for a mutual security pact. He claimed that the Americans had offered to provide the Egyptians with weapons, free of charge on one condition: a number of American experts would have to accompany the weapons which must never be used against an ally of the Americans. The proposal was returned to the Americans, with the answer: 'We want to buy the weapons with our own money; we don't want them free of charge. We also don't want the mutual security pact because it affects our independence.'

The Americans persevered, offering further pacts, in an effort to contain the Soviet Union. Nasser's group refused them all, arguing, said Sadat, that having been liberated the Egyptians did not want their freedom of action limited.

Having turned down American arms, the Egyptians turned to the Soviet Union but were rebuffed, Sadat claimed, because the Soviet leaders did not want to arm non-Communist countries. However a meeting between Nasser and Chou En-Lai at the Bandung Non-Alignment Conference led to Chinese mediation and the famous Egyptian–Czech arms deal which was to have fateful consequences.

Sadat played a leading role in preventing other Arab states following the lead of Iraq, Turkey and Pakistan in signing the Baghdad Pact, promoted by Britain. He travelled to see the youthful King Hussein in Amman and persuaded him to stay out, although his cousin was on the Iraqi throne. Lebanon, too, was persuaded to reject the British offer. The intense Egyptian propaganda against the pact, which Sadat saw as a British effort to return to the area after leaving the Canal Zone, angered the British government.

British anger increased when King Hussein dismissed his Commander-in-Chief of the Arab Legion, Glubb Pasha, an Englishman, after a prolonged campaign by Cairo Radio which cast doubts on Glubb's loyalty to the king and suggested that he took his orders from London. Although the dismissal was not due entirely to Egyptian agitation and the failure of the Arab Legion to beat back powerful Israeli reprisal raids (and the consequent turmoil in Jordan) it was probably a more cogent reason. The anger felt in London by Anthony Eden was one more rung in the ladder which led to the Suez War. No one was more adept at such propaganda than Anwar Sadat. He could be very persuasive.

Sadat's life took a new turn when Nasser made him secretary-general of the Islamic Congress, hardly a powerful organisation but providing him with opportunities for travel abroad. On one such trip – to India – he was astonished to notice two notable Communists embrace Nehru. Here, he thought, was an example of true democracy – opponents treating each other like brothers. Sadat tended to exaggerate the importance of gestures. He compared this conduct with the acrimonious exchanges in the revolutionary council. He was clearly pleased when the council was dissolved in June 1956, as, following a plebiscite, Nasser was elected President of the

Republic. But by then the country was pervaded by fear. There was widespread corruption and arbitrary arrests. By implication, Sadat placed much of the blame on Nasser for failing to control his ministers. Nasser appears as a frighteningly unstable personality, driven by suspicion and fears, without a coherent policy for solving the Egyptian people's tremendous problems.

Yet a misconception by Britain and the United States of Nasser's character, the fragile power that he wielded, and a lack of understanding of the needs of the Egyptian people was soon to bring about a crisis which was to catapult him into great popularity and make him the foremost hero-statesman in the Arab world. US Secretary of State John Foster Dulles's withdrawal of the offer to finance the construction of the Aswan High Dam provoked Nasser to declare in an emotional speech in Alexandria that he was nationalising the Suez Canal Company and taking control of the Canal. The ailing British Prime Minister, Anthony Eden, saw Nasser as the reincarnation of Mussolini and began planning to bring him down. France, who blamed Nasser for stirring up trouble in Algeria, was a willing partner. Israel, which had become concerned by Nasser's acquisition of Soviet–Czech arms, was keen to join in the attack. In the consequent fighting, only the Israelis emerged with credit. The delayed and cumbersome British–French expeditionary force was stopped in the midst of the battle by President Eisenhower. Eden resigned claiming ill health, which was true enough, but it was the humiliation of having to withdraw the expedition as sterling was on the verge of collapse that really propelled him out of office.

Nasser's method of ruling and making decisions is revealed in the manner he kept the news of the Suez Canal seizure from Sadat, who was merely told to listen to the radio speech. Nasser must have discussed the decision with a number of his most trusted advisers. Among them was probably Amer. But Sadat was not included in this circle. Sadat did not even express any deep resentment at this exclusion. After Nasser had made the announcement to cheering crowds and returned to Cairo a hero, Sadat mildly rebuked him, saying:

> You never told me about the decision and you have already taken it, so that's that. If you had consulted me I would have told you to be more

43

careful. This step means war and you are not ready for it. The weapons we have have just arrived from the Soviet Union. We have not been adequately trained to use the new weapons. Our training has been British and we have not had time to change our military thinking, our military orientation from Western to Eastern Europe. If you had asked me I would have told you to be careful. But now that the decision has already been taken, of course, we should all support you. And I shall be the first to do so.

This mild rebuke is tinged with sadness, rather than bitterness. Nasser, who according to Sadat, had once exploded in fury at his junior partner's assumption of superiority, could not have been too pleased with this further example of moralising. Nasser knew as much and probably more about the arrival of the Soviet weapons and how they had been incorporated into the Egyptian Army. Moreover, the implication in Sadat's remarks that a trained Egyptian Army could withstand an onslaught by Britain and even combined forces of Britain, France and Israel appears highly naive. Nasser was a gambler who often acted impetuously. There was a good chance that there would be no war and that British–French indignation would fizzle out in protests, as the Americans clearly desired. Had Anthony Eden's judgement not been affected by ill health, the dispute might well have been settled, perhaps not amicably but sensibly, under American jurisdiction.

In contemptuously rejecting the British–French ultimatum, ludicrous in the circumstances, demanding that Egyptian and Israeli troops should distance themselves from each other, Nasser undoubtedly had the backing of the Egyptian people, as Sadat claimed. Nasser showed foresight in withdrawing his troops from Sinai, once he saw that the Israeli troops were winning the battle. Nasser had little choice. Moshe Dayan had prepared a brilliant campaign, which would have succeeded if there had not been a complementary Franco–British invasion. But with British planes bombing his airports and choking the main roads, attempting to hold Sinai would have been sheer madness. But Sadat gives the wrong impression that Nasser withdrew his troops immediately the Israelis attacked. If that was so, it is difficult to understand why the Egyptian President did not save the whole of his forces, and not merely two-thirds of them, according to Sadat.

44

Sadat is not accurate in explaining the attitude of the Israelis or the prelude to the Israeli–Egyptian war. David Ben-Gurion, the Israeli Prime Minister and virtual founder of the State in 1948, adopted a hard-line policy towards Arab infiltrations into the new Jewish State. These infiltrations were motivated by different desires. There were Arabs who had lost their land and their homes and looked on enviously and with bitterness in their hearts as Jewish newcomers planted seeds on their former lands and enjoyed the harvests. Moshe Dayan, the Israeli Chief-of-Staff of the Israeli defence forces, which he helped to build up under Ben-Gurion's guidance, understood these feelings. Unlike Ben-Gurion, he was born in what later became Israel and many of his young friends were Arabs. Eulogising a young settler, killed by marauding Arabs, Dayan said:

> Yesterday at dawn, Ro'i was murdered. The quiet of the spring morning blinded him and he did not see those who sought his life hiding behind the furrow. Let us not, today, cast blame on the murderers. What can we say against their terrible hatred of us? For eight years now they have sat in the refugee camps of Gaza and have watched how, before their very eyes, we have turned their lands and villages, where they and their forefathers previously dwelled, into our home. It is not among the Arabs of Gaza but among our own midst that we must seek Ro'i's blood. How did we shut our eyes and refuse to look squarely at our fate and to see, in all its brutality, the destiny of our generation? Beyond the furrow of the border surges a sea of hatred and revenge; revenge that looks towards the day when the calm will blunt our alertness, the day when we shall listen to the ambassadors of malign hypocrisy who call upon us to lay down our arms.
>
> Young Ro'i went forth from Tel Aviv to build his home at the gates of Gaza to be a bulwark for his people – the light in his heart blinded his sight and he failed to see the sword's flash.

These are extraordinary words but they did express a genuine mood in Dayan and thousands of his fellow-Jews. It was only after thousand of lives had been lost, in Israel and in the Arab countries including Egypt, that Sadat himself understood them and spoke out in similar myth-breaking language.

When Sadat wrote his memoirs, he appeared still to be blinded by the conventional light of Arab public opinion, nor had he studied deeply enough events in Israel or the murderous series of attacks by Arab raiders into Israel and the brutal Israeli reprisals, which often exceeded in violence and scope the original offences.

Raids by Arabs who had lost their homes and their cattle could be sympathised with, to some degree, by Israeli idealists though very few indeed went so far as to condone them but when these raids became part of the state policy of Egypt, with the aim of harassing and weakening the Jewish State to such a degree that it might become a victim of an army attack, a harsh Israeli response was inevitable. Even Moshe Sharett, the gentle Israeli Foreign Minister, who worried about the effect on Western opinion of Israeli reprisal raids, admitted that some reprisals were necessary. Over 200 Jews were killed during the period of infiltration and the launching of the Egyptian-trained *fedayeen*. Israeli settlements became denuded of people and there were Israeli Ministers who warned that the country was in danger. Yet it was Sharett and several of his Foreign Ministry colleagues, such as Abba Eban and Eliahu Elath (Ambassador in London) who were the fiercest critics of the major reprisal assaults by specially trained Israeli troops.

Sadat made no reference to these events, nor did he seem to understand the so-called Lavon Affair. Sadat suggested that in order to sabotage the Egyptian–American *rapprochement*, Ben-Gurion and Pinhas Lavon, the Defence Minister, sent Israeli agents to Cairo to wreck US centres and properties to anger the Americans and thus destroy the good relations between the two countries to Israel's benefit. But the amateurish sabotage by a number of Egyptian Zionists and and Israeli agents, which did little harm, was directed against not American but British targets. The silly plot was worked out and implemented when Ben-Gurion had left the government to take a rest in his desert retreat, and the Prime Minister's post was held by Moshe Sharett. When the full extent of the failure of this ridiculous plot was realised and strong feelings were aroused after Nasser agreed to the hanging of two of the agents, there was an intense demand to discover who had actually given the order to carry out the sabotage. Lavon denied any responsibility, and so did high-level officials. When Ben-Gurion returned to the government he demanded an official investigation into the fiasco. Lavon was forced to resign and so great was Ben-Gurion's indignation that when his request for a judicial inquiry was turned down by the government he himself tendered his resignation.

The Lavon Affair was a central event in Israeli history. For Sadat to give such a short and misleading account of the affair is disturbing as well as surprising. It suggests that his investigations did not go very deeply into some historical events and he was prepared to accept accounts prepared by his own propaganda machine. It was only later that he was prepared not only to delve into his own character but also to examine fearlessly and with compassion, world, including Jewish and Israeli, problems.

There is evidence, produced by the Israeli historian, Benny Morris, that Ben-Gurion and Moshe Dayan tried to provoke Nasser into war because they feared that, because of the Soviet–Czech arms, Egypt might become too powerful. But Nasser himself, while evading Dayan's traps, failed to understand that by his promotion of the *fedayeen* murders and by hanging two of the Israeli Zionist would-be saboteurs he was creating the atmosphere in Israel that inevitably brought the war nearer.

Anwar Sadat is also rather too dismissive of the effect of the confiscation of property belonging to 'foreigners'. The peculiarity of Egyptian nationhood and the long period under foreign domination encouraged many Jews to retain British or French nationality while remaining a vital and vibrant part of Egyptian national life. Many of the large stores were owned by Jews, who had the connections and the expertise to develop Egyptian trade and industry. Jewish doctors, lawyers and writers were prominent. They were an essential part of the daily life of Cairo. So integrated were Egyptian Jews into the life of the country, so acceptable were the conditions for them that Zionism was comparatively weak in Egypt and the number of Egyptian Jews who settled in Israel was small. The impression which the botched sabotage plot gave of a strong Zionist anti-Arab movement among Egyptian Jews was totally mistaken.

By plundering the wealth of the Jewish community, by forcing many energetic and innovative young and middle-aged men to leave the country, by destroying communities which had lasted a thousand years, Nasser did irreparable damage to the Egyptian economy. This expulsion process was dramatically expedited after the 1967 disaster, so that a community which in 1947 numbered over 90,000, and which could trace its origins to Biblical times and which had as its luminary no less a figure than Maimonides, was reduced to a few hundred elderly men and women, hardly able to hold a religious service requiring ten males for the requisite *minyan*.

In a country where corruption was endemic, it is not surprising that accusations were made against Anwar Sadat by his critics and enemies. What is, perhaps, surprising, is that these accusations were not more numerous or more breathtaking. Mohammed Heikal wrote that Anwar and Jihan had been living in a modest house on the Pyramids Road in Cairo. They felt that the house was unworthy of a Vice-President of Egypt and looked for a grander one nearby. It happened to belong to a retired general. They offered to rent it but he refused, whereupon Sadat used his official powers to sequester it. When Nasser heard about this incident, he was greatly annoyed and Sadat was strongly rebuked. Sadat retired for a time to his village of Mit Abul-Kum, claiming that Nasser's anger had caused him, Sadat, to have a heart attack. However, according to Heikal, Sadat in the end was rewarded, in a material sense, rather than punished. Nasser ordered that a house on the Nile belonging to a Jewish millionaire, which had been turned into a government guest house should be made the official guest house of the Vice-President. Another version of the story states that Nasser turned the general's house into a Vice-Presidential residence.

Sadat himself mentioned that Nasser was annoyed with him because he had received a high fee for broadcasts on Egyptian radio. Sadat stressed that he never defended himself but that after a period of estrangement he and Nasser always became reconciled. Yet although Haikal makes various damaging charges about what he called 'organised looting' in Egypt as a result of Sadat's policies, he never actually accuses Sadat personally of corruption.

Even while praising Nasser for his brave behaviour during the Suez crisis, Sadat found reason for criticising him for attributing the Franco–British withdrawal to Soviet rather than American intervention. Sadat was, of course, right. While Eden was startled by the brutal Soviet threat to use nuclear arms, this was not the reason why he and his Cabinet called a stop to the operation. It was President Eisenhower's refusal to back the sliding pound sterling that forced the humiliating withdrawal from Egypt.

6 · *Road to catastrophe and renewal*

In describing the failures and misjudgements which led to the catastrophe of the Six-Day War of 1967, and the subsequent years of anguish which culminated in the sudden death of Gamal Abdel Nasser, Sadat laid the blame on a number of his colleagues, not on himself. Yet, despite his insistence that he was not ambitious and hungry for power, his influence did grow. Nasser never, apparently, explained fully why he chose Sadat as his Vice-President though he did give some kind of explanation to Mohammed Heikal.

It appears that Nasser picked Sadat because he saw in him the least aggressive of his Cabinet and the least likely to betray in order to obtain power for himself. Nasser, as Sadat often pointed out, was prey to all kinds of suspicions. He suspected that there were constant plots against him in which even his friends were involved, he worried about the aims of the Israelis and the plans of their powerful and efficient armed forces, he was irritated by what he thought were 'moralistic messages' from the Americans and disgusted by what he considered insufficient support from the Soviet leaders.

From their vantage point, the Soviet leaders, Khrushchev, and Brezhnev after him, must have felt bewilderment at Nasser's unceasing complaints. The Soviet Union had taken over from the US the formidable task of building the Aswan High Dam, spending huge amounts of money and expending vast resources. The Egyptian forces were re-armed by the Soviet Union, while thousands of Soviet instructors were dispatched to Egypt to train its soldiers and pilots. Egypt did undertake to pay for the equipment and much of the country's cotton was almost permanently utilised to pay back some of the huge debts but only a portion was ever repaid. The Soviet leaders, though somewhat unwilling to reschedule the payment of debts, never set out to blackmail Egypt through financial pressure to follow certain policies acceptable to the Kremlin.

The Soviet leaders were certainly engaged in Cold War games with the Americans. Egypt's strategic position was of immense importance in any struggle for influence in the Middle East and was a prize worthwhile possessing. But until the Yom Kippur War, when Brezhnev deceived Sadat, the Soviet leaders adopted a protective attitude towards the Egyptians, far greater than a marriage of convenience warranted. They were prepared to take considerable risks to protect the Egyptians, even chancing a serious military, including nuclear, clash with the United States.

Yet no country aroused such bitter anger in Nasser's heart as the Soviet Union, not even the US, which he was to blame for his greatest military catastrophe. When Nasser suddenly died of a heart attack, the Chinese Foreign Minister, Chou En Lai, said to the Egyptian envoy: 'Do you know who killed Nasser at the age of 52? The Russians!' Sadat commented that he believed that this charge was true. Nasser, he explained, liked to have freedom of action. However, when Nasser successively broke off diplomatic relations with the Americans and the Western Powers, Arab States and Iran, he had no friends left, apart from the Soviet Union.

Nasser, Sadat argued, was not treated with sufficient respect and dignity by the Soviet Union. This was the reason why his health was affected and why he finally developed a fatal heart disease. Sadat recalled that two months before he died, Nasser spent 21 days in the Soviet Union. On his return to Cairo, Sadat asked him whether the visit was successful. 'A hopeless case', Nasser replied. He added that he was so annoyed with the lack of response by the Kremlin to his requests for more and better arms that he told Leonid Brezhnev that he would immediately accept the American Rogers plan for settling the dispute between Israel and the Arabs. Brezhnev became very excited and asked angrily: 'Does this mean that you will accept an American solution?' Nasser replied: 'After what you have done to me I would accept a solution even if it came from the devil himself!' Apparently what infuriated Nasser was not merely the Soviet failure to supply the arms he thought he needed at the speed he required but the catastrophically misleading information he received from the Kremlin before the Six-Day War concerning non-existent Israeli divisions on the Syrian border which led him to his greatest defeat.

Yet, this account is incomplete; there are obviously missing factors. Nasser went several times to the Soviet Union as he fought to rid himself of the diseases which afflicted his body. Mohammed Heikal wrote about the occasion when Sadat congratulated Nasser on looking so much younger and fitter after a trip to Moscow. The cause for Nasser's increasing bitterness lay deeper; an awareness that, despite the great hopes of the revolution, despite the adulation he still received from the Arab masses, he was failing the Egyptian people. The great economic reforms he promised, the vibrant socialism that was to inaugurate equality among his people and spread prosperity throughout the land, had not brought about any noticeable changes. The scourge of grinding poverty was even more evident, especially among the peasants whom Nasser had particularly promised to help.

Israel was a constant thorn in his side, a bitter reminder of his humiliation and helplessness. Though warned by the Soviet leaders that he was undertaking a dangerous ploy that would rebound on him, Nasser ordered the bombardment of Israeli positions across the Suez Canal, starting the so-called War of Attrition. The thinking behind this confrontation was that as Egypt had more guns and far more people than Israel, it could safely bombard Israeli positions over a prolonged period, forcing them to withdraw. Israel, Nasser thought, could not afford to lose many soldiers. But while the casualties inflicted by the Egyptian guns were painful, Israel was determined to hold out and fight back, as any qualified observer would have forecast. The main result of the 'war' was that Egypt was forced to rely even more on Soviet arms – a humiliating development for Nasser, adding to his inner tensions.

To discourage Nasser from continuing the bombardment, the Israeli government decided to bomb targets in Egypt. Such a policy was advocated by Mr Yitzhak Rabin, Israel's Ambassador in Washington, who claimed that it was acceptable to the White House, but was opposed by some Ministers and experts. Their view was that Israeli air raids on Egypt would inevitably lead to an increasing Soviet presence in the country.

This was precisely what happened. Israeli raids on factories and occasional tragic mistakes, when bombs fell on schools or populated areas, propelled Nasser to seek Soviet anti-aircraft missiles to defend his country. With the missiles came Soviet instructors and pilots. Nasser was becoming ever more entangled in the Soviet web but the Soviet leaders were still refusing to provide him with the huge amounts of arms that he thought he needed to defeat the Israelis. Nasser's pride was hurt and his frustration grew, and with it, his hatred of the Soviet Union.

Nasser's 'socialism' was a type that could not be expected to bring prosperity to any country and least of all to Egypt. Sadat revealed that Nasser borrowed piecemeal from his friend, the Yugoslav leader, Tito. The Yugoslav model brought no wealth but provided dangerous opportunities for unscrupulous men who were able to wreak vengeance on their opponents.

Paradoxically, despite his failures, Abdel Nasser, a tragic figure, became the most revered figure in the Arab world. Arab masses thrilled to his call to unite in winning back Arab greatness after overthrowing their oppressors. His triumph over the British and the French, made possible by the Americans, whom he then abused, put him on a special pedestal. People began to compare him with no less a historical conqueror than Saladin. It was this conception of Gamal Abdel Nasser as a giant who effortlessly bestrode the whole Arab world and was beyond the petty quarrels of individual states that prompted the ruling Syrian Baath party to appeal to him – passionately – to lead a new Egyptian–Syrian union. Nasser had strong doubts about such a union, knowing well the cruelties, divisions and quarrels that afflicted Syrian society. For three days, Syrian officers pleaded with him to accept the plan and finally he accepted with a heavy heart.

He was soon to regret his decision. Within three months the Syrian–Egyptian union, with its name of United Arab Republic, began to show cracks. Amer, appointed by Nasser as his representative in Damascus, encountered jealousy and resentment from Syrian officers, as could have been foreseen. Nothing that Nasser could do could prevent the disintegration of the ill-founded union. It broke up amidst fierce recriminations. Amer was humiliated and sent back to Cairo. So distressed was Amer that he told Nasser he could no longer continue as Commander-in-Chief. According to Sadat, who was no admirer of Amer, Nasser welcomed the resignation but it was quickly withdrawn.

The picture of Abdel Nasser as a strong man is somewhat blurred by his treatment of Amer. Sadat watched as Nasser made several attempts to get rid of Amer but did not insist on his going, finally allowing this incompetent and vain man to remain at his vital post.

Sadat laid on Amer the major blame for Egypt's fatal entanglement in the Yemeni civil war, which tied up thousands of her best troops there during the Six-Day War. Sadat admitted that he favoured Egyptian military support for the Yemeni revolutionaries, fighting the ancient regime of the Imam. Sadat also saw the Egyptian intervention as a way of paying off scores against the Saudi Arabians who had led political campaigns in the Arab world against Egypt but primarily he envisaged the Egyptian intervention as a means of training the troops in modern warfare. Amer dispatched up to 70,000 troops who met stiff opposition from the Imam's fighters, who were more accustomed to the terrain and guerrilla warfare. Nevertheless, Sadat saw benefits from the Egyptian presence. The intervention helped to remove the Imam and curb the 'aggressiveness' of Saudi Arabia. Moreover, the Saudi King Fahd was removed in an internal coup and Faisal, who was to become Sadat's close friend, ascended the throne.

Sadat tended to ascribe most of the ills that befell Egypt not to Nasser but to Amer, whose 'false pride' he castigated. Amer, not Nasser, became the villain of the tragic story of how an unprepared Egypt was trapped into the 1967 war with Israel, a war which not only brought about the destruction of the Egyptian Army but also inflicted immeasurable wounds on Abdel Nasser.

Strangely, for someone who so strongly condemned the Soviet Union's role in the downfall of Egypt, Sadat was very moderate in describing the central role played by the Kremlin in drawing Nasser into the devastating war.

No one has yet successfully explained why the Kremlin repeatedly passed on false information to Nasser, Sadat and others that the Israeli Army was assembling in large numbers at the borders with Syria. There was no such concentration and the Kremlin, which had sophisticated means of checking the facts, must have known the truth. When the Israeli Prime Minister Levi Eshkol begged the Soviet Ambassador in Tel Aviv to accompany him to the Syrian border and see for himself the falsity of the Soviet claim, the ambassador promptly refused.

When Sadat visited Moscow in May 1967 he was seen off at Moscow airport by the Soviet Deputy Foreign Minister, Semenov, and the Speaker of the Soviet Parliament. They told him specifically that ten Israeli brigades had concentrated on the Syrian border. On arrival in Cairo Sadat learned that Nasser had been given identical false information. Sadat muddies the water by claiming that Levi Eshkol had subsequently stated that the Israeli forces would, if need be, occupy Damascus. This might suggest that there was a genuine Israeli threat. There was no such threat. There was no plan to attack Syria and occupy Damascus.

Undoubtedly the blunt Israeli Chief-of-Staff, Yitzhak Rabin, used unfortunate language in warning the Syrians against encouraging terrorist raids into Israel. The situation was becoming increasingly tense on the frontier. On 8 April 1967 a sharp air battle took place and six Syrian MIG aircraft were destroyed by Israeli French-built Mirages with no Israeli loss. This infuriated the Kremlin, who told the Israeli Ambassador in Moscow that Israel was guilty of aggression and would pay heavily for its success.

While statements by Eshkol and Rabin that Israel could not endure for ever the Syrian terrorist raids might have given Nasser an excuse for saying that Syria faced dangers, they were not sufficient for him to launch a preventive war against Israel. Available evidence would suggest that both the Soviet Union and Nasser misread the situation and fell into traps of their own making from which they could not escape. The Russians, anxious to gain kudos in Damascus and embarrassed by the failure of their aircraft, probably wanted no more than to persuade Nasser to make a public demonstration in support of Syria. Nasser, in assembling in public a large army and making it march through to Cairo and then equally publicly taking up position in Sinai facing Israel, probably, at least at first, thought in terms of a propaganda coup to retain his image as the protector and champion of the Arab people.

Nevertheless, Nasser was aware that he was playing with fire. When Amer proposed that the Straits of Tiran should be closed to

Israeli shipping, Nasser warned that such a step would lead to war. When he sent his large army to Sinai he thought the chances of war were only fifty-fifty. Nasser asked Amer if the Egyptian forces were ready for war and Amer gave him a categorical assurance. 'Everything is in tip-top shape!'

Probably some Arab broadcasts, such as those emanating from Amman, voicing doubts about Nasser's courage and willingness to confront the Israelis, helped to goad him into unthinking actions. Many Western diplomats were stunned when the UN Secretary-General U Thant meekly agreed to Nasser's demand to withdraw the UN Emergency Force. Possibly Nasser was as surprised as anyone. This was confirmed in May 1970 when Nasser remarked in a speech that he neither expected nor desired the UN force to withdraw from Sharm el-Sheikh.

Sadat does not disguise the fact that he himself voted for the closure of the Tiran Straits and, by implication, for the ensuing war. His argument later was that the Egyptian Army had better arms then than in the 1973 October War. Opposition came only from Sidqi Sulayman, the Prime Minister, who asked Nasser to wait, and to take into account the sad economic situation, as well as the ambitious development projects frozen as a result of the Americans cutting off aid. Nasser paid no attention to the Premier's pleas, seeking, according to Sadat, to maintain his great prestige in the Arab world.

Nasser, wrote Sadat, was carried away by his own impetuosity, overdramatising the situation and using the world media to increase the tension. The Kremlin became alarmed, pleading that events were moving too fast. Only a concerted effort by the major powers could at this point have prevented war. But neither Britain, France nor, most vitally, the United States was ready to take immediate action to force Nasser to desist from the headlong rush to war.

What is made abundantly clear by Sadat is that Nasser was not surprised by the Israeli attack. He even foresaw the timing and worried about the vulnerability of his air force. He was assured that the air force was aware of the dangers and that, at most, would lose only 10 per cent of aircraft.

Such a scenario does not conflict with Heikal's view that Nasser was reluctant to go into battle with Israel at that time, if ever. Nasser believed that Israel could be isolated and gradually extinguished or expelled from the Middle East.

There is no evidence that Israel had deliberately sought a war with Nasser at this time and had deliberately provoked him in a brilliant coup in which the Soviet Union acted as unwitting *agent provocateur*. Premier Levi Eshkol tried desperately to avoid a war. When it became certain that war could not be avoided the army generals demanded with increasing urgency that there should not be any delays and that every passing day added to the possible Israeli casualties. Although the Israeli strike was brilliantly conceived and magnificently executed – from the purely military point of view – there is no evidence that Yitzhak Rabin and Ezer Weizman had a long-range plan to draw Nasser into a devastating war.

Not only did Sadat blame Amer for not having the Egyptian forces fully prepared to challenge the Israelis but accused him of a particularly stupid act which ensured freedom of the skies for the highly trained Israeli air force in the first hours of the war, enabling it to destroy nearly all of Egypt's warplanes and thus, essentially, winning the battle. Despite Nasser's warning that the Israelis might attack on 5 June, Amer, accompanied by all commanders, boarded an aircraft and flew on a tour of inspection in Sinai. Orders were given to all SAM and anti-aircraft batteries to hold their fire while the Commander-in-Chief was in the air. During this period the Israelis attacked all the Egyptian airfields. 'We can thus say that the war began and ended while Amer was in the air.'

The implication in Sadat's statement that the Israeli victory could have been prevented if Amer had stayed on the ground and the anti-aircraft batteries were allowed to fire is not very convincing; nor is it true that no batteries fired. A number of Israeli aircraft were shot down. Israeli losses might have been heavier but victory would have been just as complete. The Egyptian air defences were not capable of withstanding the massive air attack in which the Israeli bombers used surprise approaches. Amer was convinced that the Americans had joined the Israelis in the onslaught. Nasser rejected this notion but eventually had to put the blame on the United States for the débâcle, so great was the humiliation.

The destruction of the Egyptian forces on the ground, which followed swiftly on the air force disaster, had a paralysing effect on the Egyptian leaders. There was no Churchillian response. Though he often presented himself in heroic poses, Sadat admitted that for days he was stunned and walked about as if in a dream. His sense of unreality was heightened by the sight of large crowds filling up the vast Pyramids Road in Cairo, chanting and applauding the victory they had been told by the state media the Egyptian forces had achieved. For the only time in his memoirs Sadat described himself as being broken-hearted.

It did not take Sadat long to turn on both Nasser and Amer. Why had not Nasser dismissed Amer immediately he heard of the air force disaster? Why did he not try to save the Egyptian Army from destruction? Why did he not establish defence lines in the Sinai Passes? Sadat claimed that he tackled Nasser on these questions but clearly obtained evasive and unsatisfactory answers. A broken Nasser was soon to go on the radio and announce his resignation and the handing over of presidential power to the lacklustre Zakaria Mohieddin.

Within minutes of Nasser's statement, huge crowds filled the main steets of Cairo, demanding that he should remain their leader. Sadat implies in his memoirs that the crowd's emotion was not so much stirred by the suffering of a beloved leader as by his allegation that the United States had joined their enemy and had made his position untenable. Their patriotic fervour had been aroused, just as had happened in 1956 when the foreign aggressor was seen to be Britain. Yet although Nasser returned to his presidential chair, Sadat became convinced that the 5 June disaster had dealt Nasser an almost fatal blow. His face was drawn and tense, his voice hollow. To Sadat, he seemed a living corpse. Nasser, Sadat was to write, did not die on 28 September 1970 but on 5 June 1967.

This judgement was somewhat of an exaggeration. For a dead man, Nasser showed unusual energy. He was a prominent figure at the Arab Summit in Khartoum which proclaimed the famous 'three Nos' – no peace, no negotiations and no recognition of Israel. Nasser was able to obtain large sums from King Faisal of Saudi Arabia, Kuwait and Libya for the loss of the Suez Canal revenue. Sadat implied that he was fully in support of this decision.

If Nasser needed any encouragement to take strong action against Amer, he received it from Sadat. But Nasser would most probably have acted without Sadat's prompting because he felt that Amer was now threatening his personal security. Amer assembled guns in his house and gathered several young officers around him. They demanded that Amer should remain Commander-in-Chief of the forces. Now fearing for his own safety, especially when he heard that the officers intended to march to the presidential home, Nasser dismissed Amer and appointed the dependable Mahmoud Fawzi in his place, with orders to disarm Amer's men.

After a confrontation with Nasser, Amer was detained and committed suicide. Even Nasser was surprised by Sadat's callous reaction to his former friend's death. When Nasser gave him the news, Sadat remarked: 'If this has really happened, it's the best decision Amer has taken as commander who has lost a battle. If I were him I would have done it on June 5.' When Nasser remonstrated, Sadat replied: 'Well, according to military tradition a defeated commander usually does that.'

In writing up this scene, Sadat probably did not realise that for once Nasser emerges as a much more humane person than he. But then it has to be remembered that there was a special relationship between Nasser and Amer. There is almost a Biblical quality in Nasser's obvious grief at the death of a man who was his lifelong friend. Although Sadat put it down to weakness, Nasser's long tolerance of Amer's incompetence which was to cost Egypt so dear, probably resulted from deep affection, if not love. There is a ringing sincerity in Nasser's wail that he could not attend Amer's funeral.

Despite his more decisive actions, Sadat felt that Nasser was still not providing the Egyptian people with the policies they needed. Sadat even appears to have sympathised with the student riots, which later spread to the ordinary public, when lenient sentences were passed in 1968 on the air force commanders in the war. Sadat, at the same time, took it upon himself to speak to the students and claims to have persuaded them to call off their action.

Sadat, however, enthusiastically approved Nasser's decision to rebuild the armed forces. When he thought that this had been accomplished, at least in part, Nasser launched his war of attrition against Israel. Heavy artillery, obtained from the Russians, was used to bombard Israeli positions across the Suez Canal. Israel responded with air raids deep inside Egyptian territory.

This war caused a division of opinion within the Israeli government. While the leading group advocated the deep raids into Egypt, there were others who warned that the raids would force Nasser to seek more Soviet arms, including sophisticated SAM missiles. This is precisely what happened. When Israeli bombers hit a factory at Abu-Zabal on the outskirts of Cairo in January 1970, causing many casualties, Nasser demanded from the Kremlin that it speed up the delivery of the SAM-3 missiles. In a hurried visit to Moscow, Nasser even agreed to Soviet crews accompanying the missiles. He alleged that the Soviets did not keep their promises. Yet whether delayed or not, the Kremlin did provide an air defence system for the Suez Canal which was to prove very troublesome to the Israeli planes in the Yom Kippur War.

One action taken at this time – on 19 December 1969 – did not displease Sadat. He agrees that it had far-reaching effects. 'In a good mood and in a moment of inspiration', Sadat wrote with unintentional self-mockery, Nasser turned to him and said that he was leaving for Morocco to attend an Arab Summit. As intrigues were being hatched against him, it was likely that the conspirators would get him on one of those days and he did not want the country to be at a loss after him. He did not want to leave a vacuum behind him. Therefore he had decided to appoint Sadat as Vice-President. A startled, though not displeased, Sadat wished to know whether this was Nasser's considered opinion. When Nasser insisted that it was, Sadat did not demur and agreed to be sworn in before Nasser left the country two days later.

Sadat later claimed that he had himself heard of the intrigues but, surprisingly, mentioned the Russians. One Russian physician who had visited Cairo, insisted that the heart attack which Nasser had suffered was serious and he had not long to live. Why this should be considered an intrigue is not made clear by Sadat, especially as the doctor's diagnosis proved absolutely correct. Perhaps Nasser's friends should have listened to him instead of accusing him of being part of a plot.

It is curious that Sadat should have felt so strongly about the doctor's statement in view of Nasser's obvious illnesses which became increasingly painful and distressing. At times Nasser was in such pain that the moment he was alone in his residence he screamed in agony. Nasser would not absent himself from official meetings, nor reveal that he was in acute pain. Boils appeared on his body and his legs hurt so much that standing could be a terrible ordeal. Yet it was at this point, when every effort should have been made to provide him with peace of mind, that Nasser was embroiled in a particularly bitter dispute. After he announced his acceptance of the US Rogers Plan for settling the Israeli–Palestinian conflict, he was subjected to a vituperative attack by the Palestinians. Sadat was correct in pointing out that no other Arab leader had done so much to bolster the Palestinian cause. He turned bitterly on any prominent Arab potentate who appeared to desert the Palestinian people. It was for Nasser a principle of faith that every Arab country should be ready to make all possible and impossible sacrifices for the sake of the badly treated Palestinians.

Thus to become the object of Palestinian insult and derision hurt him deeply. It made him feel that he was sinking in treachery and ingratitude, a feeling which deepened his normal state of suspicion and insecurity. Sadat may well be right in claiming that this unexpected dispute with the Palestinians and their attacks on him hastened Nasser's physical decline and precipitated his death from a heart attack.

Ironically, it was Nasser's desire to save Palestinian lives that led to the high-pressure summit in Cairo which was to put an intolerable burden on him. Learning of the Jordanian slaughter of Palestinians who, under the leadership of the Palestine Liberation Organisation, had made an attempt to take over power in Amman and depose or kill King Hussein, Nasser hurriedly convened the summit. At first King Hussein was not invited to the meeting and there was opposition to his being present. But Nasser was apparently keen to have the king at the talks and he was duly sent an invitation which he accepted. The talks were tense and probably acrimonious. Nasser did manage to stop the killings which were on such a widespread scale that many Palestinians escaped to Israel to avoid Jordanian wrath. The Palestinians paid the price by having to move their PLO headquarters to Beirut, together with thousands of men, thus provoking a civil war and an Israeli invasion.

These talks undoubtedly exhausted Nasser. Sadat noticed that the President was in a state of near collapse and begged him to go home for a rest while he deputised for him for the purely ceremonial duties. Sadat wrote that he offered to see off the Amir of Kuwait but Nasser insisted on travelling to the airport.

After the Amir of Kuwait had boarded the plane, it was noticed that Nasser could not move and asked for his car to be brought to him to take him home. Sadat said good-bye to him on condition that they would leave the next day for Alexandria for a rest. Sadat had hardly returned home when he got a message from Nasser's secretary that the President would call to have supper with him; however, within hours Sadat was woken up and asked to leave for Nasser's residence.

On arrival, Sadat was taken to the bedroom where he saw Nasser lying on a bed surrounded by doctors. They told him that Nasser had died an hour before. When Sadat lifted the bed-cover to see Nasser's face, it looked alive, as if the President was merely in deep sleep. Putting his cheek to Nasser's, Sadat did not feel the chill of death. Turning to the doctors, Sadat cried in a highly emotional voice: 'It is not true! What you are saying is wrong.' The doctors responded by saying that they had done everything possible to revive Nasser after he had the heart attack. Sadat still insisted, saying: 'But surely you should try again.' At this the doctors burst into tears.

As Vice-President Sadat made the arrangements for the state funeral, which many kings and presidents were to attend. But, ironically, he himself did not see much of it. The funeral cortège had hardly started when Sadat, apparently suffering from emotional stress, collapsed and had to be carried back to the Revolutionary Command Council building where the cortège started. Sadat was given several injections and fell into a deep sleep. When he woke up hours later, his first question, strangely, was: 'Has Nasser been buried?' He feared that the crowds might snatch their beloved President's body and carry it away with them.

This account given by Sadat reads true. But his critics did not entirely accept his version. Mohammed Heikal suggests that Sadat was among one of the last to be called to Nasser's death bed, and draws from it the conclusion that Sadat's standing was not very high. This version is not convincing. After all Sadat was the Vice-President and no one in Nasser's entourage would have dared to delay informing a man who was due to take over, even temporarily, the duties of President.

All Sadat's critics, however, would have agreed with his comment that Nasser's death was a tragedy that shook the entire Arab world.

7 · *Sadat the surprise President*

Anwar Sadat greatly resented the notion that Nasser chose him as Vice-President for the wrong reasons – that Sadat was perceived to be such a meek person that the neurotic President did not have to fear that he would plot against him. Mohammed Heikal, Egypt's best known – certainly in the West – journalist, editor for years of the influential semi-official daily *Al Ahram* and a personal friend and minister in Nasser's administration, believes, no doubt, honestly that Sadat destroyed the Nasser heritage. Heikal presented a very unappetising portrait of Anwar Sadat.

Heikal argued that it was only natural that Nasser in periods of great tension, particularly after the 1967 disaster, would drop in at Sadat's house, which was near to his, and have a relaxing chat with an unexacting friend. When, unknown to the population, Nasser suffered his first stroke in 1969, it was not surprising that Sadat should have been named as head of a committee to look after State affairs while the President was recovering. But the President was able to return to his post very quickly.

However, Nasser's decision to appoint Sadat Vice-President did take Heikal by surprise. Heikal tried to give the impression that Nasser's decision had not been taken with the seriousness it deserved. Heikal accompanied Nasser on the plane journey to the Arab Summit in Rabat and as they were taking their seats, Nasser remarked 'with a laugh' – notice those words – 'Do you know what I did today? Sadat was coming to see me off at the airport, so I told him to make certain that he brought a Koran along with him – I think he took the hint. I have sworn him in as Vice-President while I am out of Egypt.'

Asked by a greatly surprised Heikal why he had done so Nasser reportedly replied: 'Read these' and handed over a bunch of telegrams from an advance party sent to Rabat to check up on security. Among them was a report that the Moroccan Minister of the Interior, General Mohammed Ofkir, was collaborating with the American CIA in a plot to assassinate Nasser. If anything happened to him, Nasser commented, Sadat would be all right in the interim period. People in the Socialist Union and the Army would look after the real business. Sadat's job would be largely ceremonial. 'Besides, all the others have been Vice-President at one time or another; it's Anwar's turn', Nasser said, adding that, in any case, it was only for a week, and he did not set much store on the assassination report – he had seen too many of them.

This version of Nasser's decision to pick a new Vice-President has similarities with that given by Sadat himself but there are striking differences. The implication of Heikal's version is particularly destructive to Sadat's image. Yet even if Heikal's version reads convincingly, it should not be accepted as being the whole truth. There are obvious flaws in Heikal's version, even if Sadat had also not given a full account of what happened at their fateful meeting. Heikal's argument that it was natural for Nasser to appoint Sadat because of their relaxed friendship can hardly be taken seriously. If friendship was the only criterion, Nasser had men closer to him whom he could have chosen for the post.

Heikal implies that Nasser had a low opinion of Sadat's ability and leadership qualities, yet nowhere does he quote the President directly to this effect. It is certain that Heikal would have repeated any such remark many times had it been uttered.

It is true that the posts which Nasser allowed Sadat to hold did not provide any power bases. Neither the National Assembly nor the Islamic Congress, nor the editorship of *Al-Gumhuriya* were posts that could ever be launching-pads for a challenge for the presidency. The conclusion might reasonably be reached that Nasser deliberately avoided giving him posts which entailed making decisions affecting the life of the country because he doubted Sadat's abilities. This is what Heikal implicitly would like his readers to believe; in his eyes, Sadat dismantled Nasser's entire heritage, and imprisoned and persecuted his followers.

Yet, without accepting at face value all the self-commending statements made by Sadat, it is possible to accept a scenario closer to the one he presents than to Heikal's. Undoubtedly, Sadat was for a long time self-effacing in Nasser's highly emotional and volatile group, always jockeying for better positions around the charismatic hero.

It is significant that when Nasser, according to Heikal, spoke about Sadat's Vice-Presidency and suggested that someone in the Socialist Union or the Army would do the real work, he did not mention any names. The truth is probably that Nasser was aware that all those thrusting personalities who had tried to persuade him that they were worthy of top leadership and had built up support in the country and in the armed forces, had failed him and Egypt. Ali Sabri had not only proved an uninspiring and ineffective Prime Minister but had adopted an ardently pro-Soviet attitude at a time when Nasser was becoming increasingly disillusioned with the Kremlin's prevarications. Zakaria Mohieddin, to whom Nasser had tried, unsuccessfully, to pass over the Presidency after the 1967 war fiasco, had also proved a failure as a leader under Nasser. Amer had committed suicide after he was accused of being the main culprit in the disaster, having become corrupted by the exercise of too much power because of Nasser's indulgence. Only Sadat escaped failure and did not arouse Nasser's paranoic suspicions because he had never exercised real power for long enough, nor apparently wished to wield it.

There was a curious exchange between Nasser and Sadat when the President returned from an unsuccessful visit to Moscow where he had gone in frantic search of arms to counteract the Israeli air raids. The promised MIG-23s and electronic gear had not arrived. All the details had apparently been worked out by Sadat and Vinogradov, the Soviet Ambassador in Cairo. On leaving the plane from Moscow, Nasser had astounded Sadat by remarking: 'The Soviets are a hopeless case', adding: 'Either all the demands you had worked out with Vinogradov did not reach them or they intentionally chose to ignore them.'

Sadat was hurt by these remarks but, aware that another reason for Nasser's trip was to get treatment for his diabetes, he said: 'By Allah, you look well. You seem twenty years younger! What did they do to you?' Nasser replied, 'They put me in an oxygen cell where they treat their astronauts. But you probably hoped I would not come back so that you could stay in power!' Both men are reported to have laughed heartily. No doubt both were in a somewhat jocular mood but Nasser's remark about Sadat wishing to retain presidential power seems peculiar. It suggests that Nasser, always worried about plots against him, had for the first time given some thought to Sadat's intentions. Clearly Nasser decided that he had nothing to fear from him. But he must have realised that Sadat was a far more complex and able person than his colleagues and the public gave him credit for.

Thus Sadat made a far quicker recovery from the 1967 war disaster than Nasser. (According to Sadat, as has been mentioned, Nasser really never recovered from the shock of total defeat.) Sadat could speak to Nasser with a vehemence and directness that other members probably never dared to emulate. Thus when he entered Nasser's room and found him drawing up the letter of resignation, he turned on him: 'Why are you sitting there so complacently? You must leave for Upper Egypt where you will continue to be the symbol of the uprising while we remain here to fight. We shall prepare the people for guerrilla warfare, in the Sharkilyah and Suez districts and fight the Israelis face to face.'

Nasser: Why do you want to act in this fashion?
Sadat: Didn't you hear the announcement from the military headquarters that the Jews have crossed to the west bank of the Canal?

Nasser responded with a long explanation of the real position, accusing Sadat of falling into the same trap as everyone else, that he, Nasser, had checked out the situation and discovered that the 'useless' headquarters had misread what was happening and that he was certain that having achieved their aims, in association with President Johnson, the Israelis had no intention of occupying densely populated Egyptian areas.

This exchange is very revealing for a number of reasons. It shows Sadat, impetuous, enthusiastic, qualities which must have worried Nasser. But it also shows him in a far more combative frame of mind than the shaken president as well as revealing the disarray in the ranks of the general staff.

The suggestion by Professor Raphael Israeli that by appointing Sadat Vice-President, Nasser merely wanted to reward him for his successful leadership of the Egyptian delegation to the Islamic conference in Rabat is not very persuasive. The conference arose out of the attempt by a deranged Australian to burn down the Al-Aqsa Mosque in Jerusalem in August 1969. Israel's justified contention that the arson was the act of a lunatic was not accepted by the Arab world who claimed it was a deliberate Israeli crime against Islam. Even when it became overwhelmingly evident that a lunatic was involved, Arab politicians refused to withdraw the accusation. Saudi Arabia, which sees itself as the custodian of the holy Islamic shrines, of which the Al-Aqsa mosque is very high on the list, led the campaign to incite Muslims against Israel. Egypt quickly responded to the Saudi initiative and invited 20 Islamic states to a summit in Rabat. This was the first of many such conferences in which Islamic personalities were used to stir up hatred of the infidel Jewish State of Israel. Anwar Sadat, with his experience as the secretary of the Islamic Congress in the 1950s, was a natural choice for the leadership of the Egyptian delegation. In Egyptian eyes, though hardly in Israeli ones, he performed well at the Congress. That is not in dispute. His speech to the delegates won him a thunderous ovation. However, that such a success would impress Nasser to a degree that he would offer Sadat the Vice-Presidency seems highly doubtful.

Professor Israeli mentions another reason for the decision and himself rejects it. Leftist opposition groups claimed that Nasser had orginally promised the office of Vice-President to Abd al-Atif al-Baghdadi, a senior member of the Free Officers whom the President had once nominated as President of the National Assembly, after privately promising the post to Anwar Sadat, because he was older. However, in the hope of pressurising the Kremlin into supplying missiles and other sophisticated weapons, Nasser decided to threaten resignation, thereby leaving the post for Sadat who would deal with the Americans. This ploy worked and the Kremlin did supply weapons. But if Nasser's intention was to threaten the Russians with the American card, he would have chosen Moheddin, who was far better known as being pro-American.

Difficult though it is for Sadat's critics to accept, he was the only man of stature at this moment fit to be Nasser's successor. Heikal makes the preposterous statement that Sadat did not possess enough education to understand the intricacies of the Arab world and its aspirations. On the contrary, though he had not had a formal academic education, Sadat had a wider knowledge of Arab daily life than any of his colleagues, wider than Nasser or Sabri. Sadat had met a great variety of people, sinners and saints – very few of the latter – and had known how to survive in a harsh and cruel environment. If any one man was suited by his experience to rule a country like Egypt, with its great masses of poor, illiterate people, hard-working and suffering, ready to accept hardships, deeply committed to their faith in Allah, it was surely Anwar Sadat, born of poor parents in the village of Mit Abul-Kum.

There were those among his bitter opponents, not least Mohammed Heikal, who scoffed at Anwar Sadat's many manifestations of belief and practice of his Islamic faith. Sadat undoubtedly underwent a profound change in his personality and in his attitude towards Allah during his many years in jail. The tragedy of the 1967 war further, after an initial collapse, steeled his resolve to win back a sense of honour to the Egyptian people, to make himself an instrument of that achievement. The catastrophe also impelled him to see Islam in a new light.

Islam had been a personal faith, submission to the will of Allah. It was the faith of millions of ordinary Egyptians, peasants, workers and city dwellers. Now with his country lying prostrate and humiliated, Sadat began to see Allah in a more positive, national role. It was Allah who was going to free his country from its oppressors, it was Allah who was going to destroy the country's enemies.

In one of his speeches, Sadat declared:

> Allah has ordained us to believe. I order you to believe. We all need to fill our hearts with faith, in addition to the weapons we are carrying, so that we may enter the battle with faith, so that we may reach the standard of responsibility and of the mission that Allah has ordained. In the battle the Prophet Mohammed has equipped us with the most potent weapon – faith. It has always given us the upper hand. Arab unity is part of the campaign we are waging for the sake of Arab honour. We are motivated by faith and the mission that the Prophet has destined for us.

8 · Sadat starts a new revolution

It was a moment of rich irony when Sadat, who was claiming that he had stopped telephone tapping, discovered in May 1971 that his own telephone was being tapped. His first action was to dismiss the Interior Minister, Sharawy Gomaa. This was immediately followed by the resignation of the other leading members of the Ali Sabri group, including the head of the Presidential Office, the Director of Intelligence, the Minister of Information and others. They believed that in their absence the wheel of the government would stop, a chastened Sadat would be forced to recall them, on their terms, and then to resign.

A greater threat came from Mahmoud Fawzi, former Commander-in-Chief of the Egyptian Army and now War Minister. He sent an order to General Mohammed Sadiq, the Chief of Staff, to take action in order to take control of Cairo. Fawzi summoned the service chiefs of staff to the War Office and told them that Sadat was selling out to the Americans. Fawzi had a few days earlier, on the arrival of the US Secretary of State in Cairo, told an astonished Sadat that the Egyptian Army found the Rogers proposal and the President's counter-proposals 'unaccepable'. Fawzi turned to General Sadiq with the question: 'Are you ready?' Now fully understanding the meaning of the order from Fawzi, Sadiq turned on him, accusing him of dragging the army into politics. The armed forces, he insisted, would not get involved in politics at a time when they were preparing for the battle against Israel. Sadiq's loyalty was quickly rewarded and he was made a full general and appointed Minister of War. The coup; in which so many powerful men were involved, had failed miserably without a single shot having to be fired. Sadat had been rescued by a combination of luck and the discipline of the army, given a courageous lead by General Sadiq.

This, at any rate, is Mohammed Heikal's version of events. Heikal even mentioned that he himself passed on to Sadat a warning given to him by General Sadiq, and advised the President to communicate directly with the commander of the Presidential Guard which was nominally under the control of Sam Sharaf, one of the coup group. Sadat, Heikal argues, had emerged a hero, and the conqueror of a formidable gang of conspirators, without having to do anything at all.

This version is hardly credible. A weak, trembling, irresolute President could not have retained the loyalty of General Sadiq and the armed forces. Faced with such opposition, a weak man would have given up the struggle. But Sadat stood firm and humiliated the conspirators who all ended up in jail, their death sentences being commuted to life imprisonment. Sadat had not only dumbfounded them with his resolution, he had astonished the Americans with his ability to survive. When Elliot Richardson, President Richard Nixon's representative at Nasser's funeral, returned to Washington, he submitted a report that Sadat would not survive in office more than four or six weeks.

Sadat mentioned far more important differences with the pro-Soviet Sabri group than the meaningless loose federation with Syria and Libya. Not only were the opponents against the Rogers Plan, which was understandable as it was a blow to Soviet influence, but they were in favour of resuming the war of attrition with Israel, which was not. The Kremlin was said to be unhappy about the war, the decision for which had been taken without their approval. Sadat argued, with much justification, that 50 per cent of the Egyptian homeland was open to Israeli air raids, as had been proved during 1968 and 1969. Moreover, the Kremlin had been temporising over supplying SAM missiles. Although Sadat spoke about Egyptian weaknesses, he was well aware that the armed forces had made remarkable progress towards recovering from the 1967 débâcle. The attrition war had shown that the forces could handle the heavy artillery with effect. So much so that the Israeli commanders were secretly concerned, though, perhaps, not sufficiently, as later events proved. The impact on the Israeli public made by the sinking

70

of an Israeli submarine was considerable and was a striking sign that the Egyptian Navy could no longer be disregarded, though once again the Israelis, blinded by the devastating Six-Day War victory, did not draw the right conclusions and were to pay a very heavy price in the Yom Kippur War.

Sadat's account of his encounter with the Soviet leaders when he visited them in March 1971, makes riveting reading though one is left with the suspicion that, always the dramatist, he somewhat exaggerated the fierceness of his clashes. He was seeking, he wrote, deterrent weapons, the SAM batteries as well the replenishment of the huge amount of ammunition expended in the war of attrition. After he had presented the Egyptian case, which was reasonable enough, and included a declaration that Egypt did not want any Soviet soldiers to fight its battles, there was a sharp intervention by the Soviet Premier Kosygin and the blunt Defence Minister Field-Marshal Grechko. Why they should have been so angered that President Leonid Brezhnev had to intervene is not clear. Probably, Sadat, like Nasser before him, had complained about the frustrating delays in the supply of needed arms, particularly SAM batteries. Brezhnev promised that the Soviet Union would provide Egypt with several kinds of weapons, though not of the kind that Sadat had demanded. Nevertheless, he told Brezhnev that he would accept them, while insisting on mentioning the existence of differences.

Sadat was enraged by one Soviet proposal. The Kremlin was prepared to supply Egypt with missile-equipped aircraft and to train Egyptian crews for them, provided they were used only when prior permission was given by the Soviet Union. Sadat angrily retorted: 'Nobody is allowed to take a decision on Egyptian affairs except the people of Egypt, represented by me, the President of Egypt. I don't want the aircraft!'

An alarmed Brezhnev was reported to have taken Sadat aside and offered to send 30 of the latest and excellent MIG-25 fighter-bombers. Hearing this, Sadat declared that he would take back what he had previously said about differences, provided that the pilots took their orders directly from him. Brezhnev, according to Sadat, never sent the promised aircraft. Sadat accused the Soviet Union of using the four MIG-25s, which he agreed to receive, for spying on the American Sixth Fleet rather than in the battle against Israel. Sadat was prepared to buy them but the Kremlin refused and had them withdrawn.

In April 1971, Brezhnev did send SAM batteries and part of the ammunition that was promised, but the rest was not received until the airlift of the Yom Kippur War. And none of the promised aircraft to deter Israel was received. Commenting on Soviet methods, Sadat wrote that the Kremlin wanted to see Egyptian hands tied so that they would not be able to make a decision.

Basing himself on the Russian promises, Sadat said that Egypt was no longer bound by the cease-fire and that the Rogers Plan, which included a cease-fire, was no longer valid. He was due to resume the war of attrition but claimed that the failure of the Kremlin to fulfil its pledges put a stop to any such plan. It was probably at this period of bitter frustration that Anwar Sadat began to shape the policy which was to lead eventually to the journey to Jerusalem, though not before thousands of lives were to be sacrificed in battle. On 4 February 1971, Sadat announced a new peace initiative. He declared that if Israel withdrew its forces in Sinai from the Suez Canal to the Passes, he would open the Suez Canal, re-establish diplomatic relations with the United States, and sign a peace agreement with Israel with the aid of the UN Secretary-General's representative, Dr Jarring. Sadat commented that this was the first time in 22 years that an Arab leader had the courage to declare this.

This offer, made in a speech to the National Assembly, which he renamed the People's Assembly, when the struggle with the Sabri group was at its height, nonplussed the opposition but was welcomed by the outside world. However, the offer did not have the same impact as the offer to go to Jerusalem six years later. The truth is that the time for such an initiative had not yet come. Sadat had not prepared the United States nor, indeed, any of his own ministers for the move. There had been no diplomatic contacts behind the scenes between neutral officials and Egyptian ministers, as had happened even during Nasser's rule. Ironically, one of Israel's most formidable military and political leaders, Moshe Dayan, had suggested to the Cabinet that the Israeli troops should be withdrawn from the banks of the Suez Canal.

Israeli Prime Minister Golda Meir was not impressed by Sadat's offers, nor did she agree with Dayan's suggestion, particularly as it did not seem to require any special sacrifices from the Egyptians. It is a matter of speculation if Anwar Sadat was prepared before the Yom Kippur War to make the kind of peace with Israel which he eventually agreed to sign at Camp David. But that he was seeking some kind of accommodation with the Israelis appears clear enough. He was widely derided when his 'Year of Decision' in 1971 ended without any action and some Israelis tended to treat him almost as a political clown. But when one really studies his pronouncements, it becomes apparent that the point he was – unsuccessfully – trying to make was that peace was as much an option as war. He never made a totally definite promise to go to war during the year. He always imposed some condition. What deceived foreign observers was the strong implication in his statements that the condition of neither war nor peace could not continue. Significantly, in 1972 as five years later, he turned to exactly the same foreign leader to intervene with the Israelis – the unlikely person of Nicolai Ceaușescu, the Communist virtual dictator of Romania. Though perforce a member of the Soviet Warsaw Pact alliance, he showed surprising independence in his foreign policy, though being even more Leninist in his home social programmes. His was the only Communist State that retained relations with Israel after the Six-Day War. He allowed emigration of Romanian Jews to Israel to continue, though it is assumed that he received considerable sums of money. He established a working relationship with the remarkable Chief Rabbi Moses Rosen who helped him gain special trade concessions from the Americans. In return Ceaușescu allowed Romanian Jews to practise freely their religion and maintain several Hebrew schools.

Nicolai Ceaușescu has been universally reviled, together with his wife, since the so-called Romanian revolution of 1989, when they were unceremoniously shot in a courtyard, but he was not altogether such a vicious tyrant as he has been described. He was a man of courage, the only Communist leader in Eastern Europe who persistently stood up to the Kremlin and he undoubtedly played a crucial role in the peace treaty between Israel and Egypt.

Golda Meir found Ceaușescu (as she described in her memoirs) an attractive and energetic president when she met him in 1970. She admired him for not giving in to Arab pressure and for managing to retain diplomatic links with Israel and the Arab states. On Ceauşescu's invitation, Golda Meir willingly visited Bucharest in 1972. Ceauşescu told her that he understood from Sadat that the Egyptian leader was ready to meet with an Israeli. It could be with Golda Meir herself or with someone else but a meeting could take place. Golda stated that she told the Romanian leader: 'Mr President, this is the best news I have heard for many years.'

Both leaders were excited by the idea. There was no question in Ceauşescu's mind, wrote Golda Meir, that he was delivering an historic and genuine message. The Romanian leader even talked about details and suggested that they would not work through their foreign offices but that his deputy Foreign Minister would maintain contact with Golda through her political secretary, Simcha Dinitz, who was later to become Israel's envoy to the United States.

After so many years, it appeared that the ice was about to break. But it did not. Golda recalled that when she returned to Jerusalem 'we waited and waited in vain. There was no follow-up at all. Whatever Sadat told Ceauşescu – and he certainly told him something – was totally meaningless, and I suspect that the reason I never heard anything more from Ceauşescu about the meeting with Sadat was that he could not bring himself to confess, even to me, that Sadat had fooled him.'

In view of what happened five years later, it is sad to reflect that Golda Meir's charge against Sadat was so little justified. Curiously, Golda Meir does not mention making any effort to find out why Ceauşescu had not contacted her about the Sadat offer. She might have asked herself why should Anwar Sadat want to deceive the Romanian leader, and if an Israeli approach to Ceauşescu might solve the mystery.

Golda Meir and other Israeli leaders had cause to doubt the willingness of the Egyptian President to meet them. David Ben-Gurion, the virtual founder of the Jewish State and its Prime Minister during the 1948 and 1956 wars, offered more than once to meet Arab leaders for peace talks but was rebuffed. There have been historians in Israel, especially among the younger generation, who have doubted whether Ben-Gurion was always keen to sit down with the

Arabs for decisive peace talks. Ben-Gurion was said to believe that there was no reason for him to rush to the negotiating table when he would have to make major concessions to the Arabs and wanted first to ensure that Israel negotiated from positions of strength and not weakness. Even if this view of Ben-Gurion's real intentions is accepted – though there are powerful arguments against it – no Arab leader rushed to test his sincerity.

When she succeeded Levi Eshkol as Prime Minister in March 1969, Golda Meir made a personal appeal to Arab leaders to meet her: 'We are prepared to discuss peace with our neighbours, any day and on all matters.' She wrote that Nasser had responded saying 'there is no voice transcending the sounds of war . . . and no call holier than the call to war'. There was a similar response from Amman, Damascus and Beirut. She mentioned an article in one leading Jordanian newspaper in June 1969. 'Mrs Meir is prepared to go to Cairo to hold discussions with President Nasser but, to her sorrow, has not been invited. She believes that one fine day a world without guns will emerge in the Middle East. Golda Meir is behaving like a grandmother telling bedtime stories to her grandchildren.'

It is not surprising that Golda Meir reacted so cynically to the silence after the Ceauşescu message. But it still leaves the observer with a feeling of regret. It may be that Sadat realised that he needed more time to consolidate his position in the country. He may have misunderstood the silence by Golda Meir. There are various possibilities but the least likely was that he had set out to deceive Ceauşescu. Having decided that the year 1971 or 1972 would be a year of decision for war or peace, and realising that he could not wage war, Sadat was prepared to launch a peace initiative. Realising that the time for peace talks with Israel was not ripe, for internal and external reasons, he abandoned his initiative. He began to plan a limited war with the double intention of winning back honour for the Egyptian forces and alarming the major powers, particularly the United States, into becoming closely involved in a peace process. This scenario appears to fit Sadat's character, his vision of the future, and Egypt's urgent needs.

Anwar Sadat's relations with the Soviet Union had public and private aspects. In his speeches, Sadat frequently praised the Soviet leaders. In a significant speech on 23 July 1971, the anniversary of the revolution, when Sadat had crushed the Sabri insurrection, he told the Egyptian people:

> Over 1,200 factories have been built. In this respect I must mention with gratitude and thanks the USSR which has stood by us throughout our ordeal and has helped us in our industrialisation before and after the aggression and until this day and under the five-year agreement we concluded in March with the USSR.
>
> The USSR has helped us to build the High Dam and thereby proved to the United States and everybody else that we are not a bankrupt people . . . It is difficult to find words to express our gratitude to the USSR because every time we embark on development or on any other field, we find the USSR standing on our side, helping us and giving us the unconditional aid of a friend.

Speaking of war and peace, Sadat used the complex language which led to so much misunderstanding. It has to be remembered that hardly any of Sadat's speeches had the preciseness that people in the West expect from their leaders in addresses to Parliament. They were rambling and discursive. They might last for four hours and might consist of stories and anecdotes. His experiences as a soldier and earlier as a boy in a village provided him with a fund of homilies. In Egypt, as in every Arab country where the oratorical and homiletical use of words have a special importance and attraction, giving them almost the significance of real events, Sadat's long discourses were widely appreciated by the masses. As soon as he ended speaking, small crowds used to gather to discuss the meaning of certain expressions and stories. The earthy expressions which he had learned in Mit Abul-Kum raised smiles and provoked discussions.

Such speeches could hardly be precise. On occasions they might appear to voice contradictory sentiments. Sadat once said:

> When it comes to a decision of war or peace we must apply the maximum amount of wisdom and understand our responsibility perfectly. It is not a question of a decision. There is nothing easier than saying 'I shall take the decision tomorrow and that is that and we enter the battle'. No, there is such a thing as world opinion, other powers and so on.
>
> The USSR has honestly and unconditionally given us aid without which we would never have been able to stand fast during the past four years and speak up with a loud voice today. I previously announced to

our armed forces in the Canal zone following 15th of May and I repeat the announcement to you and through you to the whole people, the world at large, and to our friends and foes: I shall not allow 1971 to pass without this battle being decided. I have said and I repeat that 1971 will be a decisive year. If the battle requires the sacrifice of one million, then we are ready to sacrifice one million.

The USSR has supported us politically just as it has supported us militarily. The non-aligned states such as Yugoslavia, India and Ceylon have supported us. The Islamic States headed by Pakistan have supported us. Western Europe, particularly France, has supported us. I truly and wholeheartedly greet President Pompidou and the French people and government for the stand which France, as a great people, has maintained in support of our right and justice. Britain's attitude also has undoubtedly improved. The Conservative Party has courageously taken a line different from that of the Labour Party. We accept the UN resolution and the full withdrawal stipulated within. We support Jarring's mission.

One could sympathise with any ambassador in Cairo trying to analyse this speech and gauge Sadat's real intentions. Sadat appeared to be calling for war but, at the same time accepting Jarring's UN mission which was one of negotiations towards peace.

Sadat appeared to be genuine in his praise of the Soviet Union, yet privately he was fuming against its leaders. He feared and resented their intervention in Egypt's internal affairs. Their agents, he felt, not only wanted to remove him from power but to assassinate him. He claimed to have discovered at least one such plot which he managed to evade. He helped to overcome a Communist plot to take over the Sudan.

Sadat delighted in describing his clashes with the Soviet leaders in the Kremlin. His descriptions read at times as if written up many years later and benefiting from the inspiration of a theatrical dramatist. However, at least one of the descriptions has the ring of truth. During one of his early trips to Moscow, Sadat was told by Communist Party and state leader Nikita Khrushchev that conditions were better in the Soviet Union than in Egypt because the USSR had the benefit of Communism. Sadat's immediate riposte was that capitalism must be superior to Communism as conditions in the United States were so much better than in the Soviet Union!

Anwar Sadat's eventual public break with the Soviet Union had to

do as much with his character as with his contempt for the inefficiency of its leadership. As a proud man, always aware of Egypt's
long heritage, he was furious at the attempt by the Kremlin to
subjugate the country. He felt constantly that the Soviet Union
wished to adopt the same role in the ruling of Egypt as had been
taken by Great Britain before it was so painfully wrested away. By
delaying the delivery of promised war material, by changing the
type of weapons requested, the Soviet leaders, Sadat felt, were
deliberately attempting to take real power from Egypt's rulers. But
Sadat was quite prepared to provide the Soviet leaders with the
words and treaty that their bureaucratic souls pined for. Thus
immediately after the removal of the Ali Sabri pro-Soviet group
from power and Sadat's decision to jail them, the Soviet President
Podgorny arrived in Cairo with a request that their two countries
should sign a pact of friendship. Mohammed Heikal makes the
curious claim that it was Sadat who proposed that such a treaty
should be signed in order to reassure the Kremlin that he was
not abandoning his links with it. But this is hardly a convincing
claim.

If only to answer Western jibes, it would have been natural for
Podgorny to rush to Cairo to obtain formal assurances. Sadat
mentioned a cartoon in the Western press – which he appeared to
have enjoyed – showing Podgorny meeting Moscow's agents in
Egypt, all clad in prison overalls. Podgorny asked for a Soviet–
Egyptian treaty of friendship to be signed almost immediately.
Sadat had no objection to the treaty but he explained that the timing
was not right. Moscow's men had been arrested and not been tried
yet. Their case might be affected by the signing of the treaty. Their
reputation would be tarnished by the implication that they were
indeed Moscow's men.

Podgorny insisted that the treaty was essential. Although Egypt
was not happy with the way the Soviet Union was treating it, Sadat
said that he was ready to sign to show his country's good intentions.
'Please have confidence in us, confidence!'

Podgormy, whatever his private thoughts, appeared to be highly
satisfied and on leaving made the kind of promise that Sadat had
heard before: 'Give me four days and all the weapons you have
asked for will be shipped to you, including the retaliation weapon.'

Sadat waited more than four days. Three months passed and the weapons had still not arrived.

Sadat's opposition to the Communist attempted coup in Sudan widened the secret split between him and the Kremlin leaders. But in September 1971 he received a message from Moscow, inviting him for talks the following month. He hid the extent of his annoyance with the Soviet leaders and accepted the invitation. However, when he met them he told them: 'I don't mind if you keep me one step behind Israel but I find it a bit too much to be twenty steps behind.'

Again, wrote Sadat, the Soviet leaders made promises to send the required arms, dropping all conditions for their use. The crews of the SAM missiles, with their Soviet instructors, would no longer require approval from Moscow for their use against Israel. Even the sceptical Sadat was convinced that this time the Kremlin really intended to keep its promises. But by the end of the year, the promised weapons had still not arrived. Sadat learned of Soviet involvement in the Indo-Pakistani war and was told by the Soviet Ambassador that the Soviet leaders were very busy but would be ready to see him the following February.

In Israel and in the United States there was widespread derision at Sadat's unfulfilled claims. The so-called year of decision had passed without any significant event. Sadat was particularly hurt by an insulting remark, as he saw it, by William Rogers, the US Secretary of State, that 1971 had come and gone and no decisive action had been taken by the Egyptian President. Sadat attributed this insult to Rogers's desire to regain his standing with the American Jewish community after earlier backing Egypt. Moreover, Rogers announced that arms supplies to Israel would be increased, that the USA would start manufacturing arms in Israel and that the USA would ensure Israeli superiority not only over Egypt but over all the Arab states together.

This, according to Sadat, was a ferocious psychological campaign against him, as he had expected. And though he kept on publicly praising the Soviet Union, the Egyptian people's resentment against the Soviet leaders grew to new heights. This is not a claim that can be substantiated.

Although some weapons from the Soviet Union did start to

arrive, following yet another trip by Sadat to Moscow, he decided on a dramatic gesture. Sadat was not impressed by the visit of Field-Marshal Grechko who brought along with him a new advanced aircraft, the Sukhoy 17. What did impress Sadat was the outcome of the first summit between US President Richard Nixon and Brezhnev in Moscow in May 1972. According to Sadat, on yet another visit to Moscow, it was agreed that the Kremlin would send him an analysis of the USA–USSR summit. Soviet arms would be supplied in great quantities so that after a new US President was elected that November, Sadat would have the option of going to war with Israel if all avenues of peace were blocked.

When Brezhnev and Nixon issued a statement calling for military relaxation in the Middle East, Sadat saw it as a personal blow. It caused him, he claimed, a violent shock. Military relaxation meant that no major supplies of arms would be sent into the area and Egypt would be left 20 steps behind Israel. The decision meant 'giving in to Israel'.

9 · War and the great deception

When Anwar Sadat heard of Israeli and American reaction to his decision to expel, or as he told the Soviet Ambassador in Cairo, to 'dispense with' the services of the 15,000 Soviet experts in Egypt, he knew that his deception plan was working. The Israeli and American experts saw the expulsions as confirmation of their strongly held view that Sadat was bluffing, that he never intended to launch a war, that it was all bluff. Yet the 'expulsions' were part of an intricate deception. These experts who had not bothered to study carefully enough Anwar Sadat's personality and relied too much on his speeches failed to understand that the expulsions had a double purpose. First, he was furious with the Soviet leaders for letting him down, for making him appear like a clown on the world stage by accepting the American call for *détente* in the Middle East. It was entirely in line with his character that he would react so furiously.

According to Mohammed Heikal, Sadat saw himself as a Pharaoh. This is an exaggeration but certainly Sadat had an intense pride in the long history of the Egyptian people, with their powerful rulers, wonderful works of art, and complex civilisation. He looked upon most Arab leaders with disdain, pointing out that they owed their positions to the accidental discovery of oil. Otherwise their countries would have remained miserable collections of illiterate people, living on the charity of rich Western countries and subservient to their wishes. Thus Sadat found the conduct of the Soviet leaders a mixture of arrogance, condescension, and irritation, highly repugnant. His national pride was insulted by the lame excuses which gave the impression that the Soviet leaders thought that their lies would not be noticed by an unsophisticated people.

81

It can safely be said that no measure gave President Sadat so much satisfaction than being able to tell the Soviet Ambassador to remove the Soviet experts. Sadat writes about this episode with obvious relish. Not only did they have to leave but, to rub in the revenge blow, they had to be out of the country within a week! This, indeed, was responding with insult against insult. However, having the mind of a true conspirator, which allowed him to outwit the lawyers who tried to nail him, Sadat understood the value of the expulsion in his deception plan.

In one of the most revealing passages in his memoirs, the significance of which has not been widely noticed, Sadat remarked that he expected world reaction to the expulsions. He wanted to have the option of war or peace but the Soviet leaders would not allow him to go to war. He had therefore to teach them a lesson by expelling the experts and at the same time gain freedom of action. The reaction of the Kremlin, the Israelis and the Americans in thinking that he would not now fight served his purpose, he wrote.

His words, however, were themselves partly a deception. For the Soviet leaders were not deceived as he knew well. When Golda Meir heard of the Sadat order, her intuition told her that the move meant danger, possibly war. She rationalised her fears, saying to herself that some intuitions are wrong. She consulted all the top experts who carefully analysed the intelligence reports sent in abundance by first-class agents and they told her not to worry. So she took no action. Yet there was a double bluff concerning the Soviet Union which was to prove far more effective even than the misconception of Sadat's aim in expelling the Soviet experts.

Sadat has described how he went to Alexandria, which he had not visited since the 1967 defeat, and began to prepare for the battle with Israel – or for peace talks. He summoned Hafiz Ismail, the National Security Adviser, and told him that there was likely to be an approach from the United States and he should be ready with the necessary alternative for a dialogue which could be successfully concluded. Simultaneously he summoned War Minister Muhammed Sadiq and ordered him to convene the Supreme Council on the following day and inform it that Sadat had decided that the armed forces should be ready for fighting, for launching an attack as from 15 November 1972.

On discovering that War Minister Sadiq was less than enthusiastic about launching an attack, he quickly dismissed him and appointed Marshal Ahmed Ismail Ali in his place. Sadat accused Sadiq not only of being defeatist but of lying to him. However, other Egyptian generals held similar views to Sadiq's. Major-General Abdel Munim Wasil, who had commanded the Third Army, gave a desolate picture of the state of the Egyptian forces in confronting the Israeli forces. Wasil argued that the Egyptians were completely 'exposed', that any concentration would be immediately noticed by the Israelis, so that the Egyptians would be attacked before they could cross the Canal.

According to Wasil, the Israelis had built a huge chain of fortifications, an earthwork 47 feet high, while the Egyptian one was merely ten feet high. The Egyptians feared, said Wasil, that the Israelis had built a tremendous network of electronic equipment behind their line, made more fearsome because it could not be observed from the western, Egyptian, bank of the Canal.

To Sadat this was a major blow. Nasser, he recalled later, had left him with Defence Plan 200. Whenever the Israelis increased the height of their fortifications by three feet, the Egyptians would increase theirs by five feet. But Sadiq had failed to maintain this plan. Nasser, despite his bombast, had not left any offensive plan. At least Defence Plan 200 was a perfectly reasonable one, in Sadat's eyes, but this, too, had been abandoned.

In Marshal Ali Sadat found the right man to quell some of his anxieties. In sleepless nights, Sadat worried how Egypt could defend itself if Israel launched an offensive, however unlikely that might appear to foreign observers. Ali reactivated the Defence Plan 200, for which a large sum was immediately allocated, despite Egypt's perilous economic situation. Egyptian fortifications rose to 65 feet and the soldiers could overlook the Israeli defences which were far less formidable than had been imagined. The so-called Bar-Lev line, named after a former chief of staff, was hardly a defence line at all. It had no resemblance, even in miniature to the Maginot Line. It was merely a system of strung-out forts, defended by small numbers of troops. It was never intended to withstand a massive attack.

With Sadat there was always the fear that the Egyptian troops would again suffer the terrible humiliation of the 1967 Six-Day War. He knew that he could not survive such a catastrophe and believed that the stability of the entire country would be undermined. That was one reason why he wanted to make doubly sure that his offensive plans were feasible, though he knew that however well prepared for the limited war, his venture was still a gamble. Yet no ruler of Egypt had ever prepared for battle with such psychological skill, outwitting the most brilliant minds in İsrael and in the West.

Even in his memoirs, Sadat lays traps for the unwary. His account of the pre-war preparations for the assault across the Suez Canal is far from complete. Strangely, he gives himself far less credit for the initial success of the venture than could be expected. Any Soviet leader reading his account would have found it grossly unfair. And the wily US Secretary of State Henry Kissinger would have resented the clear implication that his remarks encouraged Sadat to break the diplomatic deadlock by undertaking a risky war. Sadat agreed that after a visit to Moscow in February 1973, eight months after the expulsion of the Soviet military experts, the Soviet leaders not only agreed to provide the Egyptians with a record amount of arms but sent much of them promptly, even in record time. Sadat claimed that they soon stopped, to be resumed only in 1975.

Sadat did not consider that one of the reasons for the cessation of the arms supplies was the Kremlin's fear that Sadat might undertake a larger attack than was thought advisable. In Soviet minds there were also doubts whether the Egyptians were capable of winning a full-scale war against Israel. In their talks with the Americans, they made no secret of their contempt for Egyptian soldiers.

The deception plan by the Egyptians and the Syrians was brilliantly executed and yet could easily have failed had the Israelis and the Americans not been totally blinded by preconceived notions. The most effective ploy was carried out by Sadat himself. He used the media and massed troops near the canal in May 1973 to give the impression that war was imminent. With Moshe Dayan's prompt-ing, the Israeli government ordered mobilisation. The crucial days passed without any attack. In August, Sadat again played the same trick, and obtained the same result. Sadat claimed that when after the October War Dayan was asked why he had not mobilised his troops on time, he replied 'Sadat made me do it twice at a cost of ten million dollars each time. So when it was the third time round, I thought he was not serious, but he tricked me'.

Sadat played on the Israeli conception that as his armed forces were still not strong enough and had no chance of winning, he could not possibly wish to start a war. So strong was this concept, made firmer by memories of the devastating 1967 war, that even the clearest evidence of Egyptian and Syrian preparation for war was ignored. Moshe Dayan had in May 1973 given a general warning to his generals to expect war by the late summer but, strangely, did not follow up this warning with appropriate measures. Even when the Syrian and Egyptian armies had been mobilised and had brought their troops to an offensive position, the Israeli generals accepted the ruse that the moves were part of the annual manoeuvres. Only on the Golan Heights did the commanding General Hoffe become uneasy and demanded and got extra tanks after appealing to Dayan.

So blind – or arrogant – were most Israeli generals, including those responsible for the intelligence services, that major leaks by the Egyptians were not properly evaluated or were totally ignored. Thus the official Mena news agency circulated a report that two of Egypt's premier divisions – which were to launch the attack across the canal – had been put on the alert. Apparently several foreign military attachés saw bridging equipment moving from near Cairo airport to the Suez road. SAM missiles were moved forward towards the canal. These facts were most probably received by army intelligence in Israel but were disregarded. No wonder the Egyptian generals were amazed at their luck. There had been an estimate that the Israelis, with their efficient espionage system (they were thought to have an effective cell within Egypt) and their first-class air surveillance system would discover the Egyptian plans at least 15 days before the attack. To their astonishment the Egyptian generals noted that the Israeli forces made no depositions to meet an attack across the canal. Despite great efforts to keep the plan for the attack – codenamed Badr – secret, the American CIA actually obtained a copy. But it did not believe that Sadat intended to put it into effect.

In this estimate, the CIA was at least partly influenced by Israeli confidence that the chances of Sadat launching a war were very remote.

Possibly the main reason why the deception plan worked so well was that almost every statesman, with the striking exception of King Hussein of Jordan, could not understand what Sadat was aiming at. When Sadat expelled the Soviet military advisers, the Israelis and the Americans saw the action as a sign that he was abandoning the military option. Only King Hussein warned the Americans that Sadat might be clearing the decks for war, having decided that the Soviet experts, on the Kremlin's orders, might try to obstruct him.

Even Henry Kissinger, with all his sophistication, was unable until the war had broken out to fathom Anwar Sadat's intentions. There was pressure on the Nixon administration and on the former and new Secretaries of State to try to solve the apparently intractable Middle East problem. While William Rogers dived headlong into the morass, emerging bewildered, having his peace plan rejected by Israel, Kissinger was much more cautious.

Although a non-practising Jew, Kissinger never forgot that 13 members of his family had died in Nazi concentration camps. He was not willing to encourage another Holocaust by forcing Israel to adopt policies which might be fatal for its security. Yet as a man who had achieved great prominence as a professor at Harvard and as a statesman after arriving as a refugee boy from Germany in 1938, Kissinger had to keep foremost in his mind the fact that he was now an American, not a Jewish, Secretary of State. Every policy had to be defended as being in the interest not of Israel but of the United States. As he noted in his memoirs, he had a special obligation, in view of the suspicions against his religion, to ensure that fair-minded people noted that he was working only as an American patriot. This caused him some painful experiences.

Strangely, it was in Israel rather than in any of the Arab countries that he was accused of acting unethically. Perhaps the most vicious were the attacks by those who mixed religion with politics and who castigated him with a double charge of pursuing anti-Israel policies and marrying a *shiksa*, a non-Jewish woman. There is, of course, a special danger for a Jew asked by his country to deal with inter-national, or even national, problems affecting the Jewish people. He may be tempted – consciously or unwittingly – into taking unwise actions to prove his non-commitment to any Jewish cause. A case in point is Herbert Samuel, appointed High Commissioner in Palestine in 1920, after he himself had played a notable role in the issuing of the Balfour Declaration promising a homeland for the Jewish people. Some of his actions were less than judicious, notably the one appointing the notorious anti-British agitator, Hajj Amin Al-Husaini, as the Grand Mufti.

Kissinger appears not to have been prone to such weaknesses. He admits, however, that he was as deceived as any of his officials or colleagues about Sadat's intentions. Yet, if his recollections in writing are to be fully accepted and not seen merely as a sophisticated version of hindsight, Kissinger had made an astute, if not profound, study of the reasons for the failures of the various attempts to solve the Arab–Israeli problem. Surprisingly, he came to the conclusion that what the Middle East needed was not a frenetic attempt to make peace between Israel and the Arabs but a prolonged stalemate that would move the Arabs towards moderation and the Soviet Union away from the centre towards the fringes of the conflict. President Nixon, fearing that the State Department under Rogers might propose solutions which would antagonise many Americans, especially in the run-up to the 1972 presidential election, began shifting responsibility to Kissinger late in 1971. This made Kissinger's private views particularly important.

For those who naively believed that Golda Meir had missed a golden opportunity for peace by rejecting Sadat's overtures in 1971 were disabused by Kissinger. He pointed out that Sadat was not ready for a bilateral agreement with Israel, which he was to accept later with Menachem Begin. Sadat sought a comprehensive peace in which all the Arab states participated. But Syria refused to make peace with Israel in any circumstances. Nor did Yasser Arafat's Palestine Liberation Organisation agree. The Iraqis had not even agreed to sign a ceasefire after the 1948 war. And Jordan's King Hussein, while prepared enough to talk directly to the Israelis – in secret – was nervous of making any deal with Israel in case he was accused by Arab radicals of surrendering to the Jews. As Sadat later remarked, what was needed was the breakdown of the psychological barrier between Arab and Jew. It needed a war and several years of bargaining under the drive and supervision of Kissinger to achieve this, and then only partially.

The famous United Nations Resolution 242 of 22 November 1967, of which the British Foreign Secretary George Brown was so proud, proved more of a hindrance than an aid to peace. The resolution spoke of a 'just and lasting peace' and 'secure and recognised boundaries', but was interpreted differently by the Arabs and the Israelis. There was even a single but vital difference between the French and English versions. In the English version, Israel was requested to withdraw from occupied territories but not from 'the' territories, an omission which was deliberately engineered by the Americans and enabled the Israelis to accept the resolution.

Kissinger may or may not have known the saying that the Arabs could not make peace without Syria and war without Egypt. The Egyptians formed the largest and most cultured part of the Arab people. They had passionately adopted the cause of the Palestinians, had fought wars and lost many thousands of young men on their behalf. Yet Egypt appeared to be the only Arab country that did not rule out peace while talking of war. Although Nasser owed his survival in the 1956 Suez War to President Eisenhower, he adopted an anti-American pro-Soviet policy which made Middle East peace an impossibility. In his vision as a pan-Arab leader, Israel had no part in the Middle East. Like most Arab nationalists he saw Israel as an affront to the feelings of the Arab peoples. He never envisaged a time when he would sign a full peace agreement with the Jewish State and receive an Israeli Ambassador in Cairo. So ingrained was this negative policy in the hearts of Arabs that it took Sadat painful years to realise that he had to make an historic break with old attitudes. A year after Nasser's death, he was still living mostly in the rejectionist world but he was beginning to give signals that were only partly understood in the West. It was fortunate that one of those who began to comprehend the special role of Egypt, if not yet of Anwar Sadat, was the US Secretary of State, Dr Kissinger.

Apart from the huge outcry which would have occurred had he wished to abandon Israel to its fate, Kissinger felt that it would be against American interests to force a settlement on Israel. That would have been seen as a victory for the Soviet Union and for the Arab radicals who were engaged in a bitter struggle with the moderates for control of the Arab states.

It is curious that Sadat totally omitted to mention the two-track negotiations which he conducted with the American government when Kissinger was the National Security Adviser and William Rogers was Secretary of State. Sadat's special envoy, Hafiz Ismail met officially the Secretary of State and his advisers but they did not know that he was meeting Kissinger at secret locations. The State Department was pushing an interim agreement which President Nixon disliked and which Sadat opposed. But a comprehensive agreement was also not an achievable objective, even when discussed theoretically at secret meetings. Sadat was ready to sign an agreement, provided Israel met the conditions of the other Arab groups – a sheer impossibility.

While immensely impressed by Golda Meir's formidable character, Kissinger appeared to think, though he never said so specifically, that her approach to the Arab–Israel conflict was simplistic. The idea of giving up any land was almost physically painful to her. She considered Israel so strong that there was no need to make any concessions to the Arabs, especially giving up territory. She was prepared to sign an interim disengagement agreement with Egypt along the Suez Canal as a step towards a final settlement but would not agree to final boundaries before the negotiations started, a stand from which Israeli governments have never wavered and that seems reasonable enough.

The secret talks between Kissinger and Ismail were bound to fail because the United States was not in a position – nor was it willing – to provide Sadat with a comprehensive settlement which he sought as an entrance ticket for meaningful talks with the Israelis. Such a condition would at the very least have entailed Israel agreeing to give up all the territories conquered in the Six-Day War, including east Jerusalem, clearly an impossibility at any time but even more so when Israel felt so superior to and contemptuous of the Arab states.

Sadat, as Kissinger saw it, was placed in a dilemma from which he was unable to extricate himself by diplomatic means. The Israelis refused to negotiate with him on his terms. If he accepted a step-by-step approach he would lose the support of the Soviet Union and of Syria. If he went for a separate peace with Israel, he would be ostracised by the Arab world and most probably overthrown in his country by his outraged people.

Kissinger later felt that Sadat chose a limited war to obtain his diplomatic ends. It is difficult to argue with Kissinger on this point; he makes a very powerful and convincing case. He might also have mentioned that the former young officer who felt so humiliated by the 1967 débâcle and spoke so passionately to Nasser about a guerrilla war against the Israelis, was also seeking an opportunity for the Egyptian forces to regain their honour in combat. He would then be able to prove to the Egyptian people that he was not negotiating with the Israelis from a position of weakness and defeat but from strength, a matter of great importance to an Arab nation.

Yet Anwar Sadat's words, while undoubtedly stressing his commitment to fighting, also imply that almost until at least the mdidle of 1972 he was still hoping that he might regain Arab territories without launching a war. Sadat could be a very passionate man and he could be moved almost to tears when speaking about the justice of the Arab case. His deep faith in Allah might well have encouraged him to hope for a miracle. Only when he became totally convinced that Egypt would have to fight to regain its honour and to have a chance of negotiating for the return of Arab territories in general and Sinai in particular did he give the order for launching the Yom Kippur War.

10 · How Soviet leaders joined in Sadat's deception game

After the Yom Kippur War, Arab leaders ridiculed the notion that there had been a degree of collusion between Anwar Sadat and the Soviet leaders. There was, it appears, less certainty about the Kremlin's collusion with President Assad of Syria.

In his public statements and in his memoirs, Sadat condemned the Soviet role in the war, accusing the Kremlin of pressing him almost from the start of the offensive to seek a ceasefire and of not providing him with the promised arms. Yet, apart from new evidence revealing that the Kremlin knew of Sadat's and Assad's war plans, there are some awkward questions for those who still argue that the Kremlin was kept in darkness about the Yom Kippur or (as Sadat called it) the October War.

There is, for example, the curious story of Arab terrorists capturing in September 1973 a group of Soviet immigrants bound for Israel. Two gunmen broke into one of the trains taking the immigrants to Austria and to the transit camp at Schonau. The gunmen informed the Austrian government of Chancellor Bruno Kreisky that if the government did not cease to give aid to the immigrants from the Soviet Union and closed down Schonau, not only would the kidnapped people be killed but there would be acts of violence against Austria.

To the horrified astonishment of the Israeli government, Chancellor Kreisky quickly gave in to the terrorists' demands and announced that he would close Schonau. His decision was seen as particularly outrageous and cowardly as Kreisky was himself a Jew who had suffered during the Hitler period. Golda Meir saw Kreisky's act as such a blow to the immigration of Jews from the Soviet Union, as Austria was at the time the major exit point, and such a triumph for the Arab terrorists that she felt compelled to appeal to him personally. But Kreisky remained adamant and refused to abandon the decision to close Schonau. Golda graphically remembered that her mouth felt as if it were filled with ashes.

This was the week before the fatal week when war broke out. The news of the terrorist kidnapping and of the Austrian decision filled the Israeli newspapers to the almost entire exclusion of reports of what was happening in Egypt and Syria. Golda Meir's mind was filled with thoughts of the double outrage. Commentators asked later whether this incident was deliberately staged by Sadat and Assad to draw Israeli attention away from the critical points. It was certainly a very useful diversion. But a more interesting question was how did the armed Arab terrorists manage to get on the train as it was passing through Czechoslovakia? It is inconceivable that the Czech Communist authorities would not have been aware of the presence of two armed foreigners on a train in their country. It must be assumed that the Czech Communists worked together with their colleagues in the Soviet Union to ensure that the Arab terrorists had freedom to act against the hapless Jewish immigrants. The incident could, of course, have been a coincidence but it is far more likely that this was part of the larger war deception plan.

Against this is the curious action of the Soviet leadership almost on the eve of the battle. Sadat had agreed with Assad that on Thursday, 4 October, he would inform the Soviet Ambassador in Cairo of the precise date of the attack. But on that very Thursday, Sadat was told that the Ambassador wished to see him urgently. Sadat thought that the Ambassador wanted to give him the reply from the Kremlin to his request for arms. Instead the Ambassador stated that the Soviet leadership sought permission for four large Soviet aircraft to arrive in Egypt to take the families of Soviet civilians, who had worked in factories and civil establishments, out of the country. Strangely, in view of his intricate deception plan, Sadat did not protest against this request which normally would have alerted the Israelis and the Americans that an Egyptian attack was imminent. Sadat merely felt disappointed that the Ambassador did not bring news about Soviet arms. He also saw it as a bad omen that the Soviet Union believed he was heading for defeat.

Possibly Sadat thought it better to allow the families to leave than try to keep them in the country until the war started. A dispute with the Soviet Union at this juncture could, indeed, have proved harmful. Had he been able to listen in to the discussion in the Israeli Cabinet he would have felt satisfied. In her memoirs Golda Meir does not refer to the evacuation of Soviet families from Egypt but to the families of Russian advisers from Syria. This is possibly an oversight but shows how little importance was attached by the Israeli leaders to the episode, an astonishing lapse, even in the atmosphere prevailing in Jerusalem. Golda claimed that she was worried by the report. It reminded her of what had happened before the Six-Day War but nobody else appeared perturbed. She asked the Minister of Defence (Moshe Dayan), the Chief of Staff (General Elazar) and the head of intelligence whether they thought this piece of information was very important. No, they told her, the report had not in any way changed their assessment of the situation. She was assured that Israel would get sufficient warning if real trouble was coming. In any case sufficient reinforcements were being sent to the fronts, the Premier was told. However, to the end of her days she blamed herself for not listening to her intuition but relying on the advice of her ministers and military leaders.

Much of the behaviour of the Soviet leaders becomes logical if both Sadat and they pursued a double-track policy which deceived the Americans and the Israelis. But Sadat proved himself far tougher and braver than the Kremlin imagined.

David Kimche, a former senior member of Israel's Mossad intelligence agency and later Director-General of the Foreign Ministry, rejected in his book *The Last Option* the notion, accepted by Western observers, that it was Sadat who insisted on the expulsion of the Soviet military experts in 1972. Kimche argued that it was a fundamental Soviet strategic decision, first taken by Brezhnev in 1970. In answer to questions after the publication of his book, David Kimche informed me that there were eleven distinct sources, two of the most important being first-hand records in Foreign Minister Mahmoud Riad's memoirs and General Shazly's diaries, and one based on documents by the head of the Egyptian Department of Naval History, Commodore Mohrez Mlahmoud el Husseini, whose account was confirmed by Egypt's War Minister and Chief of Staff.

According to Kimche the sequence of events leading to the Soviet decision is important. Riad stated in his memoirs, *The Struggle for Peace in the Middle East*, that on 19 June 1970, US Secretary of State William Rogers sent him a message which encouraged him to believe that the United States was about to adopt a more pro-Arab point of view. Thus encouraged, Nasser asked his Chief of Staff, General Fawzi, for a military assessment which would allow Egypt to revert to a military solution, so as to liberate Arab territories in the spring of 1971 at the latest.

Riad advised Nasser to consult Brezhnev. On 30 June 1970 Nasser met Brezhnev in Moscow. According to Riad, Brezhnev asked whether Egypt was planning to resolve the crisis by peace or war. Nasser replied that no peace with Israel was possible until Egypt could impose its terms on Israel by force.

At a further meeting with Brezhnev in Moscow on 16 July 1970, Nasser told Brezhnev that the Soviet Union must become involved in the war against Israel. This statement evidently worried Brezhnev. He instructed Marshal Zakharov, chief of the Soviet general staff, to consult with his Egyptian opposite number, General Fawzi, and to request Nasser to work towards ending the presence of most of the Soviet experts, especially in the field of air defence missiles, and replacing them with Egyptian personnel. This, in turn, worried Nasser and he asked that the withdrawal be postponed for six months until Egyptian experts had completed their training.

On 1 October 1970, after Nasser's funeral, Soviet Premier Kosygin met the new acting President Sadat, leading members of Nasser's Cabinet and heads of the armed forces. Kosygin insisted that the Egyptian government should make every possible effort to replace Soviet personnel with Egyptians before battle commenced.

Throughout 1971 Brezhnev and Marshal Grechko, says Kimche in his special memorandum, stressed to Sadat that they already had overwhelming numerical superiority over Israel in men and arms. Where Egypt was inferior was in training and organisation. This would have to be corrected before Egypt could go to war against Israel. Grechko gave specific facts and figures, supported by Fawzi, to bear out this concept.

Though prepared to help Egypt with arms Brezhnev became alarmed at the prospect of the Egyptians launching a war before they were ready. This concern reached a peak during the Moscow meetings with Sadat in February and April 1972. Brezhnev was preparing for the Moscow summit with Nixon and Kissinger, with *détente* as his prime objective. But Sadat was pressing ever more for war and threatening to urge a US–Soviet confrontation to help him with the liberation of Israel-occupied Arab lands.

Secret Soviet–Egyptian preparations for war with Israel had gone on throughout 1971, without the Americans being aware of it, judging from Kissinger's memoirs and other contemporary sources. Kimche says that it is evident from the accounts by Riad, Shazly and Hussini that Brezhnev and Grechko had believed that they could regulate and delay the Egyptian war plans by controlling the flow of arms to Egypt. But when Brezhnev realised in April–May 1972 that Sadat was prepared to disrupt the Soviet plans for *détente* with the US he decided to withdraw Soviet troops and advisers before they could be involved in Sadat's planned war with Israel.

It was, adds Kimche, a two-tier move. The withdrawal of the Soviet advisers would delay Sadat's plans while the simultaneous increase in Soviet military aid would reassure Sadat and encourage him to wait for more of the promised help. Brezhnev thought that he had ensured his *détente* with the US and the delay of Sadat's military action until all the plans for launching the attack across the Suez Canal were in place. The decision to withdraw the Soviet military advisers was taken during the Moscow talks of 27 April–10 May, Kimche stated. Sadat had wanted Brezhnev to agree to a face-saving joint Soviet–Egyptian statement announcing the Soviet withdrawal and expressing Egyptian gratitude for the Soviet help. Brezhnev declined, insisting, to Sadat's surprise and pleasure that Egypt should handle the situation as it saw fit but alone. Sadat did this in his own inimitable manner. Brezhnev did not like the story that his men were being expelled by a furious Sadat, but it had the advantage of reassuring the Americans.

Reflecting on Sadat's version of the expulsion of the advisers, Riad wrote that the Russians welcomed their expulsion from Egypt, as shown by the speed with which the operation was implemented. The Kremlin was very reluctant to maintain its military presence once the war was bound to erupt. That was the reason why the Soviet Union continued, after the departure of the experts and units, to support Egypt militarily. In fact, the Soviet Union supplied Egypt with more sophisticated arms than were made available earlier and continued to do so after the October War of 1973 started.

Having been informed about 9 July 1972 of Sadat's 'decision to expel the Russians', Shazly remarked: 'I found myself reflecting seven years later, why now? In his memoirs Sadat claims that he took the decision as an instant response to a Soviet rebuff. But in the light of all that has happened in the intervening years, I am certain that the decision was in fact calculated, pre-arranged with others whose role Sadat is still anxious to conceal.'

There were, Shazly said, only 7,752 Soviet personnel in Egypt at the time, not 15,000 or 20,000 as assumed by the Americans. Some 2,590 had left by the end of July 1972. The remaining 5,162 left by the end of August. They did not return to the Soviet Union but were transferred to Syria to assist in the switch preparations for the October War. According to Kimche, there was indirect confirmation of this version. Thus General Sadiq, then still the Egyptian chief of staff, told the Armed Forces Supreme Council after a meeting in Moscow with Marshal Grechko: 'Moscow wanted to keep the international scene quiet for at least another six months until after the US presidential election.'

Sadat reported to the Council, according to Shazly, that the Russians had told the Egyptian Prime Minister Sidky that the Soviet–US *détente* would never affect Soviet relations with Egypt. It was Soviet policy to continue its support for Egypt including supplying weapons.

Twelve months after the supposed expulsion of the Soviet advisers, General Samakhodsky, the new principal Soviet liaison officer in Cairo, told Shazly that General Sapkov and 63 Soviet special advisers would be arriving within eight to ten days to train Egyptian personnel. A month later Shazly noted that the new Soviet military mission had begun training an Egyptian missile brigade while Soviet equipment was flooding in.

In December 1972, Kimche pointed out, within months of 'ending Soviet interference', Sadat renewed the agreement giving the Soviets continued naval facilities for another five years until December 1977. This allowed unhindered Soviet use of Egypt's naval facilities at Alexandria, Sollum and elsewhere, and of the attached airfields, targeted on the surveillance of the US Mediterranean fleet.

The shipment of Soviet arms continued to arrive throughout the summer and autumn of 1973. This, according to Commodore el Husseini, led Sadat to comment on the Soviet attitude: 'All taps have been fully turned on. It looks as if the Soviets want to push me into battle!'

In his book *The Last Option*, Kimche sees Brezhnev, rather than Nasser or Sadat, or Assad of Syria, as the man who deliberately orchestrated the 1967 and 1973 wars. In this view Kimche, of course, goes against all the analyses that have come from Israeli, American leaders as well as most academic historians. Kimche claims that Brezhnev was shocked by the Egyptian débâcle in 1967 and planned a revenge war against Israel which would wipe out Soviet as well as Arab humiliation.

Brezhnev, according to Kimche, had a double policy in which he gave a leading role not to Egypt but to Syria. Brezhnev had become convinced by the arguments of the former Soviet Ambassador to Israel, D. Chuvakhin, that Egypt would not be able to strike a decisive blow against Israel so long as the Egyptians were not in control of the Sinai Peninsula. However, Syria could do so – under certain conditions. It was, therefore, the Soviet role to provide Syria with those conditions. Despite opposition to this concept by the Soviet military establishment, which had invested huge amounts of weapons in Egypt, Brezhnev acted on it, at first stealthily, with the vital support of Marshal Grechko.

Syria's armed forces had been devastated in the Six-Day War of 1967. At its end, Syria had only 25 serviceable aircraft and fewer than 200, mostly ageing, tanks, and had lost most of its artillery. Hardly a year later the Syrians had 150 aircraft, 800 tanks and 700 guns, supplied by Brezhnev. Soviet technicians, advisers and troops were sent to Syria even before they entered Egypt. They were already having a significant effect on the Syrian forces when the air force commander, Hafez Assad, seized power in 1970, retaining it until this very day. Assad was able to consolidate his power, despite being a member of the minority Alowite sect, with the aid of the powerful arms he was receiving from the Soviet Union. By the end of 1971, he possessed 1,200 of the Soviet Union's most advanced tanks.

As the Syrians and the Egyptians, together with the Soviet

Union, began the planning of the next war, the approach and out-come of which was to be so different from the Six-Day War, a prime consideration, Kimche stated, was to keep the Americans and the Israelis unaware of what was happening.

No doubt Henry Kissinger was horrified to learn later the allega-tion that he himself had unwittingly played a leading role in the disinformation campaign. Kimche sees Sadat as the main source for the contemporary history of the period. And it was Sadat, acting on the suggestion of the Soviet advisers, who hinted to the American representative in Cairo, Don Burgos, that he would like to have a private channel of communications with Kissinger. When this was accepted by the Americans Sadat, benefiting from President Nixon's doubts about the State Department and placing greater reliance on Kissinger, nominated, as has been mentioned, Hafiz Ismail, a presentable officer in his forties, whom both Kissinger and Sadat found acceptable.

Before going to Washington, Hafiz Ismail had been to Moscow and discussed his mission with Brezhnev, Grechko and Kosygin. He informed them of the message that he was carrying from Sadat, to the effect that Egypt was deeply frustrated by Soviet conduct and was unhappy with its leaders. Brezhnev liked the idea, for it fitted in with his concern to neutralise Kissinger whom he saw as a danger to Soviet interests. Kissinger apparently swallowed Ismail's version of Soviet–Egyptian relations. The result was what the Kremlin and Sadat had hoped for – the attention of the Americans and the Israelis was turned away from the actual preparations of the war.

There was, Kimche stated, a degree of genuine Egyptian dissatis-faction with the Russians, which made the disinformation so much easier to pass on and to be believed. Sadat had learned of the huge supplies of arms being sent to Syria but he still needed the Soviet Union for his own plans. Sadat accepted with reluctance the Soviet war plan. Egypt, still incapable of liberating the Sinai Peninsula, would be used as 'meat grinder' that would badly maul Israel's forces on the Suez Canal, while the offensive role, aiming at landing a crucial blow on the Jewish State, would be given to Syria. As it happened, on the eve of the Yom Kippur War, Israel had only 12,000 men and 170 tanks along the entire northern front, facing 60,000 Syrian troops, with 1,300 tanks, 1,000 guns, 500 launchers and 300 combat aircraft. This powerful force, ten miles from Jordan, was to strike into the heartland of Israel. In the event, it came close to succeeding.

There were, however, different concepts, according to Kimche. Sadat accepted the limited military task for his forces but he had a much wider diplomatic project. For him it was, in effect, an extension of the idea of using war to stir diplomacy. Without telling Brezhnev or Assad he was hoping that the great shock to the Israeli forces, and its heavy losses after the Egyptian crossing of the Suez Canal, would induce Israel and the great powers to intervene and force a ceasefire, allowing Sadat to control the canal and reoccupy a significant part of Sinai. A weakened Israel, with its forces no longer perceived as invincible, would eventually be forced, by political means, to abandon all the conquests of the Six-Day War – the rest of Sinai, the West Bank, Gaza, the Golan Heights and east Jerusalem.

In his effort to co-ordinate the actions of the two Arab armies, Brezhnev went to great lengths. He was well aware that Sadat was trying to trick him by adopting a less militarily demanding plan, the so-called Granite 2, instead of the much more ambitious Granite 1 which had been taken to Moscow but the Soviet leader, in fact, accepted the change. Egypt's lesser role meant that the Soviet plan of giving priority to Syria and using the Suez front as a trap to tempt the bulk of the Israeli forces while the Syrian front was denuded, was being given an even better chance of succeeding. President Assad was given an apartment in the Kremlin during his frequent trips to Moscow, so that he could have quick access to Brezhnev. The training of the two Arab armies, now plentifully supplied with the most modern arms, went ahead with urgent speed, under Soviet supervision. To make absolutely certain that the crossing of the Suez Canal would take place as planned against a weakened and surprised enemy, Egyptian troops were trained in crossing a replica canal on a site on the distant Karakoum Canal to the southeast of Tashkent.

There were still last-minute diplomatic efforts, primarily by Kissinger. In the spring of 1973, barely six months before the outbreak of the war, Kissinger told Golda Meir that from messages he had received from Sadat, through the special secret channel, a substantive Israeli peace initiative would receive serious consideration in Cairo. Mrs Meir persuaded her Cabinet to go beyond the offer she had made earlier in the year to Nixon and Kissinger. Sadat was told that he could have back the whole of the Sinai Peninsula in return for a peace settlement with Israel. Sadat, says Kimche, replied that Israel would first have to withdraw from all occupied territories to the 1967 boundaries. In return, Egypt would abandon the state of war but no more. There would be no recognition of Israel and no diplomatic relations. Kissinger commented that Egypt had handed the power of veto to the PLO and they did not want peace. Kimche insists that at this point, Sadat's mind was set on war, not peace.

Every detail had been worked out by Brezhnev. He proposed to Assad but not to Sadat that he would request a cease-fire immediately after the initial Syrian breakthrough, so as to forestall the expected Israeli counter-attack, especially by the air force. The Kremlin expected that within days, Syrian armoured divisions would have entered Galilee and a cease-fire would leave them there. Brezhnev planned not merely to take revenge for his humiliation in the Six-Day War, not merely to win the immediate battle with Israel but to inflict such wounds that it would never again be able to embarrass the Soviet Union.

11 · *The October explosion*

So devious were Anwar Sadat's methods of misleading the Western and most of the Arab world that not even today is it certain beyond any doubt that accounts given by the most respectable and respected historians, generals and experts can be accepted. For one thing, they vary so much. Even Arab commentators disagree.

As has been seen, Dr Henry Kissinger does not accept that there was full collusion between Sadat and Brezhnev. Sadat himself denied that there was any collusion whatever and stressed that he fought the war despite Soviet discouragement. David Kimche, on the other hand, has amassed evidence which satisfies him that the Yom Kippur, October, War was planned and largely executed by Brezhnev, but that there was so much trickery by all sides and so much Israeli bravery, even beyond what one could expect from the Jewish State, that the Kremlin's and the Syrians' aims were thwarted.

The self-deception which the Israelis inflicted on themselves continued almost to the moment when the Egyptian troops began to cross the Suez Canal, and the Syrian tanks began to move on the Golan Heights. Only in the early hours of 6 October did the Israeli government receive information that finally convinced the Prime Minister and Defence Minister that the Egyptians and Syrians intended to attack that very day. But they still got the hour of the attack wrong – a mistake which was to cost many lives. They expected an attack at dusk but Sadat and Assad had decided on a different time, after a sharp dispute. The Egyptians wished to attack at a moment when the setting sun would be in the eyes of the defenders on the east bank of the Suez Canal. Such a time would give the advantage to the defenders on the Golan Heights and there were suggestions that the Syrians might start earlier. But this would have meant a loss of surprise and Assad finally accepted the 2 pm co-ordinated onslaught.

Sadat had at the very beginning chosen Yom Kippur in October as the best time to start the war. Yom Kippur is the holiest day in the Jewish calendar, when even non-religious Jews respect the solemnity of the day. Most Jews are in synagogues and fasting for 24 hours. The country closes down, except for the most essential services. It is the most difficult time to get in touch with anyone. For Israel, dependent as it is on mobilisation within 48 hours, as the vast majority of its soldiers are reservists, Yom Kippur is the worst day for a quick call-up.

In carrying out their attacks, Sadat and Assad attempted to adopt what they perceived as successful Israeli tactics. Israel, Sadat believed, had to rely on a quick war – which was true enough – because it was numerically so much smaller than its Arab enemies and could not survive a long struggle and heavy casualties. Israel had, therefore, to aim at an initial knock-out blow when most of its power was used to the most devastating effect. The Arabs had the advantage, in themselves launching the attack, of not only concentrating all their power in one place for a decisive strike but also of being able to lose many more soldiers. Sadat had, in fact, boasted that he was prepared to lose one million soldiers.

For Sadat and Assad there was not only the intellectual arrogance in the higher reaches of the Israeli government and armed forces which set the scene for the tremendous surprise of the first days of the Yom Kippur War. There was also the change in the intelligence and in the army field commands. General Aharon (Ariele) Yariv, a brilliant and perceptive head of army intelligence, had been succeeded by General Ze'ira, who looked more distinguished but did not possess such a flexible mind. Ze'ira was obdurately of the opinion that there was not going to be a war, ignoring all the evidence, an attitude that was to lead to his dismissal after the fighting. There is a story that while he was briefing war correspondents on the very day of the war, and discussing the position on the canal front, the director of his office gave him a piece of paper. He looked at it and said: 'They tell me a war may be starting any minute.'

He went on with the briefing. After a while another piece of paper was handed to him. Ze'ira looked at it, left the room, came back, and said: 'Gentlemen, the meeting is over.' As the correspondents left the Defence Ministry building in Tel Aviv, the air raid sirens were sounding.

Another unexpected event for the Arabs was the appointment of General Shmuel Gonen as commander of the southern front facing the Suez Canal. He was a splendid combat general with many outstandingly courageous actions which won him the respect of his troops. But he was not a strategist and not of the same calibre as Ariel (Arik) Sharon who combined brilliant combat ability with great strategic sense. Gonen, too, was to be dismissed from his post.

Sharon was later to be astonished and disconcerted to find the faulty disposition of Gonen's forces as the Egyptians attacked. A division of regular troops, with 300 tanks, covered the canal. But they were not prepared in time to meet an Egyptian assault. Two hundred of the 300 tanks were 60 miles away, instead of the agreed 20 or so miles. Equally destructive for Israel was that Gonen did not fulfil the plan to withdraw the men from the Bar-Lev Line as soon as the Egyptians attacked. Large numbers of casualties were thus unnecessarily incurred by the Israeli forces.

Had he known it, Anwar Sadat would not have felt any nervousness as he launched the attack. From his own description, it appears that Sadat had no notion of the overwhelming superiority in numbers, in weapons and in men.

Against General Avraham (Albert) Mandler's division with its 294 tanks, the Egyptians had assembled five infantry divisions, three mechanised divisions, and two armoured divisions. They marshalled between them over 1,400 tanks. The Israeli Army had been prepared to deal with a three-to-one disadvantage but this ratio was far larger. And to this had to be added the priceless asset of surprise. Yet surprise alone and massive superiority in numbers did not explain the Egyptian successes. In the first few days, Israeli forces used bad tactics. Tanks were used piecemeal to try to retrieve a tragic situation, as had happened on the Western Front in the First World War. Sharon complained bitterly that tanks were not used as a powerful force to drive back the Egyptians. Sharon also argued that Chief-of-Staff David Elazar and Gonen should have used two divisions – Adem's division was moving up quickly – to strike at the bridgeheads in the very early hours. But this is more a matter of debate by military experts.

General Gonen appears to have totally misunderstood the role that the Bar-Lev Line was to play in any future confrontations with the Egyptians. This was not a defence line at all, but merely a system of outposts, seven miles from each other, providing excellent sight of the Egyptian positions across the canal and giving protection to Israeli soldiers from Egyptian artillery barrages. Sharon had opposed the construction of the 'line', urging instead the use of mobile forces to deal with any emergency. But the building of the line was speedily undertaken from 1969 when Nasser intensified his war of attrition and in one barrage managed to kill 18 Israeli soldiers.

Sadat made sure that the whole Arab world would back his apparently dangerous undertaking. He travelled to several Arab countries, telling them of his intention to wage war against Israel but without giving any definite date. Now and then he gave hints that the war was near, as when he suggested that Palestinian volunteers should arrive in Egypt by the beginning of October. But these visits and hints had no effect on the watching Western intelligence services. They took their line from Israel.

Ironically, the Western intelligence chiefs were right to trust the Mossad, the Israeli espionage service, but wrong to believe that the military–political men who evaluated the information from the agents would not be blinded by fixed concepts. The Mossad had an effective espionage group in Egypt which reported regularly about the concentration of Egyptian troops on the canal and on many other – and obvious – signs of the urgent preparations for war. But just as Stalin discounted the many warnings he received of an imminent Nazi German attack in June 1941, so Golda Meir disregarded the equally compelling indications of war in October 1973.

At exactly 2 pm on 6 October 240 Egyptian aircraft flew low into Sinai, strafing and killing Israeli troops resting on Yom Kippur. Egyptian troops on the ground had been given special dispensation to have a meal, despite it being Ramadan. They had been fired up

104

by quotations from the Koran to go and eliminate the Jews and now they were encouraged by the sight above. Wave after wave crossed the waterway. They were amazed how little opposition they were encountering. They struggled up the dyke and around the Israeli strongpoints. Soon the Egyptian flag was flying on top of one of the strongpoints, surrounded by cheering soldiers shouting excitedly 'Allah Akbar'.

The first air strike was soon followed by another, equally success-ful. Few Egyptian planes were lost, among them one piloted by Squadron Commander Atef Sadat, the president's brother. Sadat was not immediately told of the identity of the dead pilot.

The Egyptians fought well, far better than the Israelis had expected. There were aspects of the Egyptian preparations of which they cannot be proud. Sadat himself at that time still possessed anti-Jewish prejudices. He boasted that he knew that the Israelis had a weakness for spending money and played on that in preparing the deception plan: they would not want to have too many call-ups. The troops under both Nasser and Sadat were told that the Israeli Jews were enemies that had to be crushed, as the Prophet Mohammed had crushed their forebears.

Far more than Nasser, Sadat saw the necessity of thorough training. Egyptian officers and men were better trained and better educated. University graduates were conscripted into the forces, the Egyptians having learned many of the lessons of the Six-Day War when the Israeli soldiers were shown to be better educated and far more strongly motivated.

As masses of Egyptian troops began to cross the canal, the out-numbered and initially outmanoeuvred Israelis were astonished by the amount of weapons that the attackers possessed. Because the Egyptian generals assumed that their infantry would be vulnerable to Israeli armour which moved forward to the banks of the Canal in the event of an emergency, there was a huge increase in the anti-tank weapons, far beyond what could have been expected. These included RPG rocket-assisted grenades, and Sagger anti-tank mis-siles. A large number of Israeli tanks were knocked out by these weapons. Egyptian engineers were also able to demolish the Israeli sand ramparts which made the east bank of the canal impassable for any armoured vehicles. It was found that high explosives would not be sufficient to remove them. The engineers discovered a solution whereby very high-pressure jets of water would cause the sand walls to disintegrate.

So well were the Egyptian troops trained and so thoroughly had they studied the problem of crossing the Canal that they overcame the disadvantage of being as surprised as the Israelis when told only shortly before the crossing that they were engaged in war and not in manoeuvres. A survey carried out among the 8,000 Egyptian prisoners in Israeli hands discovered that only one knew on 3 October about the date of the war and that 95 per cent of them learned the facts only on 6 October, the day of the attack.

Moving exactly as they had been trained, Egyptian troops stormed across the Canal, encountering strong resistance in some places and little in others. Egyptian generals had estimated that the crossing would entail 25,000–30,000 casualties, including 10,000 dead, but the actual figure was far less than they ever imagined – only 208 killed.

The initial Egyptian attack had achieved much more than its generals had hoped and the Israeli Defence Minister had expected. Egyptian forces had established themselves firmly on the east bank of the Canal. Hundreds of Israeli tanks had been destroyed. Many Israeli aircraft had been shot down. The situation looked bleak to Dayan. Even on the second day of the fighting, Dayan was suggesting that the army should withdraw to more defensible lines, the line of the Sinai passes. The State of Israel must be defended and, therefore, the lines had to be shortened.

So convinced was Dayan that this action was essential that he took the matter up with Golda Meir and Elazar was summoned to meet them. He argued strongly against withdrawal to the line of the passes because this would involve too heavy a cost to the Israeli forces by giving up or endangering headquarters and camps. He urged consolidation along a temporary line well west of the passes from where he would launch a counter-attack the next day. But that attack when it came proved a failure, and an Israeli brigade was destroyed. Many basic errors were made by the Israelis from which the Egyptians were able to benefit.

Addressing editors of Israeli newspapers after this setback, Moshe Dayan said glumly:

We cannot throw them back now and defeat them . . . What we should do is to deploy along new lines on this side and also in the southern part of Sinai . . . I do not believe that under normal circumstances any decision of the UN Security Council will stop [the Arabs] if from a physical, military point of view they believe they will be able to continue the war. First there will not be such a decision because the Chinese and Soviets will apply a veto. Secondly they will ignore any instruction to stop. One cannot rely on this. Israel can rely only on two elements; the lines which her forces will hold, and the continued growth of Israeli strength.

The editors were even more alarmed when Dayan described the Israeli losses: 'Hundreds of our tanks have been knocked out in battle. Part we can retrieve, part we cannot. In three days we have lost fifty planes . . .'

Dayan announced that he intended to go on television that evening to tell the truth to the Israeli public. One of the editors told him: 'If you tell the public today on television what you told us, this would mean an earthquake in the nation's consciousness.'

So sombre was the picture painted by Dayan that one of the editors burst into tears. Dayan gave the impression that Israel was on the verge of defeat and was running out of ammunition. Alerted, Golda Meir prevented Dayan from appearing on television and a commentary was given by the level-headed Aharon Yariv.

Dayan's virtual collapse at the start of the war was startling, considering the heroic image he portrayed and his undoubted achievements. Chaim Bar-Lev, the quietly spoken, deliberate former chief of staff, had a far better grasp of the situation. After the first successes achieved by the Syrians on the Golan Heights, Dayan similarly suggested a wide withdrawal. Golda Meir was comforted by Bar-Lev's assurances that the situation was far from lost. Standing her right arm on its elbow, she moved it from side to side, saying: 'The great Moshe Dayan! One day like this, one day like that!'

In comparison, Anwar Sadat met his own crisis, when it came, in a more commendable manner, from the Egyptian point of view. When others were losing their heads, he kept his own. Two events were to dash the cup of victory from his lips. In his vivid study of the fighting under the title of 'The War of Atonement', Major-General Chaim Herzog (later President of Israel) made it clear that the Israeli decision to cross the Canal from the east to the west was not, as has sometimes been thought, a brilliant innovation by Sharon. Such a possibility had been considered as a tactic even before the war broke out. Certainly, Sharon's powerful leadership of men in battle was to prove invaluable.

The tank battle which the Egyptians initiated on 14 October was one of the greatest ever to take place. Only that at Kursk in the Soviet Union in the Second World War, when the Nazis suffered a fateful defeat, was undoubtedly greater. Over 2,000 tanks took part in the battle. The Egyptians lost 264 tanks in the fighting, in addition to those destroyed by the Israeli Air Force. When the Egyptian commander, General Saad Mamoun, realised the full extent of the defeat he suffered a heart attack. This was a fateful day and marked the full recovery of the Israeli forces. The huge destruction of Egyptian armour meant that the crossing of the Canal could now be undertaken. It was on 15 October that this daring crossing took place at a strategic point known as Deversoir. Many outstanding Israeli soldiers made it possible, men like Sharon and Danny Matt. Sadat himself was later to hold Sharon in some awe. Sharon's reputation was to suffer grievously in the Lebanon war in 1982 but his vital role in turning the tide of the Yom Kippur War cannot be doubted.

Ironically, Sadat was now subjected to misinformation which he had earlier imposed on the Israelis. What made the blow greater was that the Israelis had found the most vulnerable spot in the battlefield – the unprotected junction of the Egyptian Second and Third Armies. Thanks to misinformation, Sadat did not take the Israeli crossing seriously. Altogether the Egyptians reacted with incredulity and even some amusement to the initial Israeli crossing. They believed that only a few tanks had managed to get across and that they would soon be wiped out. Sadat thought the crossing was merely a 'television operation' to boost the morale of the Israeli public.

Egyptian generals had not appreciated the strategic purpose of the Israeli crossing and the danger that the Third Army would be cut off. Only when Sadat visited the Egyptian headquarters did he realise the dire threat to the army. An element of panic crept into Egyptian behaviour. Describing the situation at the Egyptian High

Command, Mohammed Heikal admitted that the crossing 'had a considerable effect on strained nerves'.

When Sadat addressed a special session of the People's Council in Cairo on 16 October he was still unaware that the Israelis had been on the west bank of the Canal for several hours. Their tanks were roaming around the countryside knocking out surface-to-air sites, destroying tanks, and ambushing convoys. The High Command told him none of this, probably out of embarrassment, as well as a belief that the crossing was so small that it could be contained. The degree of his ignorance was shown by his remark: 'We are prepared at this hour, yes, even at this moment, to begin clearing the Suez Canal and opening for international shipping.'

This speech by Sadat had been the greatest moment of his presidency. Dressed in a splendid uniform, he was received as a national and beloved hero. He had brought back glory to the Egyptian people. He had removed the shame of the Six-Day War. His eyes glowed with pride. Who could deny that he richly deserved the applause and the adulation? Never again was he to taste the sweet fruits of a great national hero.

He had felt exultation when the first reports of the storming of the Israeli positions flooded in. Now the plaudits of the deputies set the seal on his happiness. When Sadat left the Parliament building, the cheers still ringing in his ears, he went immediately to the operations room of the High Command. He was told that a small number of amphibious Israeli tanks had succeeded in crossing the Canal at Deversoir to the west bank. However, the destruction of this force was imminent and a commando battalion had already been moved to carry out this task. Sadat told General Shazly to lay siege around the Israeli bridgehead, enabling the Israeli troops to enter but not to leave.

Three days later Sadat was summoned urgently to the operations room. Here he found a desperate Shazly. The general had personally investigated the Israeli crossing of the Canal and had come back a shattered man. 'The war is over,' he cried, 'a catastrophe has occurred. We must withdraw from Sinai.'

Sadat decided on the spot to dismiss Shazly and to appoint General Gamasy in his place. But Sadat kept the decision to himself, so as not to affect the morale of his forces. While later refusing to discuss this distressing confrontation with Shazly – because he was 'concerned about Shazly's good name' – Sadat recalled that he had warned the General Staff five days before the outbreak of the war to expect daring Israeli asssaults. Egyptian intelligence had gained a number of major successes, of a type usually associated with the Mossad. It had obtained a copy of a plan by Sharon to cross the Suez Canal near Deversoir, with the result that the area was fortified. But the actual crossing took place at a spot nearby which had been only lightly protected. Nevertheless the High Command knew what was in the minds of the Israelis. It is thus very surprising that the High Command reacted with such total disbelief. Sadat had every reason to feel furious.

His quarrel with Shazly and other generals went deeper. To them the war was a matter of fighting, gaining ground and defeating an intransigent enemy. For Sadat, despite his public bellicosity, the war had other aims.

The sharp debate between Sadat and General Ismail on one hand and Shazly, backed by many officers on the other, whether or not to broaden the Egyptian bridgeheads in Sinai was reaching a climax. Sadat, even in the moment of the triumphant crossing of the Canal, never lost sight of his limited aim to regain national honour and break the diplomatic stalemate. Backed at home by such enthusiastic Nasserists as Mohammed Heikal, Shazly felt bitterly that the Egyptian troops should have exploited their outstanding successes and immediately pushed towards the Sinai passes. Shazly argued that had the Egyptian bridgehead been extended and reached the passes, the devastating Israeli crossing at Deversoir could not have taken place. This view was supported by many in the Arab world. A typical comment appeared in the respected Beirut newspaper *Al Nahar*. Its military editor wrote: 'Had the Egyptian forces advanced in Sinai immediately after the crossing of the Canal and endeavoured to capture the Gidi, Mitla and Bir Gafgafa passes before the arrival of the Israeli reserves, the war in Sinai would not have concluded as it did.'

Ironically, as Chaim Herzog pointed out, almost the very same arguments could have been used about Moshe Dayan's 'ministerial advice', as he called it. Had Elazar and Bar-Lev accepted his advice and moved back to the passes, Sharon could not have led the assault across the Canal at Deversoir.

An objective view of the situation facing Sadat would surely justify his conduct as well as his caution. He had to strengthen his armour but, above all, he needed the cover of the surface-to-air missiles. It was this cover that held back the effective Israeli Air Force. When, as in the 14 October tank battle, he moved outside the cover, he suffered the greatest defeat of the war. Sadat complained later – and with justification – that the battle was larger in scope and took place earlier than he had wished because of pressure from the Syrians to draw Israeli forces and aircraft from the northern front. A few days earlier the Syrians sent a high-ranking officer to Egypt with a message from President Assad with an urgent plea for a major Egyptian initiative.

Curiously, while Sadat was receiving the glad news from the front, he was told that the Soviet Ambassador wished urgently to see him. The Ambassador had with him a message from the Soviet leadership that President Assad had asked for a cease-fire next morning.

Although the Syrians indignantly denied the request, the Kremlin twice more approached Sadat with the same plea, followed by the same indignant denial from Damascus. This public reaction did not necessarily mean that Assad had not made the request. This wily politician may have believed that it would be wise for him to ensure that he retained the territories on the Golan that he had conquered on the first day of the fighting and was likely to gain the next day. His overwhelmingly superior tank force was punching holes in the Israeli defences. He was very close to breaking out of the Golan into Galilee. If a cease-fire took place while he was in control of Israeli territory, as well as of the Golan, it would provide him with a tremendous triumph.

Sadat himself believed the less likely explanation that the Kremlin was seeking to undermine his alliance with Assad which might affect its own relations with Damascus. Eventually, it was Sadat's unilateral cease-fire which was to cause the public rift between him and Assad, followed a few years later by a much more genuine and momentous disagreement.

When the Soviet Ambassador called again the following day, ostensibly carrying a message from Assad, Sadat acutely embarrassed him by showing him the Syrian President's answer stressing

Syria's resolve to reject any cease-fire. When the Ambassador still insisted that the Kremlin was voicing Assad's real wishes, Sadat dismissed the message by saying that his word was final and binding.

Sadat's suspicion that the Kremlin was behind the pressure to make him agree to a cease-fire was confirmed by another incident. At dawn on 13 October he was awakened by the British Ambassador to receive an urgent message from the British Prime Minister Edward Heath. He had been asked by Henry Kissinger, now the US Secretary of State but without an embassy in Cairo, to verify a claim he had received from a Soviet envoy that Sadat had asked for a cease-fire. Sadat replied that he was determined to continue with the battle.

For Sadat, it would have made no sense to stop the fighting at that point. His armour and infantry had performed well, far better than anyone outside Egypt and, perhaps, some inside had expected. He was particularly proud of the way the Egyptian Air Force had performed under the leadership of Hosni Mubarak. Sadat heard Mubarak telling the army chiefs that the air force was ready to carry out even more sorties, reversing the normal relationship between army and air chiefs. Mubarak was said to have gone to see an Israeli pilot whose plane had been shot down and to have remarked on Israel's lower standards. 'No, sir,' said the pilot, 'it is not that our standards are lower; it is yours that are higher!'

12 · *Kissinger enters the scene*

Henry Kissinger, not usually given to expressing approval of the statesmen he encountered, makes no secret of his admiration of Anwar Sadat at the very moment when the Egyptian leader might have succumbed to despair, as Nasser did.

The period between Sadat's discovery of the extent of the Israeli success in crossing the Canal and his signing of the cease-fire could plausibly be claimed by him as his finest hour. Not that all Sadat's claims and criticisms were fully justified. Shazly may well have felt shattered and he may well have expressed acute anxiety about the strategic situation following the Israeli crossing. But it can equally be argued that he was not far wrong.

If Mohammed Heikal's version of the dramatic confrontation is to be believed – and there is no reason to challenge it as it was written when he was still friendly with Sadat – Shazly's recommendations were not at all outrageous or defeatist. He noted that a powerful Israeli force, commanded by a brilliant general, was foraging through the Egyptian countryside, destroying missile sites, and with the road to Cairo apparently wide open. He knew the situation better than Sadat or Sadat's main adviser, General Ismail. Shazly felt that some of the reinforcements that had been sent across the canal should be brought back, particularly the armoured brigade, sent to join the Third Army. He also advocated bringing back some tanks and anti-tank missiles. Unless these measures were taken, he feared that the Second Army might be encircled and the Third Army threatened.

There is no reference here to the war being already lost. From the purely military point of view, Shazly was surely correct. His fears

113

were, in fact, quickly shown to be fully justified. The Third Army was cut off and there was considerable panic. Thousands of troops deserted and were taken prisoner. Had Kissinger not intervened with the Israelis, the Egyptian troops would soon have been without food and water. Had the army surrendered, the humiliation would have been such that it could have had devastating effects on the rest of the armed forces. A catastrophe on the 1967 scale could have occurred.

Shazly was accepted as probably the most brilliant general in the Egyptian Army. Good-looking and brave, he could well have achieved political fame had he wished. Even as a general, he was still a paratrooper, and his approach to the armed forces was that of a first-class Israeli general, being both youthful and innovative.

His mistake – which was to lead to his ignominious dismissal (he was sent a message that Sadat had accepted his 'resignation') – was that he did not understand that the President was not only the commander-in-chief but also the country's political leader – and a great gambler. Sadat had gone to war because he wanted an honourable peace, as he saw the matter. Now, at this point of the most acute danger, Sadat feared that any withdrawal from the east bank would result in such convulsions that precisely the situation that Shazly foresaw would be brought about. Sadat still vividly remembered the catastrophe that befell the Egyptian Army when Amer ordered the withdrawal from Sinai in the Six-Day War.

The attitude of Sadat and of General Ismail reflected their knowledge that the Egyptian Army had not yet overcome all its traumas. Had the situation been reversed and the Israelis had felt the need of bringing back armoured units to the west bank, there would have been no opposition from politicians. It is inconceivable that any general or minister would have argued that the army would disintegrate.

For Sadat there was the equally vital argument that there was a good chance that the Kremlin and even the Americans would somehow prevent his collapse. His secret talks with Kissinger, through his security adviser, had probably given him hope that he had found the right person at last who could put pressure on the Israelis.

It was a moment of great peril for Egypt. Whatever step Sadat

114

took, there lurked immense dangers. The situation on the Syrian front had seriously deteriorated. From being in a position to launch an attack into the heartland of Israel, the Syrians had been driven back by some of the bravest military exploits in the history of warfare. The Israeli forces had decided to concentrate most of their strength on the Syrian front, for it was there that the greatest threat to the very life of their country came, before switching to the southern front against Egypt. In a few days over 600 Syrian tanks had been destroyed and Israeli troops were opening the road to Damascus. The anxious Assad could not know for certain that Israel would not wish to enter a city with a huge population.

On this fateful day, Sadat made up his mind and sent a message to Assad:

We have fought Israel to the fifteenth day. In the first four days Israel was alone, so we were able to expose her position on both fronts. On their admission the enemy have lost eight hundred tanks and two hundred planes. But during the last ten days I have, on the Egyptian front, been fighting the United States as well, through the arms it is sending. To put it bluntly, I cannot fight the United States or accept the responsibility before history for the destruction of our armed forces for the second time. I have, therefore, informed the Soviet Union that I am prepared to accept the cease-fire on existing positions, subject to the following conditions.

1. The Soviet Union and the United States to guarantee an Israeli withdrawal, as proposed by the Soviet Union.
2. The convening of a peace conference under United Nations auspices to achieve an overall settlement, as proposed by the Soviet Union.

My heart bleeds to tell you this, but I feel my office compels me to take this decision. I am ready to face our nation at a suitable moment and am prepared to give a full account to it for the action.

There are many reasons to believe that President Assad was less than honest with Sadat, certainly not in statements meant eventually for publication. There was more than an element of calculation in the public rift which Assad engineered with Sadat. There is no reason to believe that Assad was not as relieved as Sadat that a cease-fire was signed with the help of the Kremlin and the Americans. The first shots of the public argument are contained in Assad's reply.

I received your letter yesterday with deep emotion. My brother, I beg you to look again at the military situation on the northern front and both sides of the canal. We see no cause for pessimism. We can continue the struggle against enemy forces, whether they have crossed the canal or are still fighting east of the canal.

I am convinced that by continuing and intensifying the battle, it will be possible to ensure the destruction of those enemy units that have crossed the canal. My brother Sadat, for the sake of the morale of the fighting troops it is necessary to emphasise that although the enemy have, as a result of an accident, been able to break our front, this does not mean that they will be able to achieve victory. The enemy succeeded in penetrating the northern front several days ago, but the stand we then made and the subsequent heavy fighting have given us greater grounds for optimism. Most points of enemy penetration have been sealed off and I am confident that we shall be able to deal with those remaining in the course of the next few days. I consider it imperative that our armies should maintain their fighting spirit.

My brother President, I am sure you appreciate that I have weighed my words with the utmost care and with full realisation that we now face the most difficult period in our history. I felt it encumbent on me to explain my thinking to you, especially in relation to the southern front. God be with you!

When the Israeli crossing occurred, the Soviet Premier Kosygin had already been in Cairo for three days. His mission was to convince Sadat that he should agree to a cease-fire. Basing their judgement on the evidence of their satellite, which had been put into orbit at the very start of the fighting as a guide for the Egyptians and as a vital source of information for the Kremlin, the Soviet leaders became frightened. After the tank disaster on 14 October they saw the Egyptians facing a major catastrophe.

Always suspicious of Soviet intentions, even though he had to rely on them for his arms, Sadat bluntly rejected the suggestion and insisted that he would continue fighting. Now, however, a new important element entered the situation which was to set Sadat in a totally different direction.

In his arguments for accepting the cease-fire, Sadat repeatedly stressed the power of the United States. He went to extraordinary lengths to emphasise this factor and stress the superiority of American over Soviet arms. When explaining the earlier Israeli

116

supremacy in the air because of the possession of the Phantom and the Mirage, Sadat said:

> In the MIG 21 the pilot has nothing except the compass. No facilities at all. In the Mirage and the Phantom, as in the Jaguar, everything is computerised for the pilot. If he enters a missile zone, there would be a light to warn him. If anyone is going to attack him from the back, another light will tell him. He just puts a card in the computer, and it will take him to the place he chooses. It will tell him when to drop the bombs and it will bring him back to his air base. In the MIG 21 and all Soviet military gear, all this is done by the pilot which is very primitive. This is what gave Israel air supremacy.

Yet Sadat acknowledged the excellence of the Soviet missiles which protected his armies and shot down so many Phantoms. He knew that Israel's losses were so great that orders were given to avoid the missile belt. Israel tried repeatedly to draw the Egyptian forces away from the missile protection. When this happened in the tank battle of 14 October Israel was able to inflict a decisive defeat. Why earlier the American arms had proved ineffective, Sadat did not explain. Now he argued that Israel had been provided with newly invented weapons which could knock out immediately his missile batteries, which Israel had failed to do before.

When the Syrians intensified their complaints against the cease-fire, Sadat responded by saying that he was prepared to fight the Israelis but not the US superpower. To his mind, it was the US that had practically conducted the Israeli strategy. It was the US that had encouraged the TV-style counter-attack across the Suez Canal. It was the US that had provided Israel with TV-guided bombs which had never been used and which could not be combated. The new American tanks had been sent directly to the battlefield. They were taken there from Al-Arish by American crews. Such claims are reminiscent of the accusations made by Nasser after the 1967 débâcle that American planes had joined the Israelis in the air battles.

Sadat was desperate to present the war as at least a partial victory. And he was justified in claiming that there were vast differences between the Yom Kippur and October War and the Six-Day War. His armies had fought well and bravely. They had taken Israel by surprise and inflicted far heavier losses than in the 1967 fighting. They could hold their heads up. And Sadat showed that he was a true national leader when he encouraged his soldiers to fight the surging forces of General Sharon.

When the Israeli forces approached the town of Suez, Sadat encouraged a stiff defence and even spoke of the spirit of Stalingrad. And, indeed, so strong was the defence and so significant were the Israeli casualties that the Israeli generals decided to by-pass the town.

For Sadat the battle for Suez was the highlight of his struggle against the Israelis. It was a heroic stand which proved that the Egyptian people were capable of standing up against even the strongest enemy. The city had been destroyed during the War of Attrition by Israeli artillery and bombs. Its industrial plant and its oil refineries had been totally demolished. Nasser decreed that the city and others devastated by Israeli bombing should remain in their lifeless form, as they would become the future battlefields. Sadat determined to follow this philosophy. He particularly emphasised the 'sublime acts of heroism' accomplished by civilians after he gave the order that the city must not surrender, emulating Stalingrad. He claimed that the battle would go down in history as one of the bravest ever fought. He instituted 24 October National Suez Day which was to be observed as a national festival. It has been suggested that Sadat wished to establish his own equivalent of Nasser's Port Said Day, to mark his soldiers' fight against the Anglo-French attack in 1956 but this is to do less than justice to Sadat's genuine emotion and pride in the achievements of the Suez defenders.

The outskirts of Suez had not become a 'graveyard for Israeli tanks and soldiers', as Sadat claimed but the resistance was fierce enough to halt Israeli progress. The Israeli aim was to encircle the Third Army and by capturing Suez they would have cut its last link with the Egyptian heartland. When they found it hard to capture the town, the Israelis swept past it and managed to complete the encirclement of the Third Army. Already thousands of soldiers were deserting it, according to Israeli accounts.

For Sadat the trapping of the Third Army was a matter of profound humiliation. He was not able to discuss it publicly. He treated this defeat in a bombastic manner which he well knew was not convincing. It was the ridiculous aspect of the entrapment of an entire army by a smaller force carrying out a manoeuvre, expected and discussed in the higher reaches of the Egyptian Army, that was particularly galling. Privately he admired Arik Sharon for his daring. Sharon was precisely the type of general that he himself would have liked to have had. When Sadat arrived in Jerusalem in November 1977 the one person he was eager to meet was Sharon. As the two men embraced, Sadat told the general: 'I almost trapped you at the Deversoir'. Sadat was making an acknowledgement of his failure.

Nothing could have been more bitter to Sadat's ears than the jokes which the ordinary Egyptians, with their strong sense of humour and their liking for making fun of the authorities, began to make about the Third Army's humiliation. Despite stringent censorship, rumours inevitably began to circulate in Cairo that even exaggerated the extent of the Egyptian defeat. Thus it was said that over 10,000 Egyptian troops had surrendered and that the Israelis were approaching the capital. How different this was from the triumphant days when captured Israeli tanks were displayed in the streets of Cairo and the few Israeli prisoners of war were paraded!

The jokes had a special Egyptian softness. One joke said that the Israeli enclave was no longer a pocket in Egyptian territory, as was being claimed by the authorities, but an entire pair of trousers. Another joke described a conversation between Sadat and Golda Meir. She said 'Bonjour' and he unwittingly replied 'Al-Ubour' (the crossing). When he wished her 'Bonsoir', she replied 'Deversoir'.

Henry Kissinger was literally awakened to receive the news of the Yom Kippur War. He was soundly asleep at 6.15 a.m. on Saturday, 6 October 1973 in the Waldorf Towers Hotel in New York when his highly energetic and usually exceptionally wise Assistant Secretary of State, Joe Sisco, burst in with the information that Israel, Egypt and Syria were about to go to war. To the startled Kissinger, Sisco declared that he was confident it was all a mistake, with each side misreading the intentions of the other. If Kissinger told them the true position, the crisis might be averted. For once Joe Sisco was over-optimistic.

Nothing that Kissinger or anyone else could do on this day would have prevented an Egyptian–Syrian attack. Earlier that morning, Golda Meir had told the American Ambassador Kenneth Keating: 'We may be in trouble'. Keating reminded her that 12 hours earlier Israeli defence officials had assured him that the possibility of war was remote. Even though this concept had been destroyed, Golda apparently still misunderstood Arab intentions. She remarked that since the Arabs were certain to be defeated, she thought that the crisis must have resulted from their misconstruing Israeli aims. The United States was asked to inform the Soviet Union and the Arab states that Israel had no intention of attacking Egypt and Syria. Israel was calling up some reserves but, as proof of its peaceful intentions, was stopping short of a general mobilisation. For the Syrian and Egyptian generals this message must have provided welcome relief. They were not facing a pre-emptive strike, not even a limited one suggested by Chief of Staff Elazar, from the air. They could take much greater risks.

Although taken by surprise like everyone else – the CIA not being much wiser than Israel – Kissinger felt from the beginning that the US was in a good position to dominate events once the war had broken out. The Americans, Kissinger felt, had a number of contradictory aims. They had to assure the survival of Israel, they needed to maintain good relations with the moderate Arab states, such as Jordan and Saudi Arabia. There was concern that Europe, which had adopted a cool attitude to Israel, would follow different paths – which, indeed, it did. Above all, there was the worry that the Soviet Union would pursue mischievous if not dangerous policies in an effort to boost its Arab clients. The Soviet leaders could not be expected to be of any real help to put out the fires, certainly not at the beginning.

Kissinger's duels with Soviet Ambassador Dobrynin, a wily diplomatic operator, and, through him, with the still powerful Brezhnev in Moscow, provided a brilliant backdrop to the fighting on the battlefields. And all the time Kissinger had to gauge the mind of that extraordinary man, Anwar Sadat.

Kissinger was optimistic that the United States could control the situation but very nearly went astray. Without the overwhelming military power that the US possessed the Soviet Union might well have been tempted to intervene directly by sending several air divisions to the Middle East to change the tide of war. Perhaps Kissinger did not at first realise the passions – irrational and raw – which dominated so much of the Arab–Israel conflict, nor the degree of humiliation which the Soviet Union felt at the defeats inflicted by the American-armed Israelis on the Soviet-armed Arabs.

To Kissinger the position seemed clear. Israel was going to win the war quickly. But Israel must not gain such an overwhelming victory which, as after the Six-Day War, would create such resentment that no Arab leader would be able to make peace. At the same time the Soviet Union must be prevented from becoming the Arabs' saviour which, in itself, would make a peace agreement, involving major concessions, impossible.

From the outset, Kissinger insisted, he was determined to use the war to start a peace process. The question has to be asked if, without meaning to, Kissinger had encouraged Anwar Sadat to start a limited war. Sadat himself had no doubts. He had read remarks made to him by American envoys as meaning that Kissinger felt that unless the diplomatic stalemate was broken by limited Arab action there could be no peace talks. Kissinger would have been horrified if such were Sadat's analysis of his private words to Sadat's security adviser, but in the tense circumstances then prevailing such an approach appears more than likely.

Nor can Kissinger claim so confidently that the Soviet Union stopped short of encouraging the war but made no effort to stop it. Without the massive supply of Soviet arms, war would have been inconceivable, on either the Egyptian or Syrian fronts. Kissinger further commented that the likelihood was that the Kremlin believed that its interests were served whatever happened: if the Arabs did well, the credit would go to Soviet arms and Soviet support; if they did poorly, Moscow could emerge, as in 1967, the champion of the Arab world. This would strengthen the Arab radicals and even get rid of the troublesome Anwar Sadat. However, this concept falls to the ground in view of our present knowledge of Brezhnev's acute anxiety to ensure an Arab, particularly a Syrian, victory. This stand-off Soviet position is incompatible with the massive Soviet airlift.

In preparing the American response to the war, Kissinger had to take into account that the President of the United States, Richard Nixon, was a flawed personality as well as exceptionally complex. He had been badly wounded by the Watergate scandal, which was to topple him from power. Although he had appointed a former German–Jewish refugee from Nazi Germany as his National Security Adviser and Secretary of State, his attitude to Jews was far from complimentary. He felt he owed nothing in electoral terms to

American Jews who mostly voted for his Democratic opponent. And, as Kissinger himself mentioned, Nixon shared many of the prejudices of the uprooted Californian lower middle-class from which he came. Nixon believed that Jews formed a powerful, cohesive group in American society, that they were predominantly liberal, put the interests of Israel above everything else and that their control of the media made them dangerous adversaries. Nixon also believed that Israel had to be forced into a peace settlement and could not be permitted to jeopardise American relations with the Arab world.

Yet, as Golda Meir was to recognise and publicly acknowledge, Richard Nixon stood more firmly by Israel, in terms of arms and support, than any other American President, including even Harry Truman. Without the amazing American airlift when Moshe Dayan despaired about Israel's ability to throw back the Arab enemy and wondered where the ammunition for the guns was coming from, Israel's entire strategic position would have been in danger. Israel would have survived as a country but the Arab States and the Palestinians would have been so emboldened by their victory that a just peace would have been impossible to achieve. A badly weakened Israel would have been prey to further wars with the Arabs hoping, with Soviet encouragement, to wipe out altogether their hated little enemy.

It was fortunate for Israel and for the free world that Richard Nixon had such a grasp of international problems that made him break the impasse with China and force the Soviet Union to see the wisdom of détente. Nixon realised that were the Arabs to achieve a major victory with the aid of the Soviet Union against a virtual ally of the United States, the prestige of the Kremlin would vault dangerously high in the Arab world while that of the US would plummet to new depths. Moderate Arab states, such as Saudi Arabia and the other oil rich Gulf States, would have to meet new forces of Soviet-inspired radicalism and might not even survive them. The Soviet Union could well become the masters of the whole of the Middle East and its essential oil supplies. This was one scenario that Nixon could never accept.

Kissinger and Nixon began with the assumption that Israel would gain a quick and devastating victory which would make it even less willing to give concessions to the Arabs. Then there came the major surprise that Israel had sustained painful defeats on the opening day of the fighting. A day after came the first direct word from Sadat. His terms for ending the war were unacceptable, as they again repeated the demand for a total Israeli withdrawal from the occupied territories, but for Kissinger the significant fact was that Sadat was inviting the United States, for the first time, to participate in the peace process. This was clearly Sadat's first move in a complex, dangerous game. It was fortunate that Kissinger understood it for what it was.

Strangely, though, Kissinger admits that until this message he did not take Sadat seriously. Because Sadat's many threats to go to war had not been implemented, Kissinger thought of him more as an actor than a statesman. Yet the very fact that Sadat had gone to war and had so brilliantly deceived nearly everyone should have given Kissenger a different impression of the complex personality of Sadat.

However, the belated recognition was of vital importance to the Middle East. Now Kissinger understood that the grandiloquent gestures were part of a conscious strategy. Kissinger had been surprised that Sadat had not asked for a reward from the Americans for expelling the Russian advisers. It was a major move (whatever the reasons for it were) that must not be spoiled by petty demands. Kissinger suggested that the move was to remove the Soviet encumbrance to war and the tilt towards the United States. Now Sadat's ability to stick to his great aim convinced Kissinger that he was dealing with a statesman of the first order.

There is a considerable amount of hindsight in Kissinger's historical analysis. There was a frightening element of gambling in Sadat's policies. The whole roof came perilously near to tumbling down.

It was helpful, perhaps, that Israel's new Ambassador, Simcha Dinitz, arrived in Washington to take the place of Yitzhak Rabin. Kissinger clearly found 'the taciturn' Rabin, as he called him, somewhat irritating, as President Carter was to find later. As a soldier all his life, Rabin lacked the charm and small-talk of the polished diplomat. He could be excruciatingly direct, which his mentor, David Ben-Gurion, found impressive. Kissinger, however, found the warmth and brilliance of Simcha Dinitz, with his ability to tell interesting stories and make jokes, much more to his liking. The two, in fact, became close life-long friends, so close indeed that Kissinger found it necessary to insist that his outlook was not clouded by his friendship with Dinitz.

In pushing through the massive airlift to Israel when the situation dramatically deteriorated and there came urgent calls for planes, tanks and ammunition, Kissinger, always backed by Nixon, came up against considerable opposition within the administration. There were those who claimed that whatever arms did arrive would be too late. Then it was found that Israel alone would not be able to transport all the esssential arms. By guaranteeing to replace all Israel's losses, making it unnecessary to keep a high level of reserve stocks, the US gave Israel immense relief.

1 Relaxing from the cares of state: President Sadat in his garden in the company of one of his grandchildren

2 Sadat as the centre of a large extended family

3 Sadat speaking after a dinner following his historic visit to Jerusalem in 1977

4 The President meets the author, May 1979; at the time Sadat was being acclaimed for his peace achievements (*Le Journal d'Egypte*)

5 Signing the Camp David Peace Accords, 26 March 1979: President Sadat of Egypt, President Jimmy Carter of the USA, and Prime Minister Menachem Begin of Israel (Photo Levon Keshishian)

6 Madame Jihan Sadat, the President's beautiful and elegant wife, now a
   lecturer at an American university

7　After the assassination of President Sadat on 6 October 1981: confusion and outrage as soldiers surround one of the suspected assassins (above); and (below) lead another gunman away (Associated Press)

8　The President, in one of the flamboyant uniforms he loved, smiles at the
start of the military parade on the last day of his life, 6 October 1981
(Associated Press)

13 · Towards a breakthrough

Frantic and illogical – that is how the Kremlin's behaviour appears now. It does not satisfy entirely any concept, neither the idea that this was Brezhnev's war, as David Kimche believes, nor the cynical view of Henry Kissinger, nor the partisan version of Mohammed Heikal. The Kremlin was seeking a cease-fire from day one, declared Sadat. Why then did Brezhnev seek Jordanian and Algerian involvement? Why did he send such massive supplies to Damascus and then to Cairo? Why the delays in the consultations with the Americans when he believed that his clients were winning?

Brezhnev would have known the limitations of Egyptian aims, even if he had high hopes for the Syrians. Why the sudden loss of nerve which made Brezhnev threaten direct intervention which he knew well could bring about a direct confrontation with the Americans and even a nuclear war which he certainly did not desire? The answer must surely be that Brezhnev was not in control of the situation, that he was not well informed of Israeli and American intentions, that he could not fathom Sadat's complex plans, and above all, that he wished to avoid a humiliating outcome of the war which would make his own position at the summit of Kremlin power less secure. Shame and humiliation were two elements which a Kremlin leader could not handle, as was seen in the case of Khrushchev after the Cuban missile crisis defeat inflicted by President John F. Kennedy.

One Soviet official in a good position to gauge Soviet–Egyptian relations at the time was Alexander Golytsin. A fluent Arabic-speaker and with long service in Arab countries he noticed how reality was different from the versions of events that were being

125

propagated then and later. Thus he is not startled by David Kimche's revelations. According to Golytsin 70 per cent of the Soviet experts ostensibly expelled by Sadat remained in Egypt. Among them was General Okunev, chief adviser to the Egyptian Army and close to the Egyptian Chief of Staff. The partial expulsions actually led to a large increase of Soviet arms supplies. Even more important, says Golytsin, was the fact that intensive training of the Egyptian forces for battles with Israel began in July 1972 under the careful supervision of General Okunev.

Sadat, says Golytsin, had never planned to have an all-out war with Israel. His aim was to create a situation that would bring in the Americans. The Soviet officials thought that the Egyptian crossing of the Suez Canal was brilliant but that the Egyptians did not have a strategy to exploit their success. They thought only in terms of giving a shock to the Israelis and the Americans. In Sadat's mind there was the concept of peace. President Assad of Syria thought of a serious war. That was the difference between the two men and the reason why Assad, in fact, felt cheated.

If so much was known to Soviet officials, the behaviour of Brezhnev might seem bizarre. But Brezhnev did not necessarily listen to what his officials told him. Even while the huge American airlift to Israel, instituted by Nixon and Kissinger in the face of much Pentagon disbelief, was preparing to lift off, the Kremlin was alerting its air divisions for service in the Middle East. The oil-rich Arab states were threatening an oil boycott. It was indeed fortunate for Israel that the United States had nothing like the same dependence on Arabian oil as Europe. The result might still have been the same but there would have been much greater worries in the State Department and the White House. Cynics might even have argued that the size of the American airlift would not have been so comprehensive.

The effect of what are considered purely national interests, without reference to the wider needs of the Middle East, could be seen in the case of the British Heath government. An illogical arms embargo was imposed on both Arabs and Israelis, with the dire result that Britain stopped sending the ammunition needed in Israel for the British Centurion tanks. It was a callous act which could not be justified, either morally or practically. If the arms would make no difference because of American and Soviet supplies why make the gesture, and if the Israelis were not going to receive the arms from the USA how did Israel, undeniably not the aggressor, deserve such treatment which could have led to the destruction of the State? Nor was Britain in dire danger of suffering major national losses.

British policies during the war could hardly be described as diplomatically perspicacious. Thus the view of the Foreign Secretary, Lord Home, on 13–14 October was that a cease-fire was a mirage and that Sadat would not accept anything less than a commitment by Israel to return to the pre-1967 Six-Day War frontiers. The US proposals for a cease-fire would not be accepted unless the Kremlin threatened to cut off supplies to Sadat. This was highly unlikely. Instead, Lord Home proposed a compromise which would encompass a cease-fire in place, an international police force for the rest of the occupied territories, followed by an international conference.

Even a cursory examination of these ideas would have shown that they would be totally unacceptable to Israel. The implications were the adoption of the Arab solution of the conflict. As Kissinger realised, these ideas were more disadvantageous to Israel than Sadat's. The Egyptian President was demanding only an Israeli acceptance in principle of a withdrawal from the occupied territories, while Britain's idea of an international force meant, in effect, Israel giving up immediately the control of these areas.

Kissinger had no doubts about rejecting these British proposals, though he had a great personal admiration for Lord Home. Exponents of *realpolitik* would have smiled knowingly at the mild Arab response to the huge American airlift. The most surprising of all was the Egyptian response. There was no furious condemnation, no threats, but restrained criticism.

After the major tank defeat of 14 October, there was an unexpected suggestion by Sadat, sent through the national security adviser, Ismail. He invited Kissinger to visit Egypt.

The accompanying message no longer spoke of total Israeli withdrawals. Sadat was seeking a political link to a military solution. The only demand was that Egypt would not be asked to make any concessions of land or sovereignty. No wonder Kissinger saw the message as the act of a statesman, confirming his new estimate of Sadat. For he realised that nothing could now divert Sadat from his objective – an honourable peace. As Kissinger pointed out, Sadat could at this bitter moment of defeat on the battlefield have unleashed the Arab mobs against the Americans, as Nasser had done with far less provocation and justification in 1967. But such a course would have totally destroyed Sadat's long-thought-out project. Acknowledgement of defeat would have thrown the Arabs back into a vortex of bitterness when talk of peace in which each side made major concessions would have been entirely inconceivable.

That Sadat had coolly calculated his steps and was not suddenly overcome with kind feelings for the Americans and for the Western world was shown by an intense campaign – which proved successful – to persuade Saudi Arabia and other oil-rich states to impose an oil embargo. At the same time, Sadat began turning away formally from the Soviet Union though he was still totally dependent on it for arms. Probably this was a divorce of convenience because the Soviet Union may well have begun to have doubts about the benefits of a continued association with Egypt under Sadat's control.

Doubts of a different nature were beginning to afflict the European states. These doubts were transforming into virtual panic as the Europeans realised that they might soon be without a sufficient supply of oil. This panic led to desperate attempts by European politicians to ingratiate themselves with the Arab oil producers.

When the American airlift to Israel was about to begin, Kissinger discovered to his considerable annoyance that no European state was prepared to allow American planes to fly over its territory on the way to the Middle East. Portugal had to be severely pressured to allow US planes to fly over the Azores. Now the Europeans were telling the Americans 'We told you so', hardly an attitude which Nixon and Kissinger found appealing.

As soon as the Kremlin realised the extent of the Israeli bridgehead across the Canal – eight miles wide in the north and four miles in the south, with over 300 tanks – it made an urgent effort to halt the war. A crucial part of this attempt would be Kissinger's visit to Moscow.

Golda Meir, who a week earlier had agreed to a cease-fire, was now much less receptive, as the situation had totally changed. Nor could she be enthusiastic at the news that Kissinger had accepted the Kremlin's invitation. Even Kissinger began to wonder whether he had accepted the Soviet invitation too quickly. He agrees that he could have delayed the departure by 24 hours and thus strengthened Israel's military position even further. But he argues to his own satisfaction that he did the right thing, that the Kremlin would have known the reasons for his delay, and that the Arab frustration would have grown. The Israelis were less convinced of the soundness of this reasoning.

When they met, Brezhnev revealed how anxious he was for an immediate cease-fire. Kissinger, who had now full authority from Nixon to make a deal without further reference to the White House, an honour which he protested left him no room for delays, saw no objection. He felt that the Israelis could not expect further days to strengthen their stranglehold on the Egyptian forces and thus obtain better bargaining conditions. A cease-fire, without conditions harmful to either side, was agreed. Neither Sadat nor Golda Meir could complain, even if many Arabs thought that Egypt had capitulated to big-power pressure. Sadat knew that both Egypt and his whole presidency and strategy had been saved. His link with the Americans, though still very tenuous, had been forged and would get stronger.

Kissinger's decision to accept Golda Meir's invitation to travel from Moscow to Israel and his subsequent personal feelings seem uniquely to have involved his Jewishness. Nowhere else in his memoirs does Kissinger refer so specifically to his emotions in regard to Israel and his background. The visit, he wrote, ranked high on the list of the most moving moments of his government service. Yet it is difficult to accept fully his impression that the Israelis, servicemen and civilians, who greeted him with tears in their eyes on his arrival at the airport, showed a weariness which showed the limits of human endurance. His impression that the Israelis were exhausted, no matter what the military maps showed, and that the people were yearning for immediate peace was at variance with what was actually happening.

Golda Meir's and Moshe Dayan's anxieties were not about stopping the war but about what had been decided in Moscow. Was there a secret agreement to force Israel to return to the 1967 borders? Would an attempt be made to impose other frontiers on Israel? Firm assurances were given that no such deals existed.

With all his perspicacity, Kissinger does not appear to have fully understood the driving force of Golda Meir's and Moshe Dayan's arguments and their inner anxieties. He mentions that they realised that Israel had lost its protective aura of invincibility. He points out that 2,000 Israeli soldiers had been killed (and a larger number injured), the equivalent of 200,000 American dead. It was for this very reason that Israel needed at this moment a decisive victory, a shattering defeat of the Arab armies on the Six-Day War scale to regain some of the invincibility, to tell the Arabs that they would always pay an unacceptable price for an attack on Israel. Had he appreciated this point, Kissinger would not have been surprised by later events.

Significantly in his intriguing descriptions of the Israeli leaders whom he met, Kissinger nowhere considers it appropriate to refer to high statesmanship as he so easily did with Anwar Sadat. While emotionally he may have felt strongly for Golda Meir, intellectually he was much more at home with the calculating Sadat. In a memorable exchange, Kissinger asked Golda Meir if she thought that Sadat would survive the military setbacks of the last phase of the war. Golda replied: 'I do, because he is the hero. He dared.'

Sadat dared! That certainly was true. But he not only dared, he survived. He kept his forces virtually intact. Unlike Nasser, given far greater glory in the Arab world, Sadat never allowed the situation to get out of his control, never allowed another Amer to take over the running of the war, never abandoned his troops to chance or to despair.

For Sadat the aftermath of the formal cease-fire 'in place' could have been catastrophic. According to the Egyptians, as they told Kissinger, the Israelis quickly broke the cease-fire and were once again moving forward. The Israelis replied that it was the Egyptians who had broken the agreement by trying to improve their desperate situation. The Kremlin, at first complacent, became almost frantic when Egyptian complaints poured in and the evidence from the satellite showed Israeli advances.

Kissinger, too, appears to have felt that the Israelis were the greater sinners in the dispute – which they probably were. Brezhnev began to use dangerous language, accusing the Israelis of 'deceit' and of 'unacceptable' conduct. This was not just moral outrage. The Egyptians were now clearly in very deep trouble. How deep, in Soviet estimation, was to be fully revealed by Brezhnev's next step. He clearly believed that the Third Army, now completely cut off, was about to disintegrate because of lack of food and water – and ammunition supplies. It was a crisis both for him and for Sadat.

Brezhnev's next action was that of a desperate man. It is highly unlikely that it was suggested to him by Sadat because it would have negated all that the Egyptian president had planned. Kissinger, too, was thrown into a profound dilemma. Brezhnev, now speaking of Israeli 'treachery' insisted on a cease-fire. He was backed by Kissinger but Golda Meir vehemently attacked the pressure put on her to comply, seeing it as an ultimatum. For the first time Sadat appealed directly to Nixon, even suggesting that the Americans 'should intervene effectively, even if that necessitates the use of forces, in order to guarantee the full implementation of the cease-fire'. The idea that the Americans might use force against their ally, Israel, might seem preposterous, but Sadat was trying to emphasise, above all, the trust he now had in the US, and the crucial fact that the US had the power to stop the Israelis. The omission of the Soviet Union in this context was highly significant. But Sadat was soon to change his stand. As the condition of his Third Army deteriorated he called on the UN Security Council to request that American and Soviet forces be sent to the Middle East.

Sadat, at this extreme moment for him, believed that a joint American–Soviet force would be advantageous to him and might even impose a solution disliked by Israel. Such a force might have the effect of an international diplomatic intervention which he had always sought. However, what the Kremlin wanted to obtain was totally different. Brezhnev was seeking to regain partial supremacy in the Arab world which he was losing.

It is difficult otherwise to understand his virtual ultimatum to Nixon and Kissinger: join me in sending troops to enforce not merely the cease-fire but enforce an Arab–Israeli settlement or I will do it myself.

Kissinger saw it as one of the most serious challenges to a US President ever made by a Soviet leader. This was no mere verbal threat. From CIA information, it was apparent that the Soviet Union was preparing aircraft to carry some of its airborne divisions to the Middle East. The number of Soviet ships in the Mediterranean had grown to 85, the highest ever. A Soviet flotilla of 12 ships was heading for Alexandria. The Soviet Ambassador in Washington, Anatoly Dobrynin, had earlier boasted that the Soviet Union had plans to defeat Israel in two days.

The United States could not accept the Soviet ultimatum, in either form. It could not join the Kremlin in a Middle East force where all the advantages would lie with the Soviet Union. And the US could not permit the Kremlin to send troops unilaterally to the Middle East and, in effect, become the master power.

To emphasise how seriously the United States took the Soviet threat the American forces were ostentatiously put on alert, including those in control of nuclear weapons. At the same time a warning was sent to Sadat that should Soviet troops appear in Egypt they would be opposed, on Egyptian soil, by American troops. Sadat was presented with the nightmare scenario of the two great nuclear countries confronting each other in Cairo. He was asked to withdraw his invitation to Soviet troops.

There was a quick response from Sadat which, by implication, meant that he was no longer seeking Soviet, as well as American, troops. If the Kremlin now sent troops to Egypt it would be against the wishes of Sadat. Soon came the Brezhnev climb-down, though not presented as such. Brezhnev merely ignored his own earlier ultimatum.

Firm and, indeed, courageous American action had prevented a Middle East and possibly a world catastrophe. At a time when Nixon's hold on the presidency was slipping perceptibly, an immense extra responsibility fell on Kissinger. It was a moment of supreme danger for the world.

It is still not certain today on whom the blame would have been put had a major war broken out between the superpowers. There are those who would have blamed Brezhnev for encouraging the Arabs to go to war and then failing to control the subsequent events. Kissinger himself would not have escaped criticism for apparently signalling to Sadat to 'hot up' the situation in order to break the diplomatic impasse. Golda Meir would have been criticised for displaying 'intransigence' in the face of Sadat's offers and Sadat would have been accused of lighting the fuse which set off the conflagration. However, Kissinger and Sadat could claim that their mutual understanding was an important factor in resolving the world crisis. The man whom Kissinger had once called 'a clown' proved that he truly deserved the title of a first-class statesman. It was a characteristic Sadat move which also removed the last obstacle to a cease-fire. To Kissinger's obvious delight – and surprise – word came, when Kissinger was still haggling with Golda Meir (and describing the Israelis as 'mad heroes') that Egypt was prepared to accept direct talks between Egyptian and Israeli officers to discuss UN Security Council resolutions on the war. Israel was about to enter the first direct talks with Arab representatives since the establishment of the Jewish State.

First, however, Sadat sought a quick visit to Cairo by Kissinger. He had invited him earlier but Kissinger felt that there was too much anxiety in Israel for him to add to it by coming to Cairo immediately after meeting Golda Meir. Now Sadat's whole strategy depended on a speedy understanding with a man who appeared to have the innovative mind which he liked to believe he himself possessed and was moreover linked to the greatest power in the world.

As a measure of his anxiety to understand even more fully Kissinger's thinking and bring him to Cairo, Sadat dispatched his acting Foreign Minister Ismail Fahmy, who knew the United States as well, having been for years a representative at the United Nations and who had, in fact, suffered during Nasser's government from having a reputation for being too pro-American. His aim was to remove the tension in Egyptian–American relationships and to give Sadat an intelligent estimate of this unique Jewish-born American Secretary of State.

Before finalising his trip to Cairo, Kissinger had to deal with a clearly embarrassing visit to Washington by Golda Meir. She had come to seek assurances that the United States was not forcing Israel to accept solutions which would hurt its security. Kissinger tried hard to give a sceptical Golda that assurance but he could not remove from her the deep-seated resentment that the powerful United States had snatched from the mouth of little Israel the fruits of victory over the Egyptians in pursuit of an unattainable end, a peace agreement acceptable to all parties to the conflict.

According to Kissinger, the Golda whom he now saw was different from the confident, satisfied leader who had told Nixon a few months ago: 'We have never had it so good'. Now in front of Kissinger stood a woman, profoundly wounded by the disasters of the first days of the Yom Kippur War, blaming herself for accepting the complacent assurances of her experts and feeling that she herself was partly responsible for the deaths of so many young Israeli men and women. As she admitted, she never ceased to mourn and took her agonising regrets to her grave.

In such a mood, Golda Meir could not accept Kissinger's reasoning. She wanted the United States to act as Israel's ally not only in providing superior arms than those possessed by the Arabs but also by taking Israel's side in any negotations for peace. At the same time she wanted Kissinger to put pressure on the Arabs to accept the Israeli point of view. His counter argument, that the US could not possess the necessary influence in the Arab camp if it pursued all the policies advocated by Golda, made no impression on her. The sharp exchanges in which Golda almost accused Kissinger and Nixon of forcing Israel to accept an American *diktat* were a measure of her frustration, resentment and fears. To Kissinger it seemed as if the Israeli leaders had given way to panic.

Golda Meir, despite her bitterness, realised that the Israeli demand for a swap of captured territories with the Egyptians and with both sides withdrawing ten kilometres from the Suez Canal, was not realistic. Sadat could not possibly accept it. Kissinger was irritated with both Golda Meir and top US officials who, incredibly, now urged an American airlift to the trapped Egyptian Third Army. This was a measure of American annoyance with the intransigent stand, as the Defence Department saw it, taken by Golda Meir's government. It was just as well that Kissinger realised that this would be a catastrophic step. Golda, for her part, calmed down and avoided a public clash with the United States. She decided to await the outcome of Kissinger's meeting with Anwar Sadat. And Kissinger also knew that he had to be especially careful that nothing he did or said would reopen the Israeli wounds or provoke Sadat into changing his diplomatic strategy.

For Kissinger the visit to Egypt had profound personal and professional significance. It was the first time that he, a Jew, would be negotiating in an Arab country, and one involved in a war with a Jewish State helped on a massive scale during the fighting by his adoptive country which he now represented. He might encounter resentment and recrimination, as well as suspicion. Indeed, Sadat's local critics were later to stress Kissinger's Jewishness. Yet Kissinger was determined from the outset that although he could not ignore personal factors, this was going to be a thoroughly professional visit as the US Secretary of State, with a fair understanding of both sides in the long dispute.

There have been wildly different accounts and interpretations of Kissinger's historic visit. Mohammed Heikal, once Sadat's friend – though always much closer to Nasser – and later his unsparing critic, saw the visit as the beginning of the betrayal of Arab interests. Kissinger, according to Heikal, had started their conversation by congratulating Sadat on the successes of the Egyptian armed forces, which naturally pleased the Egyptian President. Sadat responded by asking Kissinger why it had taken him so long to come to Cairo. 'I have been asking for you a long time. Where have you been? I have been waiting for you to take over.' Then when Kissinger began to open his briefcase and take out some papers, Sadat said: 'What are you doing? Do you think I am going to argue about the cease-fire of 22 October or about disengagement? No, Dr Kissinger. You are a man of strategy, I am a man of strategy. I want to talk to you on the strategic level.' Then Sadat began to talk to Kissinger about matters he had never dreamed he was going to raise. But what these were he never told Heikal.

Though he admits that Sadat did not tell him the substance of the talks, Heikal then goes on to say confidently, and without any qualifications, that Kissinger, when asked what he discussed with Golda Meir in Washington, took out from his briefcase the paper on which her six points were written and which she had said Sadat would not accept. After merely glancing at the paper, Sadat, claimed Heikal, declared: 'All right, I accept.' Later when meeting journalists, Sadat claimed the six points as his own.

It is not necessary to doubt that Heikal honestly believed this account which makes Sadat out to be a simpleton. But it is not an account which can be relied upon. Kissinger's account is intrinsically much more convincing and far more interesting. Both he and

Sadat were faced with a situation fraught with dangers. Nixon, suffering the effects of the Watergate scandal, now reaching a climax, had at the end of a Cabinet meeting astonished men like Brent Scowcroft and Alexander Haig by saying that it might be necessary to put pressure on Israel to avert a serious oil shortage. Kissinger realised that if he failed in his mission to Cairo, Nixon might indeed insist on pressurising Israel to withdraw its troops from the east bank of the Canal, with disastrous consequences to any peace hopes.

For Sadat there was the paradoxically unhelpful statement from the European Community urging Israel's immediate withdrawal to the 22 October line, and fully endorsing the Arab interpretation of the UN Security Council Resolution 242 calling for Israeli withdrawal from occupied Arab lands. Such a call was embarrassing for Sadat because he could not claim anything less for the Arabs than the Europeans were demanding and he knew that this was not a practical request.

It was not capitulation that made Sadat accept Kissinger's analysis. Investing time and effort on merely returning to the 2 October line was not wise.

14 · Breaking a psychological barrier

Sadat told Kissinger at the beginning of their meeting: 'I have a plan for you. It can be called the Kissinger plan.'

Sadat realised that there was a psychological barrier between the Israelis and the Arabs which had first to be broken before any peace agreement could even be discussed. Even talking face-to-face to Israelis was an impossible venture. Israel, Arabs felt, had not only occupied Arab land, chased hundreds of thousands of Palestinians from their villages, taken their homes, occupied the homes of Arabs in towns but also had humiliated all the Arabs and all the Arab states in the process. By repeatedly defeating them in battle, each time adding more Arab possessions, the Israelis had made the Arabs feel inferior. As the people of the Koran, where they were promoted to a higher rank than the Jews and Christians, the Muslim Arabs, the vast majority, saw the Israeli claim to superiority as an insult to their religion as well as to their manhood. It was almost physical distaste which prevented many nationalist Arabs from sitting down face to face with Israelis. This distaste was great before the Six-Day War which led to the Israeli occupation of the old city of Jerusalem, Gaza, the West Bank and the Golan Heights. Any Arab leader who risked breaking this barrier was facing expulsion from the Arab home camp.

For Sadat it was clear that at this moment he had to be seen negotiating not with Israel but with the United States. Kissinger flattered himself that Sadat had adopted, without any argument, his analysis and his procedural plan. But Sadat had obviously thought out his major strategy before Kissinger had arrived.

Despite the almost unanimous fears of his advisers, Sadat felt that he could trust the Americans to ensure that supplies would reach the Third Army. It seemed to him inconceivable that, having staked their reputation on an honourable cease-fire, Nixon and Kissinger would then destroy it by a piece of pure treachery, for no obvious benefit. Nor could he see the Israelis, eager though they had been to crush the Third Army into oblivion, break their word and infuriate the Americans to such a degree that their alliance would be endangered.

The six points had one item which particularly impressed Sadat. The Israeli checkpoints on the Cairo–Suez road were to be replaced by UN checkpoints. The Israelis had not been happy about this. Golda Meir, at her meetings in Washington, had dourly accepted the essence of the six points but been overruled by her Cabinet – a rare occurrence during her premiership. For Sadat, this point was an additional assurance that his Third Army was safe. Sadat had staked his whole life on being right. Critics would accuse him of taking a gamble so great that he had no right even to consider it. But to Sadat, it fitted so closely to his conception that he knew that he would not be proved wrong. Sadat even argued that the case of the Third Army was not the heart of the matter between Egypt and the United States. He wanted to end Nasser's legacy and would re-establish relations with the US as soon as possible.

To Kissinger, this again might seem a courageous act but this decision was part of Sadat's overall strategy. It was to the United States that he was now going to look to solve the great problem of war and peace. But he considered it too early to withdraw his powerful weapon – the oil embargo. This had to wait for tangible Arab successes because the weapon was in the hands of the Arab rulers and not his. They still had to be persuaded that their sacrifices and the risk they had taken were worthwhile.

Agreements between Israel and Sadat were to be far more important in the future but the six-point understanding had a special long-term significance. It showed an Arab leader prepared to make concessions, and trying to understand the Israeli mentality. The Arabs had won an unenviable reputation for (in Foreign Minister Abba Eban's words) never missing a chance to miss an opportunity. They insisted on 100 per cent success and, as a result, ended up with nothing.

In his controversial book *Autumn of Fury*, Mohammed Heikal claims that Sadat made a number of startling statements including one that the real enemy was the Soviet Union and that Egypt had fought the last war with Israel. It is surprising that in his memoirs Kissinger does not mention these words, which were crucial to the change of policy Sadat was signalling.

Whether Heikal's recollection was faulty or not is of less importance than his theory that Sadat had a practical Arab plan and abandoned it. By deciding to diversify his arms supplies and accept American weapons, Sadat was certainly signalling that he was replacing the Soviet Union as his only arms supplier and thus removing its role as Egypt's main 'protector'.

However, by arguing that Sadat could have adopted the Arab system rather than placing Egypt in a new military alliance, Heikal displayed all the weaknesses in Nasserite thinking. Nasser had rejected and eventually destroyed the Western Baghdad Pact, sponsored by Britain, with the aim of containing the ambitions of the Soviet Union. Nasser had also opposed the Eisenhower Doctrine, a looser defence system for the Middle East.

Heikal suggests that there was an Arab system, whereby the countries of the area combined for their own defence, not committing themselves in advance to either of the superpowers. This had for more than 20 years been the aspiration of most Arabs despite many setbacks, according to Heikal. Now Egypt, the leading Arab country, was abandoning the concept. The main difference between the concept Heikal liked and the pro-Western one now being adopted by Sadat was that while in the Arab system Israel was excluded, in the second Israel, if not formally a partner, inevitably was the principal beneficiary.

Perhaps nothing reveals the extent of the self-delusion suffered by those still clinging to Nasser's dreams. The fact that Heikal is widely recognised as the outstanding Egyptian journalist and current affairs writer for at least half a century adds to the difficulty in understanding such a stand.

There never has been an Arab grouping able to stand aside from one or other of the great powers. There could never be any great power interest in keeping such a grouping, were it to exist, in existence. Nor can Sadat be blamed for splintering the Arab world into small political and geographical units squabbling with one another. Egypt, with only a few years of independence from British supremacy, could hardly be described as the modernising and unifying force in the Arab world. It was Egypt's military intervention in the Yemen civil war which led to the sharp division between traditionalists and radicals. Paradoxically, it was Sadat's breaking of the psychological barrier, by which even men like Mohammed Heikal were held back, that unified most of the Arab world in one camp of rejection.

The lack of realism among Sadat's critics is shown also in the first disengagement agreement signed by Egypt and Israel, with Kissinger's aid. Heikal mentions what to him was an appalling event during the discussions in Aswan about the agreement. It had been accepted that Egypt would keep no more than 30 tanks in Sinai but then Sadat, in a gesture of goodwill, said that these 30 could also be withdrawn.

General Gamasy, Director of Operations, who had negotiated the agreement at Kilometre 101 with the very shrewd Israeli General Aharon Yariv, was apparently stunned. 'What a heavy price we paid to get our tanks into Sinai,' he is reported to have said. 'Thirty tanks was a ridiculously low figure but to reduce it to none . . .!' He went over to a window and Heikal says that he saw that the general was in tears. Kissinger noticed Gamasy's emotion and was irritated by it. 'Is anything the matter?' he asked. 'No sir, orders are orders,' Gamasy replied.

Heikal wishes to present this as an example of Sadat abandoning Egypt's true interests. But this story is, on the contrary, an illustration of Sadat's realism, essential in any modern leader, and his critics' lack of it. Nor can Gamasy, whom Sadat was later to replace, be absolved from allowing personal emotion to take over professional judgement. How could anyone imagine that 30 tanks would provide Egypt with any safety against a powerfully armed Israel? Yet by a gesture, which had no military significance Sadat, reckoned, and probably reckoned correctly, he would be able to obtain from Israel and Kissinger far greater benefits.

How unjust was the accusation that Sadat unilaterally accepted 'Golda Meir's six points' can be seen from the reaction when Kissinger sent two envoys, Joe Sisco and Hal Saunders, to Jerusalem to tell the Israeli leaders of Sadat's decision. While Golda Meir, confronted with Sadat's acceptance of essentially her own proposals, saw the agreement as a 'fantastic achievement', her Cabinet was far less certain. It insisted on the United States agreeing on a memorandum of understanding defining exactly how Israel saw the implementation of the six points. Kissinger realised that he could not go back to Sadat and ask him to spell out specifically that he accepted Israeli wishes, such as the lifting of the blockage of Bab el-Mandeb and the Israeli control of the Cairo–Suez road.

Fortunately, a diplomatic way out was suggested by Saunders, whereby Golda Meir would, in her statement to the Knesset, give Israel's interpretation of the agreement and the United States would not contradict it. Unexpectedly, General Yariv caused a flurry of concern and possible crisis by insisting that the Israeli interpretation be publicly accepted. Both Sadat and Golda Meir could have ruined the agreement but they wisely took Kissinger's advice to go ahead with the announcement and deal later with the problems, which proved to be non-existent.

It is clear from Kissinger's recollections that he believed that without Anwar Sadat's willingness to abolish all kinds of obstacles erected by others, on the Egyptian as well as on the Israeli side, there could never have been any agreement and the long haul for a peace pact could never have started.

Although in public perception, the Geneva conference called by both the United States and the Soviet Union but with the Americans really calling the tune, was a predictable failure, this was not Kissinger's view. The conference had been called with an impossible agenda: to settle the Arab–Israeli conflict. President Assad of Syria refused to attend. For him even coming near an Israeli emissary was distasteful, if not dangerous. He had led a campaign of hatred against the Israelis and had just fought a vicious war against them. While Sadat could show the results of the fighting and could proclaim a glorious victory, giving as proof the fact that Egyptian troops were across the Suez canal, Assad could merely make proclamations about the valour of the Syrian troops and try to explain, or avoid doing so, why the Israelis were only 20 miles from the outskirts of Damascus.

Nor could the Soviet Union play a meaningful role. Foreign Minister Gromyko could merely mouth sentiments acceptable to the

Arab extremists. He could not ask less, lest he be accused of giving way to Kissinger's blandishments. By not having any diplomatic relations with Israel, the Soviet Union inflicted an impossible handicap on its already maladroit and cumbersome Middle East policy. It was to take many more years before the Soviet Union recognised the fatal mistake, but by then the Middle East had undergone dramatic changes without Soviet intervention and the Soviet diplomats no longer had a country to represent.

There was plenty of rhetoric at the conference, the most fearsome coming from the least extreme, Prime Minister Zaid Rifai of Jordan, not in the least a paradox in the Arab world where language is often used to hide meaning rather than disclose it, and words are utilised for life insurance. Even Assad had not asked that the Syrian nameplate be removed from the conference table. For the first time two Arab countries sent high-level emissaries to a conference with Israel, paving the way for President Sadat for his more daring step.

Sadat showed his versatility to perfection during Kissinger's second visit to Egypt in January which developed into the shuttle diplomacy, a graphic title coined by the ever-inventive Joe Sisco. The second disengagement plan was Moshe Dayan's. It was sufficiently perceptive and 'respectable' for Kissinger to adopt it as his own and present it to Sadat. An unfortunate mix-up in the Israeli camp, leading General Mordecai Gur, the Israeli representative at the Geneva working group, to reveal its origin, might have ruined Kissinger's mission, but Sadat pretended to be convinced by the unconvincing explanations.

While the six-point agreement, proposed by Kissinger could not, despite Heikal's sarcastic dismissal, be described as Golda Meir's plan, there is little doubt that the disengagement of troops arranged during Kissinger's first shuttle trip was Moshe Dayan's. Kissinger was even able to joke about its origin when Yigal Allon remarked that Israel acccepted it. This did not mean that Sadat had been tricked or outmanoeuvred. Sadat was aware of every trap and rejected several proposals which were not essential to a disengagement but which tended to emphasise his defeats in the second part of the war. The Israelis could be exceedingly insensitive, as when they demanded that Sadat should expel all foreign volunteers.

Though Kissinger presents a moving and highly appreciative

portrait of Anwar Sadat, it is strangely incomplete. This is surprising because Kissinger, probably more than any other foreign statesman, did try to fathom the complex character of Anwar Sadat, the underprivileged village boy, revolutionary, prisoner turned national leader of a country under great stress. But Kissinger seems to accept the facts that Sadat wanted him to see. There was the warm smile, there was the amazing ability to cut through trivia, the willingness to pay a price for benefits, an ability to think many years ahead. What does not appear in Kissinger's portrait of Sadat is the agony before the vital decision. Sadat could be highly temperamental and emotional. His anger could burst out at some perceived insult, to himself or to a guest or friend. His eyes, like Winston Churchill's, could suddenly fill with tears.

Thus when Kissinger left Egypt after his first visit in December 1973, the leader who appeared so philosophical and reasonable was actually in torment. Sadat wrote later that he was in great mental and physical pain because he could see no way out. Everything seemed to have gone wrong and he was not able to put it right because it was no longer up to him. For four days he haemorrhaged. His doctor assured him that it was all due to tension but was not really serious. He was given some medicines and the bleeding duly stopped. So tense and unhappy did he feel that he convened a meeting of the commanders of all his armed forces and he endorsed a plan to liquidate the Israeli Deversoir 'pocket'. A commander to lead the assault was appointed but the plan was never pressed home. Sadat gives no explanation for this lack of action.

Even when Sadat was negotiating with Kissinger at Aswan, after spending his birthday, as he always did, in his village of Mit Abul-Kum, he was still in mental anguish. The reason he gave was that all the powers wanted to 'negate' his victory – the United States wanted to discount it and the Soviet Union wanted to put a stop to it because the Syrians had suffered a setback despite the presence of the Soviet advisers. And, of course, Israel wanted to undo his victory.

Such attempts, Sadat stressed, did not in themselves trouble him but he wanted his victory to be 'maintained' because he regarded it as an avenue to the just peace for which he had unceasingly worked.

These are very revealing if not convincing words. They show a very proud man bitterly frustrated by the inability of his armed forces to hold on to the gains made in the early part of the war which he had minutely planned. As he implicitly admits, the dreadful disappointments came later when battle was joined, when he was no longer in total control. His greatness in the end lay in his ability to hold on to main aims even at the height of his agony. The actor was able to show a smiling face while suffering mental agonies. Peace had always been his aim but with him dealing from a seat of strength. Now he was being forced to dissimulate. Like Golda Meir, he agonised over actions that could have been taken to crush the enemy in time. Sadat had the dimensions of a fully realised Shakespearian tragic hero.

In regard to the long drawn-out negotiations with Syrian President Assad, Anwar Sadat's advice and encouragement may well have been decisive. During this excruciatingly difficult shuttle by Kissinger to obtain troop disengagement on the Golan Heights, Sadat's knowledge of Assad's devious mind, with its love of haggling, was of immense benefit. Sadat understood that there would be an agreement once Israel had decided to give up Kuneitra. Assad needed such a prize, more for his own personal prestige than for any military advantage. Kissinger described Sadat as the father of disengagement.

The term 'disengagement' is peculiarly inappropriate for Sadat. For Sadat passionately opposed a policy of drift in pursuing a national and foreign policy objective. He understood perfectly that before the Israelis and the Arabs could again talk about peace there had first to be an interval of being securely apart.

Sadat's memoirs are fascinating for this particular period, not for what they reveal but for their insight into what was going on in his mind. Clearly it projected a fantasy. He implies that he had won the war and was in a position to cut off and then strangle the Israeli bridgehead that was daring to drive into the flesh of Egypt. He makes all kinds of thunderous threats as he becomes increasingly frustrated by the prolonged negotiations between Yariv and Gamasy, neither of them fully aware what was in the minds of his leaders. However, these threats can be seen as merely the first natural reaction of a national leader. Sadat joins his readers in a kind of day-dreaming. What he actually decided to do for the sake of Egypt is what he told

Kissinger. Sadat never tried to deceive Kissinger. This was the main reason why the Secretary of State trusted Sadat so completely. One example was Sadat's attitude to Assad. He saw him as a hard, devious and untrustworthy leader. But he also acknowledged that Assad was a genuine Syrian nationalist who fought for Arab rights. Sadat could not abandon him when it came to Arab national solidarity. Kissinger was told that while Sadat wanted to accelerate his departure from the Soviet camp, he had in honour to stand by Syria so long as it sought what Arabs would consider right. If the Israelis launched a war against the Syrians, he would still have to stand by them, even if it meant the destruction of his entire policy. It would be the height of tragedy but it would be inevitable.

Sadat could also understand other views, so long as the people who held them were outstanding in different ways. Thus there is little doubt that he had an admiration for such different personalities as Golda Meir, Ariel Sharon and, later, Menachem Begin. What he admired in them was their strength of character, a strength to stand by their decisions no matter what the criticism. Among the Arab leaders there was only one that won his unqualified approval, King Faisal of Saudi Arabia, though the Sudanese President Numeiri may not have been far behind. Faisal had an instinctive belief in Sadat's aims and his honesty. Sadat valued his friendship as no other man's and took every opportunity to show it.

Sadat was generally dismissive of nearly all other Arab leaders. He disliked and distrusted King Hussein of Jordan. He thought President Gadaffi of Libya dangerously eccentric if not mad. But King Faisal was to him not merely loyal but wise, a man on whom he could rely. It was mostly thanks to King Faisal that the Arabs united for the first time in the use of their most powerful weapon, oil, during the Yom Kippur War, lifting it once no more benefits could be achieved. It was a shattering blow for Sadat – both personally and politically – when King Faisal was assassinated. Yet Faisal could be childishly simplistic. Thus he never stopped arguing at inordinate length, even in the presence of Henry Kissinger, that Communism and Zionism were in essence the same evil, working in harness, and that any notion that they were rivals was a deliberate fabrication. He once asked if Brezhnev was a Jew as his name, Leonid, had a Jewish ring about it!

Probably only a man such as Sadat with the genius of an actor and showman could have arranged and conducted so superbly the visit of President Richard Nixon to Cairo. The President was terminally wounded by the squalor of the Watergate scandal, given excessive importance and prominence by the American judiciary and politicians for a variety of complex reasons, not all of them laudatory. Now in an atmosphere of rank unreality he was living out his last days in the most powerful post in the world, with the ability to destroy all mankind with one nervous move. But here in June 1974 he was in an Egyptian capital, trying to forget his anguish, behaving as if he was still the man who deserved to be courted above all. And his hosts had to behave as if they had never heard of Watergate, the little connivances and thefts, the seedy tapes, and the inexorable demands of men set on destroying the President.

Here in Cairo was the meeting of American and Arab unreality, the world of fantasy. Seven million people lined the streets of Cairo to cheer an American President whose broad smile gave no inkling of the anguish in his soul. A lavish dinner at the ornate Qubbah Palace, and flamboyant praise for his steadfastness and honesty, completed Nixon's joyful journey. Sadat never for one moment gave the slightest impression that he was aware that he was dealing with a president who was losing power with every word uttered. Sadat spoke as if he were negotiating urgently and seriously. He insisted that the Palestinian problem was still more crucial than any other to any peace deal with Israel, though he well knew that his concept was no longer entirely valid. Regaining national honour and the return of national territory conquered by the Israelis had a very high priority and could not be excluded.

In seeking a further so-called 'disengagement agreement' with Israel, Sadat was hoping to achieve two aims. He wanted to regain more of Sinai from the Israelis and particularly to push them back behind the strategic Sinai passes. This had been his ambition in the October Yom Kippur War and he had failed. He also wished to regain the Sinai oil fields which he considered vital for Egypt's economy and essential for Egypt's national prestige.

The second, hidden, aim which the Israelis suspected, was to drive a wedge between Israel and the United States. He cleverly played on American irritation with Israeli obduracy in giving up any advantage, always fearful of their security even when they appeared so much stronger than the Arab States around them. Kissinger understood that it was sometimes to the benefit of the United States if Israel was seen to be wilful and independent, refusing to accept American pressure. The US would consequently not be blamed if Israel carried out a debatable act and would be praised if the Israelis were persuaded to accept a beneficial policy. But even Kissinger became highly irritated with the Israeli government, now no longer led by Golda Meir but by Yitzhak Rabin, the former chief of staff who was the victorious leader of the Six Day War, and who then became the independent-minded ambassador to Washington.

There is no warmth in Kissinger's references to Rabin, as there is to Golda Meir. Kissinger was frequently exasperated by Golda Meir's obstinacy, as he saw it, but was deeply impressed by her passion in defending her little country's interests. Rabin's cooler, brilliantly analytical mind appeared to jar on Kissinger. Sadat must have felt that his chances of creating a split between Israel and the United States increased when Golda resigned and Rabin took her place, the first sabra, Israeli-born politician to become Premier since the creation of the state.

Sadat was also encouraged by the arrival of President Ford after Nixon's resignation. Ford struck him as an honest, straightforward man who would understand Egypt's predicament. Ford, he said, was not a cowboy like ex-President Johnson. He came from the Mid-West where most of the population were farmers. 'In a peasant population you always find stability of character, respect for promises made, simplicity, straightforwardness and honesty. It was a pleasure to detect in him all these qualities because we are tired of the cowboy policy that the Americans conducted before the October War.'

This was the impression of the new American President that Sadat obtained, or wished to obtain, at a meeting in June 1975 in Salzburg, Austria, to which Ford invited him. Sadat appeared to have achieved one of his aims to drive a wedge between Israel and the Americans. Kissinger's 17 days of shuttling between Cairo and Jerusalem had failed to achieve the second disengagement. The Israelis were ready to give up the passes and the oilfields but insisted that Sadat give a commitment to non-belligerency. Sadat refused, arguing that if he did so he would lose the right to claim the remainder of Sinai. He castigated the Rabin government as 'weak and shaky'. Up to a point he was right, because Rabin was at odds with his bitter rival, Shimon Peres, who held the vital post of Defence Minister.

Other problems about the line of the Israeli withdrawal led to Sadat's accusing the Israelis of wishing to hold on to key positions. Despite desperate efforts by Kissinger the mission failed. There were recriminations as Kissinger appeared to blame the Israelis. This was confirmed when President Ford announced a reassessment of US policy on the Middle East, which greatly alarmed the Israelis as it was clearly directed against them.

15 · Looking to Jerusalem

In planning the road ahead, which was to take him to Jerusalem and to the Knesset, though there is no indication that he had already mapped out precisely his revolutionary initiative, Anwar Sadat tried to win legitimacy in the Arab nationalist camp, while distancing himself from the Soviet Union. He apparently thought that his hope of breaking or weakening the bonds between Israel and the United States were demolished when 76 US senators signed a petition to the President urging him not to take steps likely to weaken Israel and not to cease arms supplies to Israel.

Sadat fulminated against Israel for setting the US Congress against the presidency. He voiced his anger at the apparent ability of the Israelis to manipulate the American media, though this was far from being the full truth. Yet Sadat had succeeded for a time in creating a dangerous rift between the Israelis and the Americans. Had he been fully informed – and his memoirs make no reference to any such knowledge – he would have been surprised. President Ford was new in his job but Kissinger was the world's most adroit diplomatic negotiator. It was surprising that he could have expected Yitzhak Rabin, the former army chief, to give up the strategically vital Sinai passes without obtaining a major price for them in terms of Israeli security.

Sadat had refused to agree to non-belligerency which would have won him all he desired in regard to the passes and the Abu Rodeis oilfield. He obviously feared that the Arab world would perceive such an agreement as virtually a peace agreement. When Rabin inquired, through Kissinger, whether Sadat was prepared to sign a unilateral peace pact with Israel, he received an unequivocal refusal. Even when Israel dropped the 'non-belligerency' demand and accepted the apparently less significant 'no use of forces' substitute, there were still insurmountable problems. Rabin objected to the Egyptian insistence that the agreement would last only two years and he wished to hold on to the eastern part of the passes.

On reflection, it is difficult to understand why the Americans were so angered by the Israeli attitude. The Israelis were offering to give back the Sinai oilfields and a further large area of the Sinai peninsula. All the concessions were being made by Israel, little by little presenting a more attractive package. Without a peace treaty it was reasonable for the Israelis to request that they retain the early-warning installation at Um Hashiva and that the Israeli forces would withdraw only to the eastern part of the passes. And it would make no sense to them that any agreement should last for only two years.

Kissinger was furious at what he saw as Israeli stubbornness. He even accused Rabin of misleading him and there were fierce arguments between them. Members of the American entourage were in tears when Kissinger left Israel after the failure of his mission, for which he blamed Israel. For several months, no fresh arms deals were signed with Israel, although those already agreed upon were honoured by Washington. Rabin had some justification for complaining bitterly that the Americans were using unacceptable tactics to force Israel to agree to American wishes. Was American policy towards Israel to be 'reassessed' every time there was a disagreement? This was also a contradiction of Kissinger's claim that there was some virtue in an independent Israeli policy.

Sadat's handling of the Kissinger shuttle might appear uncharacteristic, even taking into account his wish to disrupt the Israeli – American alliance. But Sadat was faced with a number of major problems. The Rabat summit of Arab states adopted a Syrian resolution that there should not be any unilateral peace agreement with Israel. Sadat knew well that the time was still not ripe for any grandiloquent gesture. His complex relations with the Soviet Union had still not been resolved. He still relied on Soviet arms and could not disengage entirely. Visits by Egyptian ministers to Moscow proved fruitless. Much hope was placed on the planned visit to Cairo by Leonid Brezhnev but this was continually put off.

Sadat adopted a paternal attitude to the Palestine Liberation

Organisation and its leader, Yasser Arafat. But it often resembled the relationship of an indulgent father with a naughty boy. Nasser spent almost his last hours in trying to mend the bitter quarrel between the PLO and King Hussein. Nasser was furious when the PLO turned on him when he accepted the Rogers Plan. Sadat was to feel the same sense of outrage very soon. In the meantime, Sadat felt the need to promote the cause of the PLO and pushed forward the proposal that it be recognised as the sole representative of the Palestinian people. Earlier, Sadat had met King Hussein of Jordan in Cairo and both had issued a statement recognising Hussein's right to negotiate on the future of the West Bank. When the Rabat summit convened, there was overwhelming support for the PLO as the Palestinians' sole representative. Not to be totally isolated, Hussein voted for the resolution.

Rabin noted that Sadat showed no awareness of his joint statement with the king and said this provided a warning about Sadat. If Sadat could break an agreement with a fellow Arab leader, how would he treat an agreement with Israel if put under Arab pressure? This confirmed Rabin in the belief that the most important part of any agreement with Egypt was not the commitment it contained but the concrete conditions it established on the ground.

It is clear that although he says that he eagerly listened to Kissinger's descriptions of the Arab leaders, Rabin at this point still misunderstood Sadat. Rabin even made a point of mentioning that Sadat had turned towards Nazi Germany as a young officer in the Egyptian Army and that his career had been marked by a succession of sharp and sudden shifts from one orientation to its opposite, from warm friendship to violent hostility.

In 1971 he signed a treaty of friendship with the Soviet Union and a year later he expelled the Soviets and switched his affections to the Americans. In 1973 he went to war alongside his 'brother' President Assad and then consented to a ceasefire without prior co-ordination with Syria. Sadat's autobiography confirmed my impression by showing that he was flagrantly disloyal to Nasser – first showering him with compliments and then going on to shatter his image with tales of the terrible calamity he brought upon Egypt because of his unsteady nerves.

Even a superficial reading of the present reassessment of Anwar

Sadat would show how unfair this judgement is. Rabin who was later to show political bravery, to complement his military, almost on a level commensurate with Sadat's, was generous enough to admit that his early judgement, based as it was on scarce information, was faulty. Rabin came to see Sadat as the father of the whole Middle East peace process and the one who tried to bring a halt to 100 years of Jewish–Arab bloodshed.

Significantly, it was Sadat who revived the disengagement talks by saying that he wished the talks to restart. This was not Kissinger's greatest hour. The threat to go back to the Geneva conference if the Israelis did not accept the US proposals had no validity because it was not in the Americans' interest. To bring the Soviet Union back to the centre of the stage made no sense. Nor would the Egyptians, now trying to reduce Soviet influence, welcome it. Everyone knew that a Geneva conference would lead to chaos.

With new ideas coming from the Israelis, and with the Egyptians proving receptive, Kissinger was able to undertake another diplomatic shuttle with much better hopes of success. The main innovation was the introduction of American servicemen to man the early-warning systems in the areas of the passes and operate them on behalf of both Israel and Egypt. The interim agreement with Egypt was completed and approved by the Israeli Cabinet a day later.

For Rabin the agreement had many important aspects for the security of Israel. A memorandum of understanding with the US linked the policies of the two countries to a much greater degree. The US would not deal with or negotiate with the PLO. The US would not undertake any Middle East initiative without first consulting Israel. The vague UN resolutions 242 and 338 would remain the basis for peace negotiations. For Sadat the agreement made it possible to reopen the Suez Canal and remove from his sight the greatest single humiliation from the Six-Day War, a blocked, dead Canal. He regained the oil wells. He could start rebuilding the destroyed cities around Suez.

Rabin is right in claiming in his memoirs that at this momentous moment the foundations of Anwar Sadat's historic visit to Jerusalem on 9 November 1977 were laid. The Likud opposition party, led by Menachem Begin, attacked the agreement. The critics even included

Moshe Dayan. But Begin would never have received Sadat in the Knesset and won the acclamation of the world if the breakthrough had not been achieved through the agreement reached by Sadat and Rabin.

'I am never happier than when I am on the banks of the Suez Canal', Sadat was to write. For hours on end he would sit in a small log cabin watching the progress of work on new projects and the reconstruction effort. There was no happier day for Sadat than 5 June 1975 when he flew in by helicopter and then drove to a cermonial platform where he declared the Suez Canal reopened for international shipping. He thought he saw joy in the eyes of the men, women and children who had been repatriated to the area after so many years. His elation was so deep that Sadat wrote ecstatically about the occasion, eulogising the 7,000-year old Egyptian civilisation and claiming that the 'Canal people' were different from all other Egyptians. He recounted how an old man stood in front of his car and then went down on his knees to offer thanksgiving to God.

In his most splendid white uniform as Commander-in-Chief of the Egyptian Navy, President Anwar Sadat exuded happiness and composure. Yet he was taking a considerable gamble. The disengagement talks with the Israelis had failed and Kissinger had returned home in bitterness. Any moment the Israelis could have opened fire. Yet Sadat had read the situation correctly. At this meeting with President Ford he had received the strong impression that the Americans would look with favour on the re-opening of the Canal. When he first raised with Kissinger as long ago as December 1974 the possibility of receiving American aid to clear the Canal, there was an immediate and positive response. The US helicopter-carrier, the *Iwo Jima*, from the Sixth Fleet, with adequate clearing equipment was invited to anchor at Port Said. Sadat paid fulsome tribute to the Americans for their part in clearing the blocked water-way. The final signing of the Israeli–Egyptian agreement made the reopening of the Canal so much safer and accelerated the rebuilding of the Suez towns.

Sadat indignantly rejected criticism that by opening the Suez Canal to shipping and rebuilding the Suez towns he was implicitly accepting the Israeli demands for non-belligerency. Rabin was well aware that regaining the Sinai oilfields and making the Suez towns live again, Sadat would have strong reasons for maintaining the peace with Israel. Earlier Moshe Dayan had argued that by withdrawing from the Suez Canal the Israelis would provide the Egyptians with the reason to live in peace with Israel. Dayan did not receive sufficient support within the Cabinet, nor did he persevere long enough. Now Rabin, as well as Peres, felt that Israel needed a specific non-belligerency commitment from Sadat, in addition to the confidence-building acts on the ground.

There were also economic benefits to which Sadat drew attention. He, in fact, exaggerated the advantages of having the Canal open, seeing in it a panacea for many, if not all economic ills. But that there were considerable benefits could be quickly seen by the clear boost to the Egyptian economy. Sadat was justified, in the minds of impartial economists, in seeing the critics as blinded by political prejudices.

In the past, Sadat told his critics, it was in the Arab interests to keep the Canal closed. Now the situation had changed following his 'great victory' in the October War. The Arabs could reap rich benefits from a freed Canal. While pledging that he would now allow Israeli ships to use the Canal, Sadat remarked that if Israel gave the necessary concessions at the Geneva conference, he would consider granting it the use of the Canal as part of a permanent settlement. He was giving the impression of speaking from a position of strength. Israel, not he, would have to be the supplicant in future.

To the Arab critics, who alleged that by allowing the Americans to man early-warning systems in Sinai he was selling out to them and presenting them with bases on Egyptian soil, Sadat responded with disdainful vigour. Why did not these critics, he asked, allege that the Russians were occupying Egyptian land when they manned early-warning stations? For Sadat these allegations were particularly hurtful and illogical because he was elated at receiving back the oilfields and the Sinai passes. He stressed that the American-manned station was Egyptian for which he paid with his own money. 'I am free to spend my own money as I wish.'

There was a realisation now that Kissinger's step-by-step strategy had run its course. For Israel there was no great benefit from giving up more land for limited recognition. Every time a piece of land was given up, either in Sinai or on the Syrian front, Israel was left with less to bargain with in the future. Sadat recognised that the time was still not ripe for a full-scale peace treaty with Israel, though he already talked about a 'peace agreement', distinguishing sharply between the two concepts. Even for a peace agreement, which would not have entailed an exchange of ambassadors and normal relations, Sadat required that Israel accept the demands of the Rabat conference for the return of all conquered Arab lands and give rights to the Palestinians, whatever that meant precisely.

For the moment, Sadat turned his mind to the unsatisfactory relations with the Soviet Union and the explosive situation in Lebanon.

Sadat saw himself, and was increasingly seen by European leaders, as a statesman of international stature. His visits to the United States, Britain and France gave him considerable satisfaction. The warmth of his reception in France particularly delighted him. He established an unusually close friendship with Chancellor Kreisky of Austria, the Jewish socialist who had so shocked Golda Meir. As for the Americans, Sadat felt that Ford and Kissinger would now press for a reconvening of the Geneva conference where really major progress in the Arab–Israeli conflict could be made. It took him some time to realise that the Americans were not keen on Geneva, unwilling to give the Soviet Union a role.

Everyone, Sadat proclaimed proudly, was now seeking Egypt's friendship and willing to listen to its voice. Egypt, which really meant him, had even helped to reduce the intensity of the Cold War between the two super-powers and maintain a balance of power. 'Egyptian policies are the ones that ultimately prevail, determine the course of events, and serve as the focus of all inter-Arab intiatives.' Although he was still capable of making bombastic statements, this was basically a new Anwar Sadat. The 'glorious October victory' had given him a new confidence and he could speak with derision about the narrow mindedness of his opponents.

Realising what a sharp battle he had taken part in and what formidable opponents the Israelis had once more proved to be, Sadat stopped making the blood-curdling denunciations of Israel. The more Sadat was accepted in the West, the more the Western

155

media sought his views (he was superb in handling journalists and television interviewers) the more was Sadat prepared to lash out at the 'mercenary' critics in Syria and among the Palestinians against his peace moves.

Feeling himself a world statesman, Sadat was ever more keen to break the Soviet bear-hug, weak though it now was. He still needed Soviet arms and still worried about the huge debts which the Kremlin refused to renegotiate effectively. Again promises of arms deliveries were made and broken. Sadat had to look elsewhere.

He picked on two Communist countries that had troubled relations with the Kremlin. Romania was ruled by a tough, independent-minded dictator, Nicolai Ceauşescu, who was more Leninist in outlook than Brezhnev. He kept Romania in the Warsaw Pact dominated by the Soviet Union but refused to take part in the invasion of Czechoslovakia. When the Kremlin broke off relations with Israel during the Six-Day War and forced other members of the Pact to follow suit, Romania was the only Eastern European country to maintain its links with Jerusalem.

For someone who was later so vilified, Nicolai Ceauşescu showed unusual courage and understanding. He established an intriguing relationship with the remarkable Chief Rabbi Moses Rosen, allowing him to maintain synagogues, establish Jewish schools and promote mass emigration of Romanian Jews to Israel. Through his links with Sadat and, later, with Menachem Begin, Ceauşescu was to play a pivotal role in the drive to Jerusalem.

For the present, Sadat was seeking arms and it is likely that he got some from Romania. A larger and more unexpected supplier of spare parts for Soviet planes and tanks proved to be China. The Chinese, still in the midst of their prolonged quarrel with the Kremlin, were happy to provide Sadat with engines for his MIG-21 planes and a great variety of spare parts for his Soviet weapons. And Sadat was additionally delighted that the Chinese refused to take any payment. 'They do not act like other superpowers, they are not arms dealers', he remarked.

As Sadat's links with the United States grew and as he noticed increasing approval for his policies in Western Europe, in China and in Romania, the formal breaking of his treaty of friendship with the Soviet Union became an ever-closer possibility. He exaggerated in his own mind his relations with France, claiming that he had a treaty of friendship with it when there was merely good will. Although he constantly fulminated against the Kremlin for its prevarications and its inability to keep its promises, Sadat seems never to have asked himself whether the Kremlin was still keen to pour large sums of money and effort into a relationship which had given it few benefits and many headaches. Had there been great anxiety in Moscow to maintain the relationship at a high level, Brezhmev would surely have visited Cairo and the Egyptian ministers would have returned from Moscow less frustrated. When Sadat announced early in 1976 that he was abrogating his treaty of friendship with the Soviet Union there was no cry of anguish from Moscow, no desperate attempt to keep it in being.

Almost from the end of the October Yom Kippur War, Sadat felt that not enough was being made both at home and in the Arab world of the 'great victory'. He found it difficult to understand why this should be. Even if there was a controversy about the extent and value of the Israeli bridgehead across the Canal, which he persisted in describing as a 'TV operation', the planning and execution of the crossing of the Canal and the capture of the Bar-Lev Line strongpoints had undoubtedly been a triumph. Henry Kissinger had personally voiced to him the feelings of the West, of respect and astonishment. The Egyptian troops had fought well and bravely, as had even been admitted by the Israeli generals and ministers. The mask of invincibility worn by the Israeli forces had been shattered. He himself felt elated and inspired yet there was a niggling reaction among the very people who should be celebrating. He had invited the famous Egyptian film actor, Omar Sharif, to see him and suggested making a grandiose film, to equal any Hollywood spectacular, to mark the victory but nothing came of it.

Contrary to the impression held by Yitzhak Rabin, Sadat did not abandon the PLO during his meeting with King Hussein in Alexandria in 1974. He took up its cause again at the Rabat Summit, betraying Hussein in the process. This is certainly the view of historians. Sadat convinced Hussein that he had no option but to accept the PLO as the representative of the Palestinian people. When Sadat met Arafat in October 1974, he assured him of Egyptian support and informed him of the outcome of the meeting with King Hussein.

For Sadat the assassination of King Faisal of Saudi Arabia at the beginning of 1975 was a devastating blow, both personally and as President. Their close friendship had led to the formation of an Egyptian–Saudi alliance. Sadat was anxious not to give the impression that he was excluding any other Arab country because he wished to emphasise his leadership of the Arab world and the fact that all Arabs, rich and poor, had participated in the October triumph. Nevertheless, no other Arab country could give him such leverage and such prestige as Saudi Arabia, constantly being wooed by the great powers, particularly the United States and Britain. Moreover, King Faisal's loyalty and support for his policies provided an immense comfort for Sadat. The unstable Gadaffi had betrayed him during the critical moments of the war, sending back empty ships when they should have been filled with tanks. President Assad of Syria was continually complaining and was pursuing devious policies but Faisal stood by Sadat before, during and after the war. By placing the immense oil weapon at Sadat's command, he gave Egypt a vital weapon which the United States and Europe could not ignore.

When he heard of Faisal's assassination, Sadat was both shocked and alarmed. He put his armed forces on alert and sent naval units to the Red Sea to assist the royal family in case King Faisal was the victim of a conspiracy instead of a single unstable individual. Sadat was assured that there was no danger to the royal family. He was able to maintain good relations with Faisal's successor, King Khaled, but he missed the close friendship with Faisal.

Had Faisal been alive, it is possible that the campaign against Sadat would not have reached such heights of vindictiveness. Yasser Arafat relied largely on the funds he received from the Saudi Arabians and he would have thought twice before launching vituperative attacks on Sadat. In one declaration, Arafat appeared to place a wedge between the Sadat government and the Egyptian Army when he said that 'the Egyptian Army will not stand idly by if the Palestinian revolution is harmed'. Sadat became increasingly irritated with Yasser Arafat and the whole PLO leadership. He found it impossible to understand why Arafat should attack him so bitterly for having recovered Arab land, regained strategic passes and taken possession again of Arab oil wells, as well as reopening the Arabs' great asset, the Suez Canal. It seemed to Sadat that this attitude graphically illustrated the lack of common sense in Arab policy towards Israel and the super-powers. He pointed out that for 50 years the Arabs had cursed the United States and had got nothing in return. Were they going to do the same for the next 50 years?

For Sadat it was obvious that '90 per cent of the cards are in American hands' and the Arabs would achieve precisely nothing without American aid. He never stopped hammering home this point. His later achievement of signing a treaty with Israel and regaining all Egyptian land, he attributed almost entirely to holding fast to this truth.

This irritation with the PLO changed to fury when he listened to the slander and abuse levelled at him by the PLO radio station in Cairo. To Sadat this was a double affront. No country had made so many sacrifices for the Palestinian cause and no country had been more hospitable to the PLO leaders. Without Egyptian support the PLO might never have developed into an influential group and, perhaps, might not even have survived its infancy. Sadat sent a warning to Arafat not to abuse Egyptian hospitality and, when this failed, closed down the Cairo half of Voice of Palestine Radio. He was unable to act against the other half, as it was located in Baghdad. The anti-Sadat vituperation continued at a high level.

This changed from words to terrorist action when on 15 September 1975 the Egyptian Embassy in Madrid was attacked by a Palestinian Fatah gang. They took the Ambassador and two of his aides hostage and demanded an Egyptian acknowledgement that the second disengagement agreement was a betrayal of the Arab cause. Only when a number of Arab governments signed a declaration criticising the agreement were the hostages released.

Despite these verbal and physical attacks by Yasser Arafat's PLO, Sadat did not break off relations with it. He never abandoned the Palestinian cause and appeared partly to attribute PLO excesses to frustration, blaming Israel for lack of generosity and flexibility. Sadat felt less patience with President Assad and his Syrian regime. The peaceful situation in Lebanon had been transformed by the arrival of many thousands of Palestinians, expelled by King Hussein of Jordan following the 'Black September' massacre in 1970 when he quashed an attempt by the PLO to overthrow him.

With the arrival of the Palestinians, the dominance in the country of the minority Christian community, already shaken, was challenged head on by the left-wing Muslim groups, leading to fighting and a bloody civil war which was to cause Sadat much distress.

16 · Trouble at home

While there were heated debates about whether Sadat failed or succeeded in his peace policies – debates which have continued to this day – even his closest supporters would not claim that he accomplished his aim of transforming the Egyptian economy and bringing a better life to the ever-increasing millions of his people. However, it is doubtful whether the failure was as complete as Sadat's critics claim. They give Sadat little credit for undoing some of the damage perpetrated by Nasser's 'socialist' policies which included the exclusion of the country's most productive elements.

For his critics, such as Mohammed Heikal, Sadat's economic policies were not only mistaken but venal and often the cause of corruption. Heikal's case for the prosecution is well presented. His argument is that by failing to control the influx of oil dollars to Egypt and allowing immoral entrepreneurs to misuse the freedom granted to them by the regime's revolutionary open-door economic policy, Sadat effectively ruined the country's economy and helped to bring about the mass demonstrations in the streets which, in turn, prompted him to adopt destructive home and catastrophic foreign policies.

Heikal claims that the first impact of Arab oil money was relatively controlled and went on specific projects, such as the rebuilding of the devastated Suez towns. But soon the flood of new money, both Arab and Western, permeated every part of Egyptian society. Whereas the Nasser-led revolution of 1952 had wrested control of most of the commercial and industrial life of the country from foreign hands, now power was being given to new groups who could misuse their possession of foreign currency. The official policy, *infitah* (opening) rendered the country wide open to foreign financiers and businessmen, as it had been during the time of the Kheidive Ismail who ruled from 1863 to 1879 and who impoverished the country.

Egypt, Heikal charged, was not being transformed from a planned to a market economy but to a supermarket economy. Undoubtedly Heikal made a valid point when he pointed out that not more than four per cent of the young men and women leaving the universities found opportunities for employment in a country described by American financier David Rockefeller as being inspired by an alliance of Arab money, Egyptian manpower and American technology. The students under Sadat's rule were faced with permanent unemployment and homelessness (flats were very expensive) or with emigration. Egypt lost not only many of its skilled workers and intellectuals but even peasants. No fewer than a million *fellahin* emigrated to Iraq, 250,000 to Jordan and hundreds of thousands to other Arab lands, despite their deep attachment to their own land. Egyptian society had become polarised between the 'fat cats' and their hangers-on, and the rest of the population. What Heikal omits to mention is that Nasser's promise to provide employment to all university graduates was preposterously unrealistic and was to boomerang on his successor.

Despite his vivid phrases and justified criticism of some parts of Sadat's policies, Mohammed Heikal, like so many of the President's denigrators, gave only a partial account of Sadat's aim and policies. Although a more complete account does not exonerate Sadat from the charges that he failed to transform fully the country's economic life and left parts of it almost as poverty-stricken as when he took over the leadership, it does provide at least some of the reasons for the failures. To attribute those failures entirely to Sadat's open-door policy and to omit mention of Egypt's backwardness and an uncontrolled, perhaps uncontrollable, population explosion is to give a totally misleading account of the problem.

Considering the failures of much more advanced countries to deal with economic problems and their inability to provide work for millions of their citizens, Sadat's comparative lack of success deserves understanding, even some sympathy. When he became President, Sadat had to deal with a legacy which would have

162

daunted most men. Nasser left him a crumbling economy, inter-communal tension, widespread poverty, a huge, corrupt bureau-cracy, ancient and inefficient public services, gross food shortages, and, above all, an immense birth rate increasing the population by close to one million every year. Probably only the innate good nature and passivity of the Egyptian people limited the mass violence to relatively few occasions and then only when the mostly illiterate or half-illiterate masses feared that their most fundamental foods, through the removal of subsidies, would become too expen-sive for them. Once this threat was removed, the street violence, mostly confined to Cairo, quickly subsided.

Elated by his October War success, in which he profoundly believed despite the sceptics, Sadat sought to use the same shock tactics to tackle the domestic enemy. He sought to capitalise on his newly won prestige as the 'hero of the crossing'. Even the title of the plan, 'October Paper', harked back to the war. Foreign experts agreed that the paper was the most systematic, well thought-out and comprehensive plan that Sadat ever produced. This was the more remarkable in that Sadat had no training whatever in economic planning. Sadat was later to be highly critical of Nasser's clumsy state socialism and haphazard emergency measures but in the 'October Paper' he still thought it inadvisable to distance himself entirely from his predecessor.

However, it was clear that Sadat was seeking a revolution in Eguptian life. He sought profound changes in technology, com-munications and other sectors. Curiously, his phraseology echoed an earlier speech in Britain when the Labour Prime Minister, Harold Wilson, spoke of a white-hot technological revolution. Unlike Nasser, Sadat did not indulge in ideology but saw the changes as part of a commonsense strategy which Egypt urgently needed.

Both in the use of the word 'revolution' and 'socialism', Sadat projected different ideas. Not for him the red-hot messianic approach of Nasser. Sadat saw through the farcical weaknesses of state socialism as practised in the Soviet Union and as introduced by Nasser. He believed that by giving the private sector a greater role in wrenching the economy from its lassitude he would provide the necessary force for the revolutionary changes. At the same time he still believed that state planning could be a powerful tool to set the revolution going, and he pointed to the examples in the developed countries such as Austria, Sweden and Britain under a Labour Government.

Sadat was particularly struck by the successes of his friend President Kreisky of Austria. An ostensibly socialist regime was able to give encouragement to private enterprise and the country appeared to be making astonishing progress in economic recovery. This may have prompted Sadat to give ever more prominence to private enterprise which finally obtained the major task of leading the economy and bringing about a better life for the ordinary Egyptians.

For Sadat a transformation of Egyptian agriculture had a special symbolic meaning. He hoped to see modern farming methods used widely. He chose his native village of Mit Abul-Kum as one of the first places which would benefit from these transformations but did not live long enough to witness them reach their fruition.

All the time Sadat was looking for models that he could follow. His lack of economic training – not unusual in modern leaders, even of highly developed countries – forced him to rely almost entirely on the skill of his officials but he liked to give them models. Apart from Austria, Sadat saw much to admire in his friend, the Shah's Iran. There he saw large wealth, obtained from the sale of oil, used to make the country militarily powerful and to introduce up-to-date technology by collaborating with the West particularly the United States. Sadat was aware that he did not possess even a semblance of the Shah's wealth but he hoped his new stature as an Arab hero and as a friend of the United States would lead to the influx of funds which would make it possible to introduce his revolutionary changes.

For Sadat, technology was the powerful secret that would eradicate most of Egypt's ills and bring about a new era. Looking at China with its huge population increasing at a fantastic rate, he admired its leaders for their ability to make it a super-power, able to produce nuclear weapons. China, although still poor, appeared to show the way for any country with a large population to feed. There were no reports of people dying of hunger in China or even of living in intolerable conditions that would provoke revolt.

Unlike the Chinese leaders, he did see the need to liberalise his regime. He felt that he could not bring about greater economic freedom without also giving the people more democracy. But his idea of democracy was idiosyncratic, with the people's needs being given greater emphasis than the individual's. He hated to see groups meet and adopt resolutions without first consulting him, even if the demands were in tune with his desires. Thus Sadat was furious when, in 1972, ten prominent personalities in the government and the Arab Socialist Union submitted a letter to him asking for more democracy. Among the signatories was the moderate Mustafa Khalil, whom later Sadat made Prime Minister. Sadat denounced the ten, almost as if they bore comparison with the Ali Sabry group whom he had removed so effectively a year earlier. He interrogated members of the ten and insisted that their explanations hid conspiratorial plans. However, in the end, he adopted their mild recommendations.

While wishing to adopt Western economic practices, Sadat firmly believed that it would be dangerous for Egypt to utilise the Western democratic system, however much he talked about democracy. Under the system installed by the British, with competing parties and ambitious politicians, Egypt had been thrown into chaos from which the 1952 revolution had rescued the nation.

Now that he had won legitimacy in an heroic manner and won back honour and respect for the Egyptian people, he could act as the benevolent father of the nation. Opposition was necessary for the working of democracy but it had to be controlled and the wilder shoots of the system had to be carefully pruned. As he was above all personal ambition and as his aim was confined to serving his people, he would ensure that the various contenders for political influence acted with common sense in the interest of the country. He pointed with scorn at the pressure groups in Western countries, particularly the United States. There he saw the use of vast sums of money by private interests in the election of the President and accused the 'Zionist lobby' of having a horrifying effect on the American system of government.

Thus Anwar Sadat saw himself as a benign ruler, or dictator, as the West would judge him. Henry Kissinger noted during his Middle East shuttles that Sadat appeared to have dictatorial powers while President Assad of Syria was always concerned about the views of his colleagues. This is some distance from the pharaohonic portrait that Mohammed Heikal painted of Sadat. Heikal recalls Sadat telling him 'Gamal [Nasser] and I are the two last great pharaohs of Egypt'. To President Jimmy Carter, Sadat is said to have remarked that it was a mistake to regard him as merely the successor to Nasser. His real predecessor was Rameses II. He liked to be photographed in stern Ramesesian profile.

Mohammed Heikal does not even consider the possibility that Sadat was not entirely serious when comparing himself with Rameses. One sometimes gets the impression that while Sadat had a sense of humour – though not always of a kind appreciated in the West – Heikal lacked one entirely. Engrossing though much of Heikal's historical writings are, they would be more convincing had he been able to differentiate between casual, rhetorical remarks and long thought-out and deeply felt statements by Sadat.

Anwar Sadat had an interesting theory about freedom of speech, as Raphael Israeli has pointed out. Every group had a right to express its opinion but such an expression had to be part of the state institutions and the state-accepted frame of reference. Otherwise free speech would be used for subversion of state authority and illegal opposition to his elected leadership. When the student disturbances took place in 1972 and 1973, Sadat attacked them as being an attempt to usurp state sovereignty and national unity. He thought that by giving limited freedom of speech and carefully channelling it towards beneficial national aims he would defuse dangerous tensions. But he discovered, as other autocratic leaders had done before him, that those who were given a limited right to speak out were not grateful but sought total freedom and became indignant when not granted it. They became not less but more dangerous to the regime.

Sadat was exceptionally sensitive to the Western critics who pointed to the deficiencies in Egypt's democracy. He rejected the criticism and claimed that the democratic rule which he had instituted was as valid as any in the world. Perhaps, even more so, as the pressure groups which disfigured democratic life in other countries did not exist in Egypt. By neutralising the Arab Socialist Union, a body which, he felt, contained elements still hostile to him, Sadat thought he now controlled the major political force in the country. The students were given a certain freedom but strictly limited so that they would not indulge in any wild subversion. The Communists, whom he could not trust, he banned as being a threat to the stability of the state and as agents of the Soviet Union.

Totally convinced that he was on the right path to bring a better life for his people, Anwar Sadat could not but be profoundly shocked by the mass demonstrations and displays of violence in January 1975. This out-burst of discontent was the more wounding because it appeared to be directed against the President himself rather than his government. His people were attacking him for the scarcity of staple foods and expressing fears that rising prices might make them even more scarce in millions of homes. Sadat was taunted and ridiculed in the demonstrators' slogans, one of the most telling being: 'Oh hero of the crossing, where is our breakfast?' The taunt was the more biting because it rhymed in Arabic.

Shocked and furious, Sadat did not accept that he or his government deserved such condemnation. He was convinced that agitators, particularly the Communists, were behind the riots. He ordered the media to launch a campaign against the agitators and the newspapers, with only one or two exceptions, meekly submitted. He did change his Prime Minister, appointing the tough Mamdum Salem to the post. Salem had been a police chief and was known for his harsh methods of law enforcement. Sadat clearly hoped that Salem would be able to stifle the efforts of the agitators. However, the problem went deeper. This was dramatically shown when 40,000 textile workers in Mahalla al-Kubra went on strike. There were clashes with the police and many casualties. Even more disturbing for Sadat and Salem was that some of the strikers broke into the homes of their bosses and seized imported foreign luxuries, foodstuffs and drinks. 'This is how these thieves live while the people starve,' they shouted.

Though never admitting any flaw in policies, Sadat felt that he should try to raise a large amount of money to give his economy a lift. Fund-raising was something that he could do superbly but he shied away from everyday, boring details of economic progress. He decided in 1976 to make approaches to the rich powers, Western and Arab. He obtained a huge $1 billion aid programme from the

Americans and $2 billion from the Gulf States. The American aid was intended to provide more food for the hungry Egyptian masses, while the Gulf States' grants, over a longer period, were intended for the rebuilding of the ruined Suez cities. Alas, the Cairo masses whom he hoped to appease, were not satisfied. Sadat had given them high hopes of a great economic bonanza. They did not see it. Their stomachs still called for more food which did not arrive or they could not afford to buy. They could not possibly understand that Egypt needed several years of uninterrupted effort, and foreign aid, before the country's economic structure could be put on a sound basis. They wished for instant benefits which made the long-term solutions all the more hard to achieve, if they were ever really attainable. Sadat might glory in his foreign triumphs, the trips to the United States and Europe, the meeting with President Ford, the second disengagement agreement with Israel, the return of the oil wells, the regaining of more Sinai sand but the masses were not impressed. The hero of the crossing was no longer the hero of the Cairo streets.

Aware that he would be accused of 'selling out to the Americans', and this, indeed, was the explicit or implicit theme of many of Mohammed Heikal's accusations, Sadat explained that he was taking a rare opportunity to strengthen Egypt's economy. He rejected the notion that he was relying entirely on the Americans, stressing that his Arab brethren were even larger donors.

Sadat had a wide vision of the Egypt he wanted, economically viable, a well-fed, well-dressed people, literate and cultured. He spoke of the necessity to revolutionise methods of education and culture at all levels beginning with the eradication of illiteracy and the achievement of high standards of academic education and of scientific and technological research. Egypt, he declared, must 'free itself from the strait-jacket of uniform and centralised educational curriculi and adopt different levels of education to suit its varying environmental conditions'.

The emancipation of women was one of the aims that Sadat said he wished to achieve but he recognised that this and other aims, such as better conditions for the youth, better housing and health facilities, could not be attained in the over-crowded cities. Like

David Ben-Gurion, the Israeli leader, when referring to the empty spaces of the Negev, Sadat wished to see great efforts put into regaining the desert land of Egypt. If the 35 million Egyptians – the figure went up by nearly ten million in a decade – lived in only 3 per cent of Egyptian territory they could hardly expect satisfactory conditions. The situation was particularly demoralising in the capital, Cairo, where millions of people arrived from the provinces looking for shelter and work, neither of which was available. The City of the Dead, on the outskirts of Cairo, where large numbers of people lived in the tombs, side by side with the dead, using tomb-stones as tables and beds, was a highly disturbing consequence of this uncontrolled influx.

Sadat totally rejected the criticism that foreign interest rather than Egypt benefited from his open-door policy. 'All I need for the open door today are safeguards', he declared.

> I shall not confiscate foreign investments. The investors would be able to take their money out, after I had received half of it. But if they want to take out part of their half, they are free to do so. To my mind, the complications relating to foreigners and foreign occupation are, since 1952, no longer valid. The foreigners now come to work for me and my technology. As long as they work effectively, all is well; otherwise I shall repay them their money and show them the way out. Before the revolution the British were here and capitalism meddled in everything. Our government obeyed the orders of capitalism, of the king and of the British. Today, who can give me orders? Allah forbid! So the open door is simply a transfusion of new blood which will help us back on our feet.

Heikal gives the impression that Sadat silently acquiesced in the corruption that followed the open-air policy. There is even an implication that, far from fighting this insidious corruption, so apparently different from the golden days of his hero, Nasser, Sadat was not averse to personally benefiting from his autocratic rule. Yet there is evidence that Sadat was embarrassed by the corruption around him, which was not new but of long standing. Inevitably with the freer flow of funds from abroad and with an imperfect system of controls, there was bound to be a considerable misuse of funds. Foreign operators were bound to use their skills to circum-vent what were meant to be tight regulations. Sadat emphasised that he had no objection to anyone making money but taxes had to be levied on all gains. He stressed that he still believed in the values of the village, the values of simplicity and honesty, rather than those of the rich. However, the new system was far superior to Nasser's when 'everyone waited for his salary, queued up for promotion and had no other opportunities to build his life'.

As time went on and, despite all his efforts and hopes, no appreciable improvement in the Egyptian economy was noticeable and the life of ordinary Egyptians in town and village remained harsh, Sadat began to have doubts. He began to admit publicly that 'many things have gone wrong' and that 'no human being is infallible and I am a human being'. He acknowledged that many of his economic and social policies were at times 'faulty and did not produce the desired results' but he attributed that to the heavy burden of debt to the Soviet Union and to the red tape in Egypt itself which hampered his decisions for reform. Egypt, he admitted, was not 'good enough yet' and he could not assure his people that matters would be rectified within a year.

With some justification, Sadat blamed the rise in the cost of consumer commodities on the world markets. The ever-increasing state debts and ever-larger loans he attributed, again with considerable justification, to the need to subsidise basic consumer foods. Egypt had to use its meagre hard currency and loans to import food.

As an example of the incompetence with which he had been surrounded, Sadat mentioned that he understood that the country's deficit amounted to four billion dollars a year. He thought that this could be covered by foreign loans and grants. But then he discovered that the actual deficit was four billion pounds sterling, four times the sum at the exchange rates then prevailing. This was an amount that Egypt could not possibly cover. Thus there were two years of euphoria from the end of the war in 1973 while the state was actually on course for a catastrophe. Sadat said that Egypt's economy was comparable to a person 'who looked healthy but who had no blood in his veins and needed a transfusion to function again to prevent him becoming paralysed and dead'.

This lack of confidence in local officials made Sadat invite foreign experts, a course which inevitably aroused envy. At the same time he went off on his arduous travels to the Arab states and to the West to raise funds. He warned, however, that the transformation of the

170

country would take a number of years and that, in the meantime, there had to be austerity. Unless the country was developed properly, the Egyptians, and all the Arabs, would become isolated, remain backward and finally end up like 'Indians of America. We would lose our lands and houses and Israel would treat us the way America treats its Indians'.

For Sadat the teeming city of Cairo was a horrifying example of how lack of planning, uncontrolled mass migration of people, inadequate and poorly-run public services could destroy a country like Egypt. A city meant to house at most two million people now had a population of at least ten million, many of them living in the most squalid conditions. Public transport was ludicrously over-loaded, the telephone system hardly worked. The sewerage system was dangerously inadequate, as was the water supply. Even in central Cairo there were holes in the roads and the traffic lights were capricious or out of order, with the result that drivers ignored them. Yet Sadat dreamt of making Cairo a beautiful city again. Now, he realised, it was a dream which could only come true in the distant future.

Citing the example of Western Germany, which had risen from the ashes after the war to become one of the richest states in the world, Sadat pleaded with the Egyptians to show personal initiative and not always rely on the state. Egypt had been one of the world's greatest agricultural empires, providing food not only for itself but also for other peoples. Yet here was Egypt having to import huge amounts of food from abroad and having to pay with scarce dollars. Egyptians could easily grow vegetables and other staple foods, as well as raise chickens. He ignored, however, with contempt the statements by some foreign agitators, notably 'the madman of Libya' Gadaffi, that 'Egypt under Sadat was starving'.

Sadat sought to stir his people's imagination by evoking their ancient civilisation and drawing parallels with the present. Recalling the Pharaohs Thut-Moses I and Thut-Moses III, and alluding to the October War, he reminded audiences that 'when the primitive Hyksos tribes invaded Egypt the Egyptian will-power ultimately overpowered and expelled them, together with the Hebrew'. Rejecting the accusations that foreign banks were being given too many privileges, Sadat pointed out that banks had played a crucial role in bringing about the economic miracle in Western Germany. While the Marshall Plan aid was valuable, the banks' initiative in borrowing large amounts for reconstruction was essential.

Deciding to take over personally the control of the economy, Sadat travelled ceaselessly during 1976 to inspect projects of his five-year plan. He frequently flew by helicopter to the construction sites, spoke to the workers and managers and gave advice. He delighted in the friendship of David and Nelson Rockefeller of the Chase Manhattan Bank, and of Robert McNamara, President of the World Bank, implying that without this friendship they would not be so helpful to Egypt. His sights for recovery were, however, set not for the immediate future but for the 1980s.

17 · First steps to peace

Anwar Sadat's decision to break the psychological barrier between
Arabs and Jews, fly directly to Jerusalem and speak directly to the
Israeli people, did not come to him suddenly. It did not arise out of
desperation, it was not a momentary flash of inspiration, though
that was how it seemed to him and to his admirers and detractors. It
was the culmination of many years of private deliberations and
agonising self-examination. The manner and method of his stunning initiative perfectly exemplified his dramatic personality; the
actor, the visionary, the humanitarian, the innovator, the builder,
the confident leader, the breaker of taboos, the fearless creator of
new ideas. It also revealed his impatience with and contempt for the
Arab leaders who held on to old shibboleths and through fear,
ignorance and prejudice refused to follow in his footsteps. Had he
been less bold, he would never have achieved the great breakthrough; had he been more understanding of leaders like King
Hussein he might have achieved even more, but that is still a matter
of debate.

For inveterate critics like Mohammed Heikal, Sadat's journey to
Jerusalem was almost entirely due to two main causes. The first was
Sadat's desperation following the humiliating demonstrations
against him at a time when prominent foreign visitors were in the
country. From this arose a desire to divert people's attention from
their economic plight, from the corruption and from inefficiency of
the Sadat regime. The second main reason was Sadat's desire to join
the Western camp and continue on the path which he had started
with his new friend, Henry Kissinger. This is not convincing.

No doubt the economic factor was in Sadat's mind. Indeed, it is inconceivable that it was not, with Egypt's economic plight so woeful, with no signs of improvement. Sadat was always aware of the huge amounts of money used to buy arms, money that could have been utilised for improving the country's agriculture, his beloved villages and farms, as well as bringing about a technological revolution.

Two years earlier, in August 1974, he made what is believed to be the first public linkage between economic well-being with the attainment of peace. His vision of what kind of peace still appeared blurred to the American Congressmen who listened to him but from hints and remarks that Sadat made, then and later, it is clear that the outline of his audacious plan was already being drawn in his mind.

Sadat was as aware as any world economist, as aware as David Rockefeller, that an Egypt still nominally at war with Israel, with the possibility of fighting breaking out if not every minute then every month or year, the country, a high-risk area, was not an attractive proposition for most foreign investors. They would demand very high returns for their money which Egypt could not afford to give.

Sadat's critics argued that he provided attractive conditions for the foreign investors at the expense of his own people. The Egyptian economy had, according to a finance minister, become what it had been before the 1952 revolution; a cow grazing the pastures of Egypt, with its udder being sucked from outside. There was no compelling evidence to support this view, as a general situation, even if a number of disparate 'examples' of unfair practice were produced. Sadat was at this point driven by two conflicting desires. He wished passionately to rebuild his country, to see the destroyed cities alive again, to watch with pride the Suez Canal filled with shipping, to invest huge amounts of dollars, painfully extracted from the rich Arabs and the Americans, in a new technological future. Yet at the same time he worried that all the efforts of rebuilding would come to nothing if another war broke out. Only a long peace, with no constant threats of fighting and bombs, with the country's youth engaged on rebuilding the shattered factories and homes, and on building an entirely modern infrastructure, would heal the country's wounds and set it on a triumphant course. It was Egypt's glorious past, its civilisation that existed so outstandingly over 7,000 years ago that inspired Sadat, and not his supposed role as the modern Pharaoh.

Curiously he had a similar pride in his people to that of the great Zionist leader, Chaim Weizmann. Weizmann told the British leaders, whom he wanted to win over to supporting the aims of Zionism, that Zion's Jerusalem was a great city when London was still a swamp. Sadat spoke with contempt of the ignorant and arrogant Arab leaders whose affluent countries were nothing but desolate desert posts until, by mere chance, oil riches were discovered.

Neither the Arab world nor the Soviet Union could provide him with any immediate hope that they would one day help to promote a better life for his people. His disillusionment with the Soviet leaders and the Soviet system had reached a stage where any reference to them aroused his anger. As an example of Soviet barbarism he recalled the occasion when the Soviet leaders decided to get rid of the ferocious chief of the dreaded secret police, the KGB, Beria. They invited him to a meeting of the Central Committee's Political Bureau, the notorious Politburo, of which he was a member. They wanted to arrest and execute him. He had detailed testimony about each one of them, on tape and on photographs, carefully gathered by his numerous henchmen. With this testimony, he could destroy their careers and even take away their lives. But they could not ask anyone to arrest him because he was surrounded by his guards. At the Politburo meeting no guards were allowed. At the moment he entered the room, the doors were locked. At a signal, all the members, Khrushchev included, rushed at Beria, got hold of his neck and kept wringing it until he fell down dead.

When Khrushchev told this story, he suggested that the Egyptian leadership should take identical action against one of the ministers noted for his pro-American sympathies, whom he called 'the Egyptian Beria', Zakaria Mohieddin, notorious in Soviet eyes for hunting down suspected Communist agitators.

Sadat suspected Syria's President Assad of having tried to trick him, with the aid of the Kremlin, regaining the Golan Heights after Egypt had done most of the fighting and incurred most of the casualties. Sadat was even more angry with Colonel Gadaffi whom he accused of having betrayed Egypt by not fulfilling the promise to send oil and spare parts for aircraft. As an example of Gadaffi's 'madness', Sadat told the chilling story of how the Libyan leader, whom he also described as a Jekyll and Hyde figure, wished to sink a cruise ship with hundreds of passengers. Sadat had lent two submarines to Gadaffi. The commander of one of them told Cairo that he had been ordered by Gadaffi to sink the British liner, *Queen Elizabeth II* as she sailed through the Mediterranean to Israel, packed with many hundreds of American and British passengers, wishing to celebrate the 25th anniversary of the foundation of the Jewish state.

Fortunately the submarine commander radioed back to Alexandria naval headquarters every two hours. Sadat was told of the order and that the submarine was on the way to sink the liner, in an area controlled by the American Sixth Fleet. Sadat asked: 'Can you contact the commander of the submarine?' The naval officers replied: 'No, there is a radio blackout. We will have to wait until he makes his routine contact with us in two hours' time.' Sadat then enquired: 'Will the submarine have reached the objective by then?' The reply was 'No, not by then. We expect it will be some distance away.' A relieved Sadat exclaimed: 'Thank God! As soon as he is in touch with you give him orders from me personally that he is to abort the mission and head directly for our base in Alexandria.'

Sadat requested that he be told immediately when the submarine commander had received his orders. After two very long hours, Sadat was informed that the commander had made radio contact, had been given the new instruction and was sailing to Alexandria.

Later Sadat considered the shock and disgust that would have been felt in the civilised world at the murder of hundreds of innocent men, women and children. Moreover, the American Sixth Fleet would not have allowed the Egyptian submarine to escape. Its sinking would have added a military and political aspect to the tragedy. How, asked Sadat, could an Arab leader ever conceive such a mad, irresponsible action? For Sadat this action was further proof how immature most Arab leaders were.

For King Hussein of Jordan, Sadat had different feelings which made it impossible for him to collaborate with him. Sadat believed that King Hussein could not be trusted, that he was too shifty, that he changed his mind too many times. There was a strong element of contempt in Sadat's attitude towards King Hussein. Sadat could not understand why the Western powers, particularly Britain, still saw King Hussein as a courageous figure.

Sadat appeared to have little respect either for the veracity or courage of Yasser Arafat, the leader of the Palestine Liberation Organisation, whose base was in Cairo and whom he met from time to time. Sadat recalled a visit to Washington of Crown Prince Fahd of Saudi Arabia. The prince told President Carter that Arafat had agreed to accept Security Council Resolution 242 which recognised Israel's right to exist within secure borders. Fahd added: 'Here is Arafat's signature to this written document, testifying to this.' The very next day, Yasser Arafat stood up and announced that he did not recognise Resolution 242 and that he had not spoken to Prince Fahd on the matter. Prince Fahd was furious and as soon as he returned to Saudi Arabia he issued a violent condemnation of the PLO in which he referred to the signature of the document.

Commenting on this incident, Sadat remarked: 'He [Prince Fahd] had realised beforehand how he should deal with Arafat and his supporters. Unfortunately, I never followed that procedure in my own dealings with Arafat. The PLO people would sit with me and approve issues and resolutions but as soon as I announced them, they would evasively deny they had anything to do with them.'

With the tragic death of King Faisal, assassinated in mysterious circumstances by a young member of the royal family, Sadat lost the one single Arab figure whom he not only highly respected but whose advice he would have been prepared to take before undertaking the journey to Jerusalem. It is doubtful that Sadat would have abandoned the whole peace process but he might have prepared it more carefully and brought at least some of his closest advisers into planning.

Sadat attributed the start of his momentous peace initiative to a visit he paid to the newly elected President of the United States, Jimmy Carter. Undoubtedly there was an immediate rapport between the deeply religious, serious, Bible-influenced son of a Southern peanut farmer, and Anwar Sadat, the former village boy. Within a short time, Carter considered Sadat a 'close friend', ignoring the cynical pressmen. Carter was enchanted by Sadat's willingness to make apparent concessions in advance of any negotiations, in contrast to the 'inflexibility' of the Israelis, Rabin, Dayan and Begin. So great was the impression made on Carter by Sadat's honesty and bravery that he began to adopt a 'protective' attitude towards him. Curiously, Carter even thought that Begin took a similar view!

Carter invited Sadat to visit him in Washington in February 1977. The Arab–Israeli conflict, and not merely the Egyptian–Israeli dispute, was the theme of their talks. Before them, according to Sadat, were three main items:

1. The problem of the Arab lands occupied in the 1967 war.
2. Relations between Arabs and Israelis.
3. The Palestinian question, which the Arabs considered the basis of all the other problems.

Sadat himself added a fourth item to the agenda – the situation in Lebanon, where a civil war had broken out with many implications.

Sadat claimed that he and Carter did not differ greatly over Arab territory captured by the Israelis. They differed over the question of relations between Arabs and Israelis. Sadat asked Carter: 'How can you ask us to have normal relations with the Israelis while they continue to occupy our lands?' Israel, he argued, was anxious to normalise relations before a withdrawal agreement was reached in order to justify the occupation and its continuation – just as they once used Israeli security as a pretence to occupy the lands of others. The October War gave the lie to the theory of Israeli security. Because of this, the Israelis had come up with a new excuse, the call to establish normal relations with the Arabs before they agreed to withdraw. Sadat added: 'It is unacceptable for the Israelis to call upon us to normalise relations before we agree to end the occupation and draw up a timetable specifying the stages of a complete Israeli withdrawal from Arab lands. The talk of normalising relations, while the Israeli occupation of our lands continues, is unacceptable to any Arab thinker.'

This point was discussed at length but they failed to reach agreement. Carter, Sadat stated, failed to convince him of the justice of his point of view. Nevertheless, Sadat felt that the visit to Washington was a very important one. The two men pledged to work together towards solving the Arab–Israeli conflict, no matter what difficulties this created. Sadat remembered Carter telling him: 'We shall never lose hope. We shall certainly find a solution with each problem we are faced with. What is important is that we maintain contact between the two of us so that we can exchange points of view on every step we take'.

Sadat felt that Carter was sincere in his pledge and wanted to participate honestly and wholeheartedly in the search for a just and comprehensive solution, acceptable to all parties. President Carter, Sadat pointed out more than once, was the first American President to call unceasingly for the right of the Palestinian people to a national homeland, a call which had aroused the anger of the Israeli leaders. Golda Meir had doubted the very existence of the Palestinian people. Carter, Sadat went on to claim, had incurred the wrath and hatred of world Zionism which did everything in its power to destroy him. 'For Carter to have been faced with the enmity of the Zionists and the Israelis is understandable', Sadat bitterly commented. 'What is not understandable is the antagonism of the Arabs towards the only American President who called for a national homeland for the Palestinian people. No one else had given a thought to this from the days of Harry Truman in whose term the Jewish State was first created, right down to the time when Carter took over the US government'.

Carter, according to Sadat, received the same treatment from the Syrians. They baffled and bewildered him. At the beginning they agreed with him that the Arabs should attend the Geneva peace conference and deal with Israel as one delegation, rather than separate groups, as demanded by Israel. Carter asked Sadat for his opinion. Sadat, well aware of the devious manoeuvring to which the Syrians were addicted, told Carter that he rejected the proposal because one delegation would achieve nothing. The conference would be transformed into an auction of never-ending slogans.

Carter, with his touching goodwill and his lack of understanding of the intricacies of Middle East diplomacy, tried to persuade Sadat to accept the Syrian point of view. Carter noted in his diary that the Syrian idea that the Arab League should represent the PLO was a step forward, one example of how far he understood Assad's aims. Carter remarked 'It will be to the Palestinian advantage if the Arabs

179

go as one delegation. In that way the Palestinians will be represented. Israel will not object to the presence of the Palestinian representatives within a single delegation but if they go as a separate delegation, then the Israelis will object.'

Although knowing full well that this was another of the Syrian manoeuvres, Sadat agreed to Carter's request, as he wished to help him. The Syrians who never expected their proposal to be accepted, were very embarrassed. By bringing forward new objections in order not to attend the conference, the Syrians again split the Arab ranks, to Carter's bewilderment. Never had Carter met foreign diplomats as unreliable and as unpredictable as the Syrians. Sadat remarked that Carter expected that the Syrians would be as good as their word but was taken aback when he found that the word of a Syrian was a thousand and one words, and what they accepted one day they rejected the next, returning to it the following day. In total bewilderment, Jimmy Carter sent a personal letter to Anwar Sadat. He wrote it in his own hand and sent it through an intermediary. Neither the American Embassy in Cairo nor the Egyptian Embassy in Washington knew anything about it.

In this sad letter, Jimmy Carter confessed his bewilderment at these political manoeuvres whose aim he could not understand. He had been working hard towards a solution of the problem and imagined that his efforts would secure for him the co-operation of all the parties concerned. He had, therefore, been stunned by the manoeuvring. The complications had left him at a total loss.

Responding in a way that Carter greatly appreciated, Sadat assured him that he was still resolved to carry out what he had pledged to do during the visit to the White House. 'We would find a solution that would not only get us out of the vicious circle they were forever trying to keep us locked into but we would also reach a comprehensive solution to the Arab–Israeli conflict.' When he wrote these words, Sadat admitted he had no idea in his mind about the shape of that comprehensive solution. All he had were good intentions, coupled with a firm resolve.

It was at this time of Western bewilderment and Arab disunity that Anwar Sadat began to draw up the strategy for the breakthrough for peace with Israel. The descriptions of his train of thought which he gave later to a number of people, including his Foreign Minister,

Mohamed Ibrahim Kamel, and to the present writer personally, sound authentic and convincing.

Sadat realised that what he had to do was very complex. He had to break through psychological barriers and he would be misunderstood and perhaps even reviled. He was certain of that. But he knew also that he could not rely on anyone else, that if he was to retain the element of surprise and drama he would have to keep his thoughts mainly to himself.

Sadat's first idea was to call a meeting of the big five – the United States, the Soviet Union, China, Britain and France – in Jerusalem. The big five would guarantee peace and security for Israelis and Arabs. He had considered this plan as he flew over the Ararat mountains on his way from Romania to meet the Shah of Persia. However, Sadat decided not to pursue this plan. He realised that the Soviet leader Leonid Brezhnev would be among the five. While Brezhnev might be considered 'a friend' and a reasonable man – certainly in contrast to some of the other Soviet leaders – he was linked to the Syrians and to the Palestinians in such a close way that he would not be able to take a positive stand. Moreover, Sadat suspected that Brezhnev had not forgiven him for so badly damaging the prestige of the Soviet Union by the manner of 'expelling' the Soviet experts from Egypt (whatever mysteries the 'expulsion' still held).

A second consideration was the uncertainty about Communist China's position. China had totally supported the Arab cause, though not the extremist one of Gadaffi. (When the Libyan leader sent one of his emissaries with a request to buy an atom bomb from China, he was politely told that such a venture was not possible.) Chinese policies at the United Nations were not always predictable and Sadat feared that China might refuse to take part in the Jerusalem summit as it was then refusing to attend meetings of the UN Security Council.

A third consideration for not going ahead with the Jerusalem plan was that heads of state would be unable to give up several months to working on a Middle East solution. Certainly President Jimmy Carter would not have favoured such a summit, as he made clear later.

Having rejected the five-power summit, Sadat's mind then turned to considering the new Israeli Prime Minister, Menachem Begin, leader of the hard-line Right-wing Likud coalition which had won a sensational electoral victory, ousting the established Labour Party which had been in power ever since the establishment of the State in 1948. For Sadat the fact that Begin was known to be an advocate of the retention of all the conquered territories, believing particularly that the West Bank – Judaea and Samaria in Biblical times – was an indissoluble part of Israel, was not an additional obstacle.

When Sadat was asked his opinion of Begin following the election shock, he replied that as far as he was concerned, there could be no difference between Begin, Rabin, Golda Meir or any other Israeli elected by the people of Israel. Surprised by this answer, Mohammed Ibrahim Kamel, the then Egyptian Ambassador in Bonn, suggested to Sadat that he might have been more non-committal in his reply, particularly since Begin's party programme called for a Greater Israel to comprise all that remained of Palestine. Kamel went on to remind Sadat that 'Begin himself was an extremist and the terrorist responsible for the massacre at Deir Yassin.' Sadat replied that all Israelis were alike – a generalisation which Kamel could not accept.

For Sadat there were other considerations. He had been greatly irritated and possibly angered by the attitude of Yitzhak Rabin during their prolonged negotiations for the second disengagement agreement. Somehow Sadat got the impression that Rabin was a weak man, unable to make a decision. The manner of Rabin's virtual resignation from the Premiership may have added to this impression. It was discovered that Mrs Rabin had a bank account in Washington at a time when such accounts were not allowed for Israeli citizens. It was a comparatively trifling offence but Rabin felt that he must stand by his wife, who was later fined by an Israeli court, and resign. It appeared at the time that he had destroyed his political career.

Sadat underestimated Rabin, as later events proved. Rabin re-emerged to defeat Begin's successor, Yitzhak Shamir, and sign an historic agreement with Yasser Arafat.

Strength of character was what Sadat was seeking. He learned that after his election, Begin was planning to visit Romania and have talks with President Nicolai Ceauşescu. By good fortune, Sadat considered Ceauşescu one of his closest friends. He had also been Nasser's friend and had urged him to allow him to take on the role of mediator with Israel. Ceaușescu's insistence had greatly embarrassed Nasser, who told him: 'You go and speak to the Israelis instead of me.' When Sadat succeeded Nasser, Ceaușescu repeated his mediation proposal. He advised Sadat to negotiate directly with the Israelis. Sadat excused himself each time, giving the reason that the time was still not ripe for such a step.

Recalling the Romanian leader's repeated suggestions, the idea of a solution for the Arab–Israeli conflict came to Sadat. He recalled how Begin had often challenged the Arabs by saying: 'You Arabs have a problem with us. Your lands are in our possession. You have rights that you are always talking about and are always calling for. How can you regain them without coming to sit with us around the conference table?'

This was a question, Sadat said, that Golda Meir directed at the Arabs before Begin (though in neither case were the words used as suggested by Sadat). It was a question echoed by the world at large. 'Our image before the world was truly an ugly one,' Sadat added. 'We were calling for our land and we were refusing to ask it of those who occupied it. We were calling for our rights but we were refusing to sit down with those who had deprived us of them.' All the Arabs did even now, Sadat commented contemptuously, was to sit in their capitals and issue warnings to Israel and its friends. Every day one could hear an Arab leader threaten the Israeli leaders, calling on them to return the occupied lands 'or else'. Then the Arab leader would direct another warning to the United States to put pressure on its protégé Israel, 'or else'. The world heard those threats and warnings and laughed scornfully at the Arabs, making fun of the Arabs' peculiar methods of obtaining their rights and recovering their occupied lands.

By winning the October War, regaining their honour and proving themselves, the Arabs, Sadat argued, now had a golden opportunity. Why not put aside the slogans and attempt to solve the problem in such a way that the civilised world could accept and understand?

He meditated again on Ceaușescu's call to him to negotiate with the Israelis but he did not want to think of the Romanian leader as mediator, negotiating in the name of the Arabs. Sadat recalled how Ceaușescu had urged negotiating directly with the Israelis.

'I resolved that Egypt should take its problems into its own hands and not leave it in the hands of others.' Ceauşescu could be of some help to him in this respect.

Shortly afterwards, Sadat flew to Saudi Arabia, his first visit to the kingdom. He met King Khaled, Prince Fahd and other princes but he did not inform them of the plan that was crystallising in his mind, to bring an end to the state of hostilities with Israel. He explained that he still had not fashioned the final shape of his initiative.

Possibly had King Faisal still been alive, Sadat might well have broached the subject. Sadat's relationship with the Saudi Arabian royal family was correct but not warm. Whereas Faisal might have expressed some reservations about Sadat's sensational ideas but given him general backing, King Khaled found them totally incomprehensible. His reaction after the Jerusalem visit showed the depth of his disapproval. Sadat implied that he did not speak about his coming initiative because he wanted to prove to the whole world that he was a true man of peace and was not merely indulging in political manoeuvring. This is both confusing and unconvincing.

It was on the way back to Egypt from Saudi Arabia that the precise nature of his initiative began to take shape. His thoughts, he said, centred on a simple idea. Why should he go around in circles to reach his target? His obvious and only target was peace and peace could be achieved only through direct meetings between the parties in the conflict. It was a sentiment which had frequently been expressed by the Israeli leaders, from Ben-Gurion to Begin.

I was thinking on the following lines: Why should I not go to Israel directly? Why should I not stand before the Knesset and address the Israelis themselves as well as the whole world, putting forward the Arab cause and stating its dimensions? As I thought about it, I conjured up what the reaction might be to such a move, which no one would expect. It would be said that it was an uncalculated gamble. How can you venture to go to your own enemies? What guarantees do you have? Are you sure they would not shoot you on the streets of Jerusalem, as they did before with Count Bernadotte, the chief UN mediator in Palestine?

My answer was ready. This is my fate. No man can escape his fate. The day of my death is set beforehand by God. It might take place in

Jerusalem or in Cairo, on a bridge or under a bridge. The hour is coming, have no doubt. How can we forget the words of God Almighty? 'Wherever you may be, death shall overtake you, even though you may be in fortified castles.'

These moving words were uttered just months before he died in circumstances almost uncannily forecast by him. They have a prophetic quality as well as a searing sincerity, however much his critics might scoff at them.

While the frustrations of the latter part of the October War made Sadat physically ill with a mysterious malady, the realisation that he had hit on a tremendous truth struck him. First, he said, he felt an intellectual strain and then happiness overwhelmed him, a happiness previously unknown to him. It was a different happiness from that he felt when he learned that his troops had successfully crossed the Suez Canal and had stormed the strongpoints of the Bar-Lev Line. That happiness had a strong element of relief and pride – relief that the long planning and preparations had not failed, pride in the bravery of the Egyptian soldiers. The present happiness had a special, unalloyed, almost heavenly quality.

Having made the decision, Sadat never wavered. Throughout history, Egypt had suffered many horrors – martyrs, destruction, delays in development. Egypt had become a backward country because of the slogan 'war is supreme'. He believed that without peace, Egypt would revert to the old attitudes. He wanted to create an atmosphere that fostered development, so that Egypt could survive and become a partner in the twenty-first century before it was too late. Why, he asked himself, did he think he could achieve so much through peace?

He calculated how much war had cost Egypt and the Arab world since 1948 when Israel was established. Until the October War, 90 per cent of the economic burden was borne by Egypt. Even after the October War, when the Arab world made a lot of money out of oil (the price of which was greatly increased) and thus added to its wealth, Egypt was drained of its resources. So whenever the Israelis created problems during the peace negotiations, Sadat said his thoughts went back to the burdens Egypt had to carry and he would opt for peace.

In perhaps the most revealing and, in the circumstances, most surprising remarks he ever made, in view of his grandiose claims after the fighting, Sadat stated: 'I also thought of the direct results of the October War. What did the war achieve for us? We regained a very small portion of Sinai and we managed to re-open the Suez Canal. Against this we have to set the cost to Egypt of 14 billion pounds, plus all the losses in men and equipment. We all know that Israel was taken by surprise in the October War. But it also taught us that we could gain less by war than by our peace initiative.' Moreover, in the October War, Sadat argued, the United States had sided militarily with Israel and the Egyptians knew that they could not fight the United States. They also knew that the Soviet Union would never side with an Arab country as the United States had sided with Israel. A war with Israel would have set Egypt back more than a century. As a ruler, he felt he had a responsibility before God and his people, even though it would have been easier to act like any other Arab leader 'and drag my people to destruction while acting as a hero of slogans'.

18 · Mixed fortunes

It is curious how two of the three main actors in the Camp David peace epic deliberately avoided delving into the fascinating preliminaries to the venture which stunned the world. Anwar Sadat remained silent when questioned by his new Foreign Minister, Mohammed Ibrahim Kamal. The story that Sadat wanted to be known was short and simple: after the Romanian leader Nicolai Ceauşescu had confirmed that Menachem Begin was a strong man, Sadat decided to challenge the Israelis in the Knesset. Yet the journey might never have taken place if some Israelis, Moshe Dayan and Begin foremost among them, had not had the foresight and courage to investigate beforehand the possibility of an Egyptian–Israeli peace pact.

The Begin–Dayan partnership was a highly unusual one. Begin, the perpetual loser in Israeli elections, seen by David Ben-Gurion as virtually a fascist, had emerged as the sensational new Israeli leader. In the eyes of his followers he was more than a leader. His power was virtually that of a dictator of the Herut Party, the successor of the Revisionist New Zionist movement founded by his teacher, the brilliant and charismatic Zeev Jabotinski. He had been imprisoned by the Russians and switched to full-time leadership of the underground Irgun after arriving in Palestine during the Second World War with units of the Polish army. Several actions by the Irgun, notably at the Palestinian village of Deir Yassin, the hanging of two British soldiers and the blowing up of the King David Hotel in Jerusalem, led to his being described by the world media as a cruel terrorist. During the war a large price was put on his head by the British Army but he managed to evade arrest by disguising himself as a rabbi and living in a secret compartment in a Tel Aviv house, tended by his ever-loyal wife.

Menachem Begin never saw himself as a terrorist. He refuted the charges that the Irgun had deliberately massacred hundreds of Palestinian villagers at Deir Yassin. He blamed the British for most of the casualties at the King David Hotel because they refused to heed the warnings that bombs had been placed in it. Begin saw himself as a patriotic Jew who had to fight the British because they were cruelly preventing the rescue of the remainder of European Jewry killed by the Nazis in the Holocaust. His view of himself was shared by a large section of the Israeli public, though the Israeli Labour leaders looked upon him with deep suspicion. At one time, Ben-Gurion suspected Begin was planning a right-wing coup. In the midst of Israel's War of Independence, Ben-Gurion ordered his troops to fire on and sink an Irgun ship, the *Altalena*, packed with arms.

By the time that Begin won the 1977 election, his violent past was no longer a factor in Israeli political life. Even a man more extreme than Begin, Yitzhak Shamir, a leader of the so-called Stern Gang (known in Israel as Lehi, freedom fighters) entered political life without any difficulty. Shamir was to become Speaker of the Knesset, Foreign Minister and Prime Minister. The Israeli public was prepared to throw a veil over actions by their leaders against the Arabs and the British in the days preceding full independence.

In 1977 it was almost impossible to conceive of Menachem Begin as a terrorist. Immaculately dressed, with the manners of a Polish nobleman, he presented an image of a respected European lawyer, which, indeed, he was. He could be as pedantic as any small-town lawyer, a trait which greatly irritated Dayan, but he could also speak with the fervour of a fundamentalist religious preacher. With most of his family having been murdered by the Nazis and with an acute sense of the dangers still facing the Jewish people, Begin saw every moment of the day the fruits of the Holocaust. Some Labour critics even accused him of ignobly using the Holocaust theme for political ends, as when he passionately opposed the Reparations Agreement signed by Israel with Western Germany.

Revered by his own followers and detested by the opposition, Begin was a formidable personality, as Ceauşescu realised. He was totally convinced of the justice of his view that every part of ancient Israel had to remain within the new Israel: that Judaea and Samaria (which others referred to as the West Bank) were as much part of the Jewish State as Jerusalem and Haifa.

His unexpected electoral victory, after an unbroken chain of defeats since the establishment of the State, was, however, not entirely due to his own undoubted appeal to a large section of the Israeli public, including the Sephardim, the Jews born in or originating from Arab lands. Most of them felt a kinship with Begin. Like them he had been an outsider in Israeli society, a loser. They applauded his attacks on the 'rich kibbutzim' created by the Ashkenazi (European-born) founders of the State. However exaggerated these claims and criticisms they nevertheless had a profound effect on the Sephardim, especially the poorer sections and the religious.

Corruption within the Labour Party was another vital element that brought Begin to power. Long years as the only ruling party in Israel had badly weakened the moral fibre of the Labour Party. A leading party figure, who was due to become the Governor of the Bank of Israel, had been jailed for taking large bribes and for fraud. A Cabinet minister had committed suicide after being accused in the press of corruption, though it was never proved.

Begin surprisingly admired Dayan. Some even said that he was in awe of the general-politician, the only person in the world of whom this could be claimed. Begin admired Dayan's dashing generalship, displayed in the Suez War of 1956 and the Six-Day War of 1967, his courage, his independence, his ability to project new ideas and find solutions where none appeared to exist. Begin was delighted – and surprised – when Dayan accepted his offer to become his Foreign Minister. For Dayan, one of the most famous figures in the Labour movement, to join Begin's government was a great shock for his former colleagues. But Dayan had also undergone a profound transformation. He was bitterly accused of being the major culprit in the early reverses of the Yom Kippur War. This criticism turned to disgust and fury when the Agranat report on the causes of the failures cleared Dayan, though he had been Defence Minister, and saddled the unfortunate Chief of Staff, David Elazar, with all the blame. But with characteristic indifference – or arrogance, as others saw it – Dayan dismissed the criticism with contempt. His agreement to join Begin, though elected a Labour member of the Knesset, emphasises this contempt. Dayan knew that he was brilliant and thought it illogical not to continue serving his country, even though the Premier was the leader of a different party. Country before party was his slogan, he claimed. His ex-colleagues accused him of giving up principles for office. Yet strangely, Dayan retained a great deal of respect and admiration in sections of the Israeli public. He still epitomised to them the vibrant Sabra (Israeli-born) tough, independent and individualistic. He had lost the myth and much of the charisma. He was a wounded lion but still a lion to be feared.

It was Moshe Dayan's ability to propagate new ideas that was to prove of crucial importance for the Sadat peace initiative. He was a man of moods, frequently in pain from his sightless eye, lost so long ago when fighting for Britain against the Vichy French. He could be morose and offensive but he also could be joyful and charming, as many women could attest. Though seen by the Israeli public as powerful and decisive, Dayan could be riven with doubts. Throughout the Yom Kippur War he was in a state of shock and pessimism. A famous Israeli cartoonist, Zeev, saw him rightly as an Israeli Hamlet. He projected brilliant ideas, as he did when suggesting that the Israelis should withdraw ten and even 40 miles from the Suez Canal. But when he encountered strong opposition, he quietly accepted the situation.

Dayan had come to the conclusion that if he was to be effective as Defence Minister, he had to have the support of the formidable Prime Minister Golda Meir. She was by far the strongest, the most stubborn personality in the Cabinet, or, as her admirers remarked, the only 'real man' in it, an evaluation which she did not particularly like, seeing nothing wonderful in being male. Though unquestioningly and passionately desiring peace and often in tears at the sacrifices in young lives caused by the constant fighting with the Arabs, she doubted whether the Arab leaders really shared her desires. She suspected them, including Sadat, of wishing to trick Israel into giving up land without achieving real peace. That is why she rejected both the withdrawal from the banks of the Suez Canal and Sadat's 1971 peace initiative.

Criticism of her policies was not confined to Arab and Western leaders. Abba Eban, her Foreign Minister, was frequently at odds with her, and so to an even greater extent, was Gideon Rafael, Israel's representative at the United Nations, Ambassador to Britain and Director-General of the Foreign Ministry. Rafael, perhaps the only Israeli official to see through Sadat's clever war and peace tactics, was critical of Golda Meir's stubborness. He clearly would have liked Eban to have resigned rather than accept Golda's total control of foreign policy. Even such a level-headed general and politician as Chaim Herzog, who had an outstanding double term as President of Israel, wrote that 'her doctrinaire, inflexible approach to problems and to government was to contribute to the failings of the government before the war'. She was very much the overbearing mother who ruled the roost with an iron hand. Of course, as Herzog perceptively agrees, these very qualities proved of immense value once the war broke out.

It will always be a matter of debate whether the Sadat visit to Jerusalem would have taken place if Golda had still been Premier. Sadat believed that he could have made peace with 'the old lady', as he called her, though not with Rabin, a judgement not universally accepted. However, it is highly doubtful if an Egyptian–Israeli peace agreement could ever have been achieved without the partici- pation of Moshe Dayan and, to a lesser extent, of Ezer Weizman, a nephew of the great Chaim Weizmann, a former RAF fighter pilot and commander of the Israeli Air Force which dealt Egypt a devastating blow at the very start of the Six-Day War.

Far from impetuously deciding to visit Jerusalem, with only his friend the Shah of Persia knowing what he had in mind, Anwar Sadat had carefully prepared the ground. As Mohammed Heikal remarked, Sadat could be impetuous in small matters but not in great. Strange as it might seem, he allowed his Foreign Minister, Ismail Fahmy, to voice views on policy towards Israel and relations with the Soviet Union that were opposed to his and would have made peace with Israel inconceivable. In an interview on British television, Fahmy fully endorsed the PLO claims made by Yasser Arafat at the United Nations. Fahmy went beyond them, calling on Israel to accept the boundaries which had been proposed in 1947. He suggested that Israel should disappear as a Jewish State by transforming itself into a democratic Palestinian state with Muslims, Christians and Jews – and with the Arabs as the majority! Even that was not enough. Israel would first have to make good the losses suffered by the Palestinians for the past 26 years and recompense Egypt for its losses in oil production and other damage suffered in the 1967 war. Moreover, Israel would have to undertake to freeze its population at the 1974 level. There had to be no more Jewish immigration for 50 years.

Sadat probably allowed these and other pronouncements favouring links with the Soviet Union for two main reasons. He wanted to show that he had to fight opposition within Egypt to his peace policy and wished to use Fahmy's curious statements as a cloak to hide the sensational announcement that was being prepared. Causing a surprise was ever Sadat's great enjoyment. However, this time Sadat did not surprise Israel; he colluded with it. He surprised the Egyptian people and the whole Arab world. He astonished his new-found friend, Jimmy Carter.

Sadat, like a skilful crime writer, had laid clues to his thinking all along the way. After Fahmy had visited Moscow, ostensibly to renew the old relationship with the Soviet Union, Sadat signalled that a new road had to be taken, the road of friendship with the United States. He revealed the real state of the Egyptian economy in 1973 before the outbreak of the October War. The economy had reached rock bottom, he confessed. On one occasion it was not possible to provide bread for 1974. 'Really and truly, it was the $500 million we received immediately after the battle (from the USA) which propped us up and helped us through the painful tribulations. Our economy had been completely drained during the six years which preceded the battle.' He implied that whatever the Arab leaders discussed at their conferences and summits they would not help to feed the Egyptian masses. Nor would help come from the Soviet Union. A new scenario had to be written into the script.

For a time the Israelis were confused by the conflicting statements that were coming from Egypt, either from Cairo or their representatives in Washington. Fahmy announced that Egypt would request the immediate convening of a Geneva conference that would seek a comprehensive peace in the Middle East, after all the Arab states

192

and the PLO had been fully consulted and acted together. The war with Israel would not end until Israel withdrew from all Arab lands and a Palestinian state was established. But Sadat was gradually coming to the conclusion that achieving a comprehensive peace through a Geneva-type conference, with the Syrians and the PLO competing with each other and with Egypt by making extreme demands, was a mirage and a dangerous one at that. While all the nebulous talking continued, Egypt's problems would intensify and fester. Israel began to realise that Sadat's ultimate solution was a *de facto* alliance with the United States. No one else could help Egypt to overcome its desperate social and economic problems. No one else could put enough pressure on Israel to come to an acceptable agreement with Egypt. But it was Israel that had to help him establish an alliance with the USA. It was a huge paradox which he had, somehow, to resolve.

Another paradox facing Sadat was the US unwittingly preventing the realisation of his plans. He had regretfully, come to accept the departure of his friend 'Henry', knowing that, in any case, the time for step-by-step policies and shuttle-diplomacy had passed. He had seen possibilities in a relationship with the 'honest' President Gerald Ford. Now Ford had been superseded by the earnest Bible-quoting, human-rights champion Jimmy Carter, with his new set of advisers, with the Polish-born Brzezinski trying, inadequately, to fill the place of the German-born Jew Henry Kissinger.

Far from following in the footsteps of Kissinger and learning from his mistakes, as well as from his considerable successes, Jimmy Carter decided that his own 'New Deal' for the Middle East was the only way forward. Nor could he learn much from the Europeans who insisted on issuing pious statements in which Israel was implicitly, and sometimes, explicitly admonished for not carrying out the resolutions requiring her to withdraw from Arab lands and calling for a comprehensive peace settlement that would satisfy all the parties.

Israel was still smarting from the decision by the British government, led by Edward Heath, to stop sending spare parts and ammunition for the Centurion tanks, bought from Britain, during the Yom Kippur War. The argument that this ban was part of a general arms embargo for the Middle East added to the derision in Jerusalem. Only later, under the leadership of Margaret Thatcher, was Britain to adopt a more sensible policy towards Israel and the Arabs, a policy continued by Foreign Secretary Douglas Hurd under John Major's premiership.

An example of European and Arab blindness, and the willingness to adopt political stands at the expense of humanitarian measures occurred at the United Nations. The Europeans supported an Arab sponsored resolution in the UN General Assembly on 23 November 1976, two months before Carter assumed the presidency, ordering Israel to halt an ambitious and imaginative plan to rehouse tens of thousands of Palestinian Arabs living miserably in the UN refugee camps in the Gaza Strip. David Kimche in his book *The Last Option* makes a pertinent comment on this blocking action:

> The majority – 118 states voted against the Israeli proposal – did not do anything to alleviate the abject conditions of the refugees, which Israel had sought to do on many occasions, but they had at least the consolation that, more than a decade later, the continuing misery of these refugees provided convenient propaganda fodder for politicians bent on condemning Israel, such as the then British Minister of State at the Foreign Office, David Mellor, or the British Labour Party's spokesman on foreign affairs, Gerald Kaufman.

No such criticism could be directed at Lord Jakobovits, the emeritus British Chief Rabbi, who has frequently voiced deep sympathy with the plight of the Arab refugees and implicitly demanded more Israeli action on their behalf.

At first Sadat, always an optimist in those years, always looking for a way out, saw benefits in the arrival of Carter. He became convinced that Carter's new policy for the Middle East could at long last open the doors to a true peace agreement, advantageous for the Arabs generally and for Egypt specifically. Although Sadat brought to his meeting with Carter in April 1977 an extremist Arab plan for settling the conflict with Israel – a Palestinian state, total withdrawal from the occupied territories as a price for ending the war with Israel, not a peace pact – Carter was delighted with his visitor. The Sadat charm could be irresistible. Compared with the solemn Rabin, Sadat was warm, flexible, understanding, sympathetic. 'It was as if a shining light had burst on the Middle East scene', Carter felt. When Rabin left, Carter was angry, describing the Israeli Premier as stubborn, unimaginative and unwilling to take positive steps or risks for peace with Egypt. In contrast, it hardly mattered what Sadat said. Carter was fascinated by the magnetism of the Egyptian leader. 'He was a consummate actor', William P. Quandt, one of Carter's leading advisers, was later to remark of Sadat.

The euphoria which Sadat created was bound to disappear, as Carter's new Secretary of State, Cyrus Vance, who was quickly to develop into a diplomat of stature, realised. Sadat's plan had no chance whatsoever of succeeding. Carter's impatient question to the Israelis, whether they were ready to withdraw from the conquered territories, merely emphasised his ignorance of the deeper strands of the Arab–Israel conflict.

Sadat could not possibly have believed that his demands would meet with a suitable response. His long negotiations with the Israelis under Kissinger's guidance would have told him what to expect. Sadat told Carter that he was opposed to concluding a formal peace treaty with Israel. He was seeking instead a 'peace agreement', out of which normal relations with Israel would gradually develop after a full withdrawal from the Arab territories. Even if Israel withdrew from the territories, including Jerusalem, there would still not be an immediate normalisation of relations, no open borders and no exchange of ambassadors. Why Israel should accept such terms, Sadat did not explain.

What Sadat was doing was testing the Washington waters. How far was Carter prepared to go? How committed was he to obtaining a Middle East peace? How strong was he in resisting Jewish pressure? (Sadat had an exaggerated estimate of the power of the 'Jewish lobby'.) What genuine concessions could he wrest from the Israelis, what funds could be allocated to save the ailing Egyptian economy?

From the purely Egyptian and Arab point of view, Sadat was clearly right to pose those questions. Carter had jumped into the sea without first learning to swim. He demanded that the Israelis hold rapid negotiations with the Arabs, including the PLO, while making it known that it was willing to withdraw from the occupied territories. So sure was he of the absolute fairness of his attitude that without even consulting his staff, Carter pronounced 'there has to be a homeland provided for the Palestinian refugees'. When Brzezinski and Vance sought to fudge this statement, already imprecise, so as to assure the Israelis that there had not been a fundamental change in American policy, they received strict instructions from Carter that no elaboration or clarification about the precise meaning of 'Palestinian homeland' was to be issued. While Carter found Sadat almost irresistible, his National Security Adviser, Brzezinski was less impressed. In his diary he described Sadat as a 'man who could not distinguish fact from fiction'. Without writing or stating it, Sadat might have wondered how well Carter, and his two top aides, Vance and Brzezinski really understood the Arab–Israel conflict and why it had not been susceptible to any solution.

While the Americans were seriously considering the role that the PLO would play at the Geneva peace conference, the organisation was meeting in Cairo and openly proclaiming that it wished to see the elimination of the state of Israel. Meeting the Americans only a few days later, Sadat must have been astonished to discover that they were apparently ignorant of the PLO resolutions and spoke about a comprehensive peace agreement in which the Palestinians would participate.

When Sadat returned to Cairo, he still had to wait a few weeks to learn the outcome of the Israeli general election. It is doubtful whether he mourned the disappearance of Rabin or felt particular unease at the sensational emergence of Menachem Begin. He may well have felt a certain kinship for Begin who, though a mere prime minister in a democratic country, wielded unusual powers and brooked no opposition. Sadat understood where Begin stood but he could never fathom the cool, logical, military-political, analytical mind of Yitzhak Rabin.

For the Americans, the election of Begin, 'the hard-line extremist', was a shock. This shock was not entirely removed when Begin visited Washington. Yet whereas Begin saw Carter's formulation of US Middle East policy as totally negative – withdrawal from the occupied territories – Moshe Dayan, who was present, saw the positive side. The Americans would not impose a settlement. The Israeli borders would have to be negotiated by the parties themselves and would have to be defensible. Peace had to include open borders, diplomatic recognition and full normalisation of relations, as Israel had demanded. And the US was opposed to the establishment of a Palestinian state, favouring instead a 'Palestinian homeland', whatever that meant, linked to Jordan.

Without a Kissinger by his side to stress the realities of the Middle East morass and with a splendid confidence in his own ability to comprehend and solve the most complex of problems, Carter alarmed both Sadat and Begin. A comprehensive settlement sounded logical and magnificent, with all the Arabs agreeing what they wanted and Israel making the necessary concessions for the sake of peace. Then why not go in unison to Geneva and settle all the problems in the manner of humane God-fearing men? Carter did not seem to realise – and none of his advisers hammered home the truth – that the Arabs did not want the same thing, that they distrusted each other and that what they meant by 'peace' was totally different from what the Israelis meant by this term. Even Sadat began by believing that 'peace' meant a cessation of hostilities and that normal peace would take generations to achieve. He, too, had to break the psychological barrier.

Sadat was not particularly convinced by the diplomatic tricks by which Brzezinski and others tried to get the better of the Israelis. The collusion plan, consisting of a concocted mini-crisis in which Sadat would make extreme demands, which would be whittled down by the Americans, who would then put great pressure on a grateful Israel to accept the new reality, did not appeal to him. Knowing the Israelis far better than the Americans around Carter, Sadat appreciated that they would never fall for such a trick.

Convinced that the Americans with their naive thinking were, paradoxically, becoming a greater obstacle to a peace agreement than Sadat, Dayan suggested a revolutionary idea to a worried Begin. Why not approach Sadat secretly without the knowledge of the Americans? After some hesitation, Begin agreed.

Sadat, whose estimate of Carter and his team was almost identical to that of Begin and Dayan, was also seeking an end to his frustration. Carter's approach was totally unrealistic. Sadat was beginning to believe that direct talks with the Israelis, without the involvement of Carter, might break the stultifying impasse.

Dayan realised that an influential intermediary had to be found quickly. Romania's Nicolai Ceauşescu might have been suitable but with the KGB so heavily represented in Bucharest the secret would not have lasted long. Dayan's mind turned to King Hassan of Morocco, who had many friends in the Jewish community, and kept links even with one or two who had settled in Israel. He was known to be a moderate when it came to the Arab–Israel conflict. He was one of the very few Muslim leaders who did not join in the condemnation of Sadat for the second disengagement agreement with Israel. Dayan travelled to Marrakesh and suggested to the king that he arrange a meeting between a representative of Sadat and Dayan. The suggestion went to Cairo and with almost incredible speed – seven days only – came the positive reply. On 16 September 1977, Dayan met Sadat's representative, Hassan el-Tuhami, Deputy Prime Minister, with King Hassan as host. Tuhami, with his beard and piercing eyes, had been chosen for one main reason; absolute devotion to Sadat. Foreign Minister Fahmy knew nothing about the meeting.

Dayan gave a special written message to Sadat. The three-line message, which no one was to see before Sadat, stated simply and succinctly, that Israel was prepared to return the whole of the Sinai Peninsula to Egypt in return for a full peace treaty between the two countries, open boundaries and normal relations between two independent countries.

When shortly afterwards Dayan visited Washington, he was subjected to sharp criticism by Carter, Vice-President Mondale, and Vance who still hankered after a Geneva conference and a comprehensive settlement of all problems. Dayan thought it wise to inform Vance of his meeting in Marrakesh with Sadat's envoy.

In Cairo, Sadat also informed the American Ambassador, Hermann Eilts, of Tuhami's meeting with Dayan. Reporting to Washington, Eilts offered the opinion that if Sadat had been serious he would not have chosen a man like Tuhami.

To Dayan's amazement – and probably to Sadat's – there was no American reaction to the Marrakesh talks. They were not seen as marking any vital progress or doing any harm to the US policy. The Americans were somewhat annoyed that Israel had made an independent foray into secret diplomacy. Nothing was expected to come of it. This feeling must have been strengthened when two days after Tuhami's meetings with Dayan, Sadat sent a message to Carter to get the Geneva conference under way and stop haggling about details. The Israelis were also bewildered when they learned about this message and about Fahmy's proposal that Carter should ignore Jewish pressure and meet the PLO leader, Yasser Arafat. Fahmy told Carter that 'Arafat rightly feared that if the PLO accepted that clause [UN Resolution 242] it would in practice recognise the State of Israel and its right to live in peace.'

This explanation told as much of Fahmy's attitude to Israel as Arafat's. Sadat's real attitude became apparent when Carter, in his well-meaning innocence and ignorance, fell for a Soviet suggestion for a joint Middle East statement. Had Kissinger still been around, it is inconceivable that such a blunder, bringing the Kremlin, now totally sidelined, into the centre of the stage, could ever have been issued. Dayan, who was visiting Washington, was justifiably furious, especially as the Americans had withheld vital parts of the statement from him and particularly as the statement did not refer to peace as an objective in Geneva but only a 'settlement'. For a marathon seven hours, Dayan was closeted with Carter and Vance, until he obtained an American–Israeli 'working paper' which virtually scuttled the American–Soviet statement. The Kremlin was apparently stunned by Israel's power to reverse in one day a move over which many painstaking weeks and intense effort had been spent.

For Sadat the American–Soviet declaration was the final proof that nothing could be expected from the Americans at this moment. They had to be taught a lesson. He sent an urgent letter to Carter urging him 'that nothing be done to prevent Egypt and Israel from negotiating directly . . . either before or after the Geneva conference'. Yet nothing appeared able to lift the blinkers from Carter's eyes. He wrote to Sadat, humbly asking him to back publicly his proposals. Sadat remained silent. Another letter from Carter proclaimed that the US and the USSR would jointly convene the Geneva conference under UN auspices. By stressing that he would personally urge the settlement of the Palestinian question and Israeli withdrawals from the occupied territories, Carter appeared to be offering to ditch the Israelis in return for Sadat's support for the Geneva option.

This, for Sadat, was a most unhelpful letter. He knew that Carter totally misunderstood the situation. Above all, Sadat realised that this policy would never win him back Sinai. Something much more radical, more sensational, had to be produced.

Sadat was famous for the improvisations in his speeches. He had somewhat curbed this tendency after the Yom Kippur War but when he addressed the National Assembly on 9 November 1977 he appeared to revert to the old style. The many Arab foreign dignitaries present were used to his asides and often enjoyed them. So there was no immediate reaction, no walk-out by Arafat or any other radical, when Sadat remarked, after a long tirade against Israel, that for the sake of peace he was prepared to go 'to the end of the earth . . . even to the Knesset in Jerusalem'. The audience applauded, not realising the momentous bomb he had just exploded.

The reverberations were to win him fame and the Nobel Prize. He would become one of the great seminal figures in modern history. But he would also incur calumny and hatred before his vision was accepted as the only possible path for the future.

19 · *Hero in Jerusalem, villain in Damascus*

When Anwar Sadat offered to go to the Knesset he remarked that 'Israel will be astonished' to hear his words. The astonishment was mixed with puzzlement. The Israelis still did not understand fully his complex personality. When later Sadat, as well as Begin, received the Nobel Prize for Peace, Golda Meir remarked that she did not know whether they deserved this prize but they certainly deserved Oscars. This puzzlement was well expressed by Yigal Allon, the former Foreign Minister and one of the most brilliant generals in Israel's War of Independence. Allon asked what had happened to Sadat between May Day 1972 and November 1977. Five years previously Sadat had told his audience that he would crush the intolerable arrogance of the Israelis. He was prepared to sacrifice one million Egyptian soldiers in the next war. Now he was prepared to go to Jerusalem to 'prevent a soldier or an officer of my sons from being wounded – not killed but wounded'.

Most probably, Moshe Dayan was much less surprised. The element of the theatre that was contained in the dramatic offer and journey was shown in the conversations that took place between Walter Cronkite, the celebrated presenter of CBS News, with Sadat and Begin:

Cronkite: When will you go to Israel?
Sadat: I am just waiting for the proper invitation.
Cronkite: You must get something direct from Mr Begin, not through the press.
Sadat: Right, right.

Cronkite: And how would that be transmitted, sir, since you do not
    have diplomatic relations with Israel?
Sadat: Why not through our mutual friend, the Americans?

The only condition he would make, said Sadat, 'is that I want to
discuss the whole situation with the 120 members of the Knesset
and put the full picture and detail the situation from our point of
view'.

Begin, for his part, told Cronkite on the air that 'I will during the
week ask my friend, the American Ambassador in Israel, to find out
in Cairo from his colleague, the American Ambassador to Egypt,
whether he will be prepared to give us his good offices and transmit
a letter from me to President Sadat inviting him formally and
cordially to come to Jerusalem.'

When asked about opposition by Arab leaders to his proposed
journey, Sadat remarked:

> I did not tell any of my colleagues and I did not ask them to agree or
> disagree upon this. I felt that my responsibility and my responsibility as
> President of Egypt is to try all means to reach peace. And I took the
> decision. For sure there are those who are against it. But as much as I am
> convinced that this is the right way and my people back me, I shall be
> fulfilling the whole thing. We are at a crucial moment. There has never
> been a suitable time in the Arab world to reach a genuine peace but there
> is now, so I want to put the facts before them and at the same time we
> want to discuss what will be the alternative if we cannot achieve peace.
> It would be horrible. Believe me, horrible.

However, misunderstanding and even suspicion coloured some
of the picture of the thrilling visit to Jerusalem that captivated
millions of television viewers. Israel's Chief of Staff, Motta Gur,
worried that this was a clever ploy by Sadat as a prelude to another
1973 scenario. In a newspaper interview, which infuriated his
political superior, Defence Minister Ezer Weizman, Gur said: 'We
know that the Egyptian army is in the midst of preparations for
launching a war against Israel towards 1978, irrespective of Sadat's
declared willingness to come to Jerusalem.' Immediately after a
tense confrontation with Gur, Weizman was badly hurt in a car
accident but insisted on being taken to the Knesset to hear Sadat's
speech.

Weizman had at first thought of the whole idea of Sadat's visit to Jerusalem as a kind of fantasy. He even joked at the very idea of the hard-line stern Menachem Begin kissing the hand of Sadat's wife. Weizman was apparently only partly convinced by the arguments of the intelligence chief, Moshe Gazit, who used a memorable simile. Sadat, he said, was like a hurdler who bypasses all the obstacles, heading straight for the finishing line.

The Israeli public was stunned with amazement – and hope. As they watched on their television sets the Egyptian President emerge from his plane at Ben-Gurion Airport to be greeted by a long line of the top Israeli personalities, Menachem Begin and Golda Meir among them, many Israelis felt as if they were seeing the beginning of a Messianic era. There were cheers along the route taking Sadat's cavalcade to Jerusalem, cheers from people who only four years earlier had suffered casualties inflicted by the same President's troops. No wonder President Sadat felt somewhat bewildered as well as moved.

In Cairo, too, there was excitement and dazzlement. Crowded around television sets in homes and cafés, the Egyptians were amazed by the courage of their President in entering the den of their foremost enemy. It was as if they were watching a magnificent Hollywood epic but with their own President as the main star.

Perhaps no one in Israel saw Sadat in a more imaginative manner and more as the President saw himself than Ezer Weizman. Personal tragedy had apparently transformed this rough, tough ex-RAF fighter pilot who enjoyed using four-letter words. A head injury to his son, caused by a sniper's bullet in the War of Attrition, had made Ezer Weizman rethink his attitude to war with the Arabs, so it was said. Now, hardly able to sit in the Knesset as he was racked with pain, Weizman saw a dream being fulfilled.

Though aware that Sadat was not enamoured of the Israelis, Weizman felt that the Knesset rostrum was to be occupied by a man of extraordinary character, possessing a rare courage and great political élan. Only a man like that could have ventured a leap of such enormous dimensions. By taking it, Sadat was risking his life.

Yet Weizman, like many in the Knesset, was soon to feel a sense of disappointment. Sadat opened his address in rich-sounding

203

Arabic with a moving declaration: 'Every person who meets his end in war is a human being, irrespective whether he is Arab or Jew.' But Weizman did not like at all the subsequent remarks which he considered intransigent and even menacing. Sadat, he thought, was restating the unyielding position to which Egypt had adhered since 1967 – complete withdrawal to the old, dangerous borders, without granting Israel full peace.

'I did not come here to sign a separate peace between Egypt and Israel,' Sadat announced. 'A separate agreement between Egypt and Israel cannot guarantee a just peace. Furthermore, even if peace is achieved between Israel and all the confrontation states, without a just solution of the Palestinian problem it will not bring that just and stable peace for which attainment the whole world is pressing. I have not come here to submit a request that you evacuate your forces from the occupied lands. Total withdrawal from Arab land occupied after 1967 is self-evident. We shall not countenance any arguments about it nor will we go begging to anyone.'

When Weizman heard these words, he scribbled a note to Begin: 'We have to prepare for war.' Begin read it and nodded.

Probably it was this note that prompted Begin to make a response to Sadat's initiative that was less than imaginative. There is general agreement that Begin, normally so aware of dramatic undertones, did not totally rise to the uniqueness of the occasion. He, like Weizman, did not at this moment realise how constricted Sadat was, how he had to speak not merely to the Israelis but to his own people and to the Arab world. He could not, for one moment, give the impression that he was a traitor to the Arab cause; he had to set out the maximum of the Palestinian demands. Begin's somewhat legalistic response was not appropriate though it did no great harm. Weizman came to realise that his first impressions of Sadat's speech were misleading. What he brought to the Knesset were not the conditions for a new war. Moreover, Weizman came to appreciate later that what Sadat had done in addressing the Knesset was unique in the long, blood-stained history of relationship between Jew and Arab. What Sadat was offering in return for his terms was, he thought, full peace, not an interim arrangement but a completely normal relationship. Since the establishment of the Jewish State every Israeli leader had sought such a development and waited in vain. Now it was being unambiguously presented to the people of Israel in their own Knesset.

Fortunately, only experts spent much time in analysing Sadat's speech. Even Ministers joined in the general jubilation. Even Ezer Weizman forgot for the moment his fears. Arriving painfully in Menachem Begin's office to greet President Sadat, he hauled himself out of the wheelchair and grasping his walking stick, he swung it up in a quasi-military salute. This gesture caught Sadat by surprise. He began to laugh. It was also the beginning of a friendship which was to signally affect the tortuous negotiations for a peace pact. It is doubtful whether it was as deep as Weizman thought. Sadat never allowed personal friendship to affect his judgement, as he showed in the case of Henry Kissinger. Cynical diplomats and journalists also suspected that Weizman was being somewhat naive and was in danger of being manipulated.

Yet the jublilation in Jerusalem and the consternation in Damascus could not be fully justified, if the analysts were to be believed. Sadat's priorities were not those which Israeli leaders sought. First, there was to be a peace agreement based on Israel's withdrawal from all the Arab territory occupied in 1967. Next would come the fulfilment of Palestinian aspirations, including the setting-up of a state. Then would come the right of all nations in the region to live in peace, the non-use of force and, finally, the ending of the state of war.

Sadat did not mention open borders, diplomatic relations and full normalisation of daily contacts between Israel and its neighbours, particularly Egypt. Such a development was apparently a matter for the future, in ten years' time perhaps. Some Israeli experts even suspected that the main reason for Sadat's visit was to force Israel into a corner, so that he could speak directly to the Americans and to his fellow Arabs. To the Americans he was the man of peace, to the Arabs he was to be the hero who challenged the enemy in his own Parliament. However, this judgement by some of the experts was to be proved utterly false.

A far more convincing reason was given by Sadat himself. He had to break the psychological barrier that was stopping every drive for peace.

By psychological barrier I mean that huge wall of suspicion, fear, hate and misunderstanding that has for so long existed between Israel and the Arabs. It made each side simply unwilling to believe the other . . . I have, therefore, tended to compare that barrier to the Australian Great Barrier Reef, which is so dangerous to navigation in the southern hemisphere. We had been accustomed to regard Israel as taboo, as an entity whose emotional asssociatipns prevented anyone from approaching it. So I decided that any possible change should occur to the substance of that attitude itself. If indeed we wanted to get to grips with the substance of the dispute – with the basis of the problem – in order to establish a durable peace, I reasoned we ought to find a completely new approach that would bypass all formalities and procedural technicalities by pulling down the barrier of mutual mistrust. Only thus, I decided, could we hope to break out of the vicious circle and avert the blind alley of the past.

Sadat several times repeated this theme of the psychological barrier. He genuinely believed that he had broken it by visiting Israel – and in large measure he did do so, as the future was to show. However, he misunderstood the Israeli needs. They were grateful to him for breaking the taboo but they wanted more. Cyrus Vance, the American Secretary of State, a shrewd judge of people, noted that Sadat believed that the Jerusalem odyssey had given Israel 'her fundamental requirement'. The leader of the largest Arab nation had given Israel 'legitimacy'. Israel had been, according to the Arabs, an illegitimate intruder in the Middle East. Now it had been accepted.

This was surely, Sadat felt, a tremendous gift which should bring joy to every Israeli. He felt sad and astonished that Begin and so many Israelis appeared to reject this gift. How could Begin be so ungrateful? As Sadat at first saw the situation, according to experts at the Israeli Foreign Ministry, his gift of legitimacy would so impress Begin that he would grant all or most of the Arab demands.

According to David Kimche, the former Director-General of the Foreign Ministry, this flawed assessment by Sadat was rooted in innate Egyptian self-assurance of national, if not racial, superiority over the Jews, Zionism and Israel, which had survived the defeat of 1967 (after it had been rationalised away) and the failure of the

October 1973 war (which had been transformed into triumph and success by a similar perversion of history). 'Sadat expected that Begin and Israel would agree to all his demands with alacrity and gratitude in return for the honour bestowed upon Israel by the President of Egypt condescending to come to Jerusalem and bring us this message in person.' Yet David Kimche, after giving the cool, cynical assessment of the Foreign Ministry, was far-sighted enough to recognise the greatness and uniqueness of the Sadat odyssey. He concluded: 'However much it had been misread by Sadat – and by us – at the time, it was a glorious and unique moment in history and, undoubtedly, the cornerstone in the making of the peace between Egypt and Israel soon to be consummated.'

Vilified in the Arab capitals for breaking the Israeli taboo, Sadat discovered that barriers still existed to achieving his aims. Begin, too, was to find that he had to do a great deal of painful re-thinking.

20 · *The rocky road to Camp David*

With so many conflicting currents, so many misunderstandings, so many attempts to lay mines under the peace vehicle, it is astonishing that any agreement was ever reached and signed. It is certain that without Anwar Sadat's single-mindedness and his almost brutal disregard of the vehement advice he received from his ministers and officials, no accord could have been achieved. Even those who criticised Sadat for initially not appreciating what the Israelis really wished could not but stand in wonder at his courage in single-handedly taking Egypt away from war to peace, even if the peace remained a cold one.

However, the roles of Menachem Begin and Jimmy Carter should not be underestimated. Begin had to make very painful decisions, changing his stand on concepts which had been part of his ideology. For this transformation most credit must go to Moshe Dayan and, to a lesser degree, Ezer Weizman. Jimmy Carter, too, had to rethink his entire strategy and had to abandon many conceptions and to acknowledge his ignorance of the complex issues which made a comprehensive peace, involving all the Arabs, an impossibility. It was an injustice that he did not join Sadat and Begin as a winner of the Nobel Peace Prize.

There are both painful and farcical aspects to the aftermath of Sadat's trip to Jerusalem. In much of the Arab world there was consternation but opposition was by no means unanimous. The Saudi Arabian royal family had frequently called for a comprehensive settlement including the Palestinians, but this was probably as much out of fear of PLO gunmen as concern for the plight of the Palestinian people.

Nevertheless, there was a strong reaction in Saudi Arabia. Sadat's journey occurred on the very day of Eid el-Adha (Feast of the Sacrifice) commemorating Abraham's willingness to sacrifice his son, Isaac. The ruler of Saudi Arabia goes to the mosque in Mecca and unlocks the door of the Ka'aba, Islam's most sacred shrine. King Khaled remarked later: 'I have always before gone to the Ka'aba to pray for somebody, never to pray against anyone. But on this occasion I found myself saying: "Oh God, grant that the aeroplane taking Sadat to Jerusalem may crash before it gets there so that he may not become a scandal for all of us". I am ashamed that I prayed in the Ka'aba against Muslims.'

According to Mohammed Heikal, King Khaled added that never again would it be possible for him to put his hand into Sadat's. If political necessity ever made contact necessary, that would have to be done by his brother, Prince Fahd. 'But for me, never. Sadat has made himself a scandal for all Arabs and all Muslims'. Yet the Saudi reaction was very muted. According to Foreign Minister Kamel, Saudi Arabia did not, in contrast to several other Arab states, break diplomatic relations with Egypt but joined Jordan and the Gulf States in adopting 'a non-committal stance and chose to await the turn of events'. This does not suggest deep indignation, at least not by the whole of the royal family.

Another group of Arab states was favourably disposed to Sadat and his dramatic visit. It was led by King Hassan II of Morocco, not surprising in view of his vital role in setting up the contacts between Sadat and Begin. Morocco was joined by Sudan, whose leader, Numeiri, had a close friendship with Sadat, and by Sultan Kabous of Oman.

Leading the opposition to Sadat were the radical states, Syria, Iraq, Algeria, Libya and South Yemen. They were joined by the PLO and became known as the Steadfastness Front. They took an extremist, hostile view of Sadat's initiative, claiming it was a betrayal of the Arab cause and merely a plot by Sadat to seek a separate peace with Israel. A contemptuous Sadat reacted by severing diplomatic relations with them.

Sadat had managed to keep to himself his plan to visit Jerusalem. Even his wife, Jihan, was surprised by his statement in the National Assembly. When she tackled him about his secrecy, he admitted that he had been pondering over the issue for months and had come to the conclusion that this was the only way to regain Sinai and to remove the psychological barrier that separated Jews and Arabs. Many people telephoned her to persuade Sadat to change his mind but in vain. Among the strongest opponents were Foreign Minister Ismail Fahmy and his deputy, Mahmoud Riad, who duly resigned. In appointing Mohammed Ibrahim Kamel as Fahmy's successor without even discussing the matter with Kamel Sadat made a mistake. But, in any case, he paid little attention to the views of his Foreign Ministry staff and he quickly learned that the man with whom he had shared prison in their conspiratorial youth was not the tough, level-headed diplomat he had imagined.

If Sadat ever wanted to point at an influential Arab who still suffered from the psychological barrier dividing Jew and Arab, he could not have chosen a better example than Foreign Minister Kamel. His memoirs reek with his prejudices. His incomprehension of Sadat's aims and Israeli arguments is almost farcical. It is also sad. Yet the mass of Egyptians were delighted with their leader's initiative and courage. Forgotten were the demonstrations calling for more and cheaper food. Sadat was hailed as the 'hero of peace'. He was thrilled by the adulation he was now receiving from his people, greater than he had expected. Israelis and Jews from abroad, so long the object of vilification and dehumanisation, were welcomed in Cairo. Egyptians began to dream of a better life made possible by American money. The slogans of 'no more war', 'no more widows and orphans' caught the mood of the ordinary people. They were also in tune with the writings of famous authors such as Mahfuz.

Newspapers in Egypt all joined enthusiastically in praising Sadat and his courage. The army and the bureaucracy expressed their approval. Sadat's own mouthpiece, the *October* magazine, branded the rejectionist Arab leaders, such as Gadaffi and Boumedienne of Algeria, as 'mice and monkeys'. Sadat himself described them as 'pygmies'. Even Kamel, who was appalled when he learned of Sadat's plan to address the Knesset, could find, at that time, no justification for the Gadaffi-type vituperation. What after all, Kamel asked, did Sadat say in Jerusalem? Sadat had unflinchingly, coura-geously and honestly interpreted the principles of international law and UN resolutions on the Arab–Israeli conflict. It was Begin, according to Kamel, who tried to trick Sadat. Israel should have accepted Sadat's offer with alacrity. Therefore Egypt must not make any more concessions, must not discuss sovereignty of Arab land and should only discuss matters of security, co-existence and peaceful relations. Clearly, Kamel did not have in mind a full peace agreement and normal relations between friendly neighbours. He worried that Sadat would be cornered and would sign a separate peace with Israel.

Kamel derived some comfort from an analysis of the situation: either Sadat's initiative would succeed in achieving a just and comprehensive agreement, in which the Arabs would get back all their land, or Israel would be shown up to the world to be an aggressor state. The implication of this was clearly that the world would force Israel to give up her conquests. However, said Kamel, he overlooked then a factor which was undermining Sadat's initiative and working for its destruction.

> This unknown factor – the last thing that could have occurred to me – was Sadat himself. His bouts of enthusiasm, his precipitate action and his exaggerated concern to succeed were bound to defeat his own objectives. He had fallen victim to stimulants that few could fail to succumb to, all stemming from his initiative: the hopes that millions pinned on peace; the fierceness of the attacks from brother Arabs; the inflexibility and perfidy of Begin; his straying from the Arab fold; and finally, the fact that he seemed to be mesmerised by the deceitful American mirage he was vainly pursuing.

This summing up is more revealing of Mohammed Ibrahim Kamel's state of mind and his narrow vision than of Anwar Sadat's outlook. But it provides a notion of the type of opposition that Sadat had to face, even from so-called moderate Arabs. Characteristically, Sadat appeared to enjoy the commotion that he was creating.

The euphoria began to lessen when Sadat called for a peace conference to be held at the Mena House hotel, facing the pyramids, a month after his Jerusalem visit. The conference was to be attended by the superpowers, all the countries bordering Israel and the PLO. However, although many Arab flags flew, including that of the PLO, only Israeli and Egyptian delegates turned up. They presented their conventional stands. No progress whatsoever was made.

When Ezer Weizman visited Sadat shortly afterwards he found him still optimistic about a settlement. But there were already signs that Sadat was becoming impatient at the failure to move forward. Being constantly attacked by the 'pygmies' of the steadfastness front, Sadat was eager to prove that his visit to Jerusalem was both courageous and statesmanlike. He told Weizman that he would be prepared to accept full normalisation of relations with Israel, provided Begin agreed in principle to evacuate all Arab territories and provide a solution to the Palestinian problem. Sadat was still living under an illusion that Begin could respond in such a comprehensive manner. Weizman, who was visiting Cairo as Defence Minister to take part in talks with General Gamasy, his Egyptian counterpart in the Military Committee, found less optimism – and less welcome – in the military establishment.

The summit held in Ismailia between Sadat and Begin made the situation not better but worse. Sadat chose this small town because he was not sure what type of reception Begin would receive in Cairo from the Egyptian people. (The likelihood was that it would have been quite warm, so amazed were they still by their President's venture.) There were no Israeli flags to greet the Israeli visitors, no Egyptian crowds to wave and cheer. Yet Sadat showed exceptional patience in trying to come to some fundamental agreement with Begin. Even the keenest supporter of the Israeli cause cannot avoid some criticism of Begin's behaviour at this juncture. Having displayed great courage in inviting Sadat to Jerusalem, Begin appears to have decided that he must adopt a hard-line attitude so as to avoid giving the impression to his followers that he was becoming soft and was being outsmarted by the Egyptian superstar.

One feels some sympathy for Sadat (if Kamel's account is accurate) for the way the President was harangued by Begin with a barrage of questions. 'Did you not mass Egyptian army forces in Sinai in 1967? Did you not close the Straits of Tiran? Were there no demonstrations calling for Israel to be driven into the sea? Were there no posters in Cairo calling on the Egyptian army to enter Tel Aviv in three days? Did you not ask the UN Emergency Force to withdraw from Sinai?' Sadat answered yes to each question posed by Begin. He waited for Begin to end the questioning and then remarked: 'We are sitting around the negotiating table to forget the past and establish a lasting and comprehensive peace.' Begin, according to Kamel, responded by saying: 'The war of 1967 was an aggression on your part. Israel was in a state of legitimate defence. Consequently, it is entitled to keep the territories it occupied while defending itself against aggression.'

Begin had announced that he was bringing with him two projects. The first was a withdrawal from Sinai, the second an autonomy plan for Judaea and Samaria. Begin reportedly said that when the peace agreement was signed the Egyptian Army could be established on a line which would not reach beyond the Mitla and Geddi Passes. The rest of Sinai would be demilitarised. Israel would retain the military airports as well as the early-warning stations. The Israeli settlements between Rafah and El Arish, and Elath and Sharm el Sheikh would remain and become civilian, protected by Israeli troops. Begin claimed that his plans had been approved by President Carter and the British Prime Minister James Callaghan. Kamel, who had just been installed as Foreign Minister, could hardly restrain his anger. It was not a propitious start to his short ministry.

Responding, Sadat stressed that much had been achieved through his visit to Jerusalem. But differences still clearly existed between the two sides. Sinai was Egyptian territory and he could not accept Israeli forces or troops there. Were he to tell his people that his friend Begin wanted to retain settlements in Sinai and forces to protect them they would stone him. Anyway, agreement on peace could not be reached in one meeting. What really mattered was that the talks should continue.

Later, at a press conference that fully revealed the failure of this particular meeting, Sadat astonished his temperamental Foreign Minister by using the Israeli term for the West Bank – Judaea and Samaria. It was, indeed, an unhappy start for Kamel. Sadat, in a spontaneous gesture meant to show his Israeli guests that a new era of comradeship had arrived, suggested to Kamel that the swearing-in to office should take place in the presence of the Israelis. The astonished Kamel showed his displeasure. Kamel claims that the ceremony took place in a part of the room away from the Israelis, but Weizman did not notice any such concession. Yet in most respects, Kamel's and Weizman's accounts do not differ materially. Weizman wrote of the impatience which he and Dayan felt at Begin's interminable description of his peace and autonomy plans. So oppressive had the atmosphere become that Sadat's command to a waiter to open a window in the smoke-filled room was a matter of general relief. When the occasion called for an imaginative elaboration of great principles, Begin had insisted on concentrating on the smallest detail of his plans, quoting extensively the legal opinions of the international lawyers, Lauterfacht and Oppenheim.

According to Ezer Weizman – whom Sadat strangely insisted on calling Ezra – the Egyptian President had learned the contents of Begin's autonomy and peace plans from the Americans. Yet Sadat never interrupted the grinding discourse which wearied even the Israelis. Possibly Sadat was also aware of a stunning claim by Weizman. While President Carter had merely said that the autonomy plan was 'very interesting', his aides had commended it. The reason for this was that when examining it they came to the conclusion that it inevitably presaged the establishment of a Palestinian State. Begin, wrote Weizman, had fallen into a trap, and returned from the United States boasting of a brilliant success. So much did he misunderstand Carter's real attitude that he remarked: 'I have not met such an intellect since Jabotinsky', the greatest accolade that Begin could bestow.

A real opportunity for progress had been lost at Ismailia. Sadat had gone out of his way to be affable. He mentioned that it was his 59th birthday and was happy to receive Begin's formal congratulations, though he baulked at the idea of living to 120 years as proposed in Jewish good wishes. Sadat remarked: 'This may be the first time we have sat together since the time Moses crossed the Red Sea, not far from here. We are sitting together to tell the whole world that we are working for peace and that we shall establish peace and love. Love will always guide our relationship – instead of the bitterness and hatred of the past thirty years.'

Perhaps for the only time during this abortive meeting, Begin found the right words. Responding, he said: 'When Moses led us out of Egypt, it took him forty years to cross the Sinai desert. Today we did it in forty minutes. Not only will we make peace, we will become friends.'

However, this meeting ended in stalemate. Even the establishment of the political and military committees announced by Sadat after a private talk with Begin, was to prove fruitless. Though Weizman was happy that Sadat had agreed that Jerusalem be the venue of the political committee, this very fact led to a dangerous confrontation. No wonder the Israeli delegates, with one surprising exception, were gloomy as they flew back to Israel. Only Begin was in high spirits, exchanging jokes and witticisms with journalists covering the summit. He was soon to learn that his euphoria was misplaced.

As Weizman perceptively noted, what Sadat wanted from Begin, and what Begin refused to give him, was a ringing endorsement which would impress the Arab hounds who were after his blood. Sadat was being venomously described as a traitor to the Arab cause, of selling out to the hated Israeli enemy, yet Israel was keeping him at bay, refusing to join him in declarations of friendship and making demands which he could not possibly accept.

There was no doubt that both Sadat and Begin wanted peace but their methods and aims were at that moment totally at variance. Sadat spoke like a poet, Begin like a lawyer, the one in magnificent phrases, the other in boring detail. For Begin, Sinai was the only place where meaningful concessions could be made. The land of Judaea and Samaria was sacred and was to be protected by making concessions and creating 'new facts' elsewhere. For Sadat, regaining every inch of Sinai, his territory, was the start of a process of withdrawal and accommodation by Israel.

Not only was Sadat clashing with Begin but he was constantly hearing complaints from his new Foreign Minister Kamel and his staff. Kamel's ideas were diametrically opposed to those of Sadat. His whole outlook was still that of the traditional Arab politician to whom Israel was an evil newcomer, an outcast holding on to Arab land. Kamel gives the impression that he found it difficult even to talk in a friendly fashion with Begin or Dayan.

How quickly the whole peace drive would have disintegrated had it not been for the patience, perseverence and sensitivity of Sadat was fully revealed when Kamel travelled to Jerusalem to begin the work of the Political Committee. The Israelis and the Egyptians had prepared totally contrasting proposals, while the

Americans submitted a neutral agenda. When Sadat invited Kamel to a meeting of the National Security Council there was an open clash, which astonished the members. For the first time, Kamel was told that he was to leave for Jerusalem that very afternoon. He was to use the American proposals which he had not yet seen. Offended, Kamel said that he must first make an adequate study of the American draft before he left. According to Kamel, Sadat flew into a rage and shouted: 'Are you afraid of going to Jerusalem?' To this Kamel says he replied that he feared nothing and nobody!

Sadat was suddenly called to the telephone. He returned elated, saying that he had spoken to President Carter who told him that the American delegation, headed by Secretary of State Cyrus Vance, would arrive in Jerusalem the following day and would participate in the talks of the Political Committee, along with the Egyptians and Israelis. Kamel commented that apparently Sadat's tension was the result of his uncertainty about Vance participating in the meetings of the Political Committee. But Kamel made a condition for going immediately to Jerusalem. He would deal only with the opening item, concerning a declaration of principles, unless an agreement was reached on it. This was hardly a harbinger of success. A much more serious obstacle was in the way. The Egyptians received reports, soon confirmed, that Israel was creating 'new facts' by building settlements in Sinai. However, the situation was more complex than Kamel imagined.

Weizman described the sudden apprehension that was aroused in Israel when the stark fact that Israel would have to give up the Sinai peninsula stared the country in the face. Everyone, civilian and soldier – and in Israel the two are often the same – had become accustomed to having Sinai as a protection against a sudden Egyptian invasion, as nearly happened in 1967. Many leading Israelis realised that they did not really trust the Egyptians. Weizman himself became an object of criticism. Why was he so friendly with Sadat and the other Egyptians? Where were the clever Jewish brains that could deal with the trickery of Sadat? Even Weizman, with all his passionate desire for peace, with all his profound understanding of Anwar Sadat, had reservations. He was prepared to give up Sharm el Sheik, ignoring the famous remark by Dayan 'better Sharm el Sheik without peace than peace without Sharm el Sheik'.

But Weizman wanted to retain the two large airfields in Sinai, Etzion and Etam.

It was largely this mood of mistrust, wrote Weizman, that made everyone in Israel seek ways of tightening the grasp on Sinai before it was too late. Ariel Sharon, now Agricultural Minister, a post he presumably held because of his farming background but still hankering after the Defence Ministry, now proposed that something be constructed in Sinai to create 'facts on the ground'. Moshe Dayan lent him support. This might seem strange in view of Dayan's crucial role in promoting the Sadat–Begin summit by telling the Egyptians that Israel was prepared to give up Sinai for peace. But Dayan's thinking was always complex and sometimes unpredictable. It was he who suggested the establishment of the Yamit town in Sinai which flourished with its flowers and vegetables, fulfilling the poetic vision of making the desert bloom but which was to end in recriminations and tears. Now the plan was different. Not real but dummy settlements were to be established. Sharon most probably saw them as an obstacle to any agreement while Dayan merely considered them valuable as bargaining counters.

When Weizman learned of the proposal it struck him as a stab in the back of the peace process. Like others, Weizman saw Sharon as a great strategist and possibly the greatest combat commander of modern times. But Sharon had become too much of a politician with a politician's easy way with the precise truth. As was to be seen in Lebanon a few years later, Sharon's combination of military skills and a politician's duplicity could be a very dangerous mixture. Begin's remark that Sharon would one day send his tanks to surround the Prime Minister's office was dismissed as a rather rueful joke but there was undoubtedly a considerable amount of truth in it.

When Sharon, armed with maps, as was his wont, put forward the dummies proposal it was quickly accepted by the majority of the Cabinet. The view was that if the Egyptians acquiesced to the Israeli 'colonisation' the trick would have worked and if they refused, the Israelis would make a gesture of giving them up in return for the right of retaining the existing settlements.

Predictably, the Egyptians reacted furiously. Even Sadat, who had shown so much forbearance up to now, expressed his indignation.

In an interview with his magazine *October*, Sadat said it seemed that Israel had failed or had refused to understand that he had offered, in his visit to Jerusalem, more than it had ever dreamed of – recognition and legitimisation of its existence by the Arab States and peaceful coexistence with its Arab neighbours. Sadat declared that he would not allow a single Israeli settlement to remain on Egyptian soil. If Begin wished to burn the settlements before their evacuation, he was free to do so.

Kamel claims that Begin flew into a rage and said that only Nero burnt cities. Sadat responded by saying that he had not said 'burnt' but 'ploughed', two words that could easily be confused in Arabic. In commenting on this exchange, Kamel remarked that it was immaterial which word was used. Yet the right use of words was very vital in the controversy and his failure to do so was to cause many problems. Kamel wrote that the dummy settlements idea 'was a revival of the age when precious stones, gold and ivory was bartered for alcohol, bead necklaces and cheap mirrors. This was an insult, and I could not see what more Shylock could have done than Begin had he lived in our age'.

Kamel went on to quote Weizman as writing: 'And now we were to adopt the guise in which the most venomous of anti-Semites have always depicted the Jews; crafty petty traders, slyly cashing in on every available opportunity, and reneging on their undertakings whenever it was profitable'. In quoting those words, Kamel characteristically failed to realise how close he himself came to adopting precisely that prejudicial anti-Jewish attitude.

Most that subsequently happened in Jerusalem might almost have been foreseen, given Kamel's temperament, feelings of outrage and pomposity, which he unwittingly reveals. On arrival at Ben-Gurion airport he was met by Dayan, who invited him to say a few words. In reporting his prepared speech, Kamel shows surprising naïveté.

I mentioned that there were basic facts to be confronted with courage and foresight. These facts were that peace could not be established while the lands were occupied or while national rights of the Palestinian people, particularly their right to self-determination, were denied. A lasting peace could not be established unless the peoples of our region

strove to create conditions conducive to living together peacefully and
securely.

Kamel was astonished to receive a coded message from Sadat 'who
apparently considered my airport speech violent and was now
asking me to control myself, refrain from outbursts and show
patience in the negotiations'.

The inaugural session was, as might have been expected, totally
fruitless. Kamel saw Dayan as a 'cunning fox'. The two sparred
suspiciously. Sadat must have had special reports of Kamel's
unhappiness. Through Vice-President Hosni Mubarak, Sadat sent
a message to Kamel expressing the hope that 'you will maintain
your calm and that your speech will be deliberate and controlled'.
Kamel was instructed to consult Cairo when a difficulty arose.
'This astonished me since my calm had not deserted me', Kamel
remarked. Clearly, Sadat was beginning to be worried about his
new Foreign Minister. More than once Sadat stopped Kamel from
responding sharply to Begin's statements. The air was filled with
misunderstanding. Begin believed that Sadat was prepared to listen
to his plan to retain Israeli settlements in Sinai and was astonished
at Sadat's strong reaction. Kamel was angry because on the day of
his arrival, Israel Radio quoted Begin as saying that Sadat had told
him that the PLO leaders were Soviet agents. Kamel even tackled
Begin about this, seeing the story as an affront to Egypt and
assuming, from his experience of a controlled radio service in
Egypt, that Israel Radio was ordered to broadcast it. The surprised
Begin told Kamel that these were precisely the words Sadat had
used when speaking to him and that the story had got to the radio
station by a roundabout route. Kamel was hardly convinced, forgetting that Sadat was capable of precisely such remarks and that
Israel Radio had considerable freedom in its news broadcasts.

Neither Begin nor Kamel emerge with total credit from the row
which occurred at the banquet given by the Israeli government to
the Egyptian delegation. As Cyrus Vance remarked later, Begin had
been less than tactful, but it is certain that had Sadat been present
the occasion would not have ended in discord.

In a long, rambling speech which, in typical style, began with
references to the beginning of the Jewish nation and dwelt on the

Holocaust, Begin expressed surprise that Kamel had suggested the redivision of Jerusalem, the capital of Israel. How could Kamel ask for the withdrawal by Israel to the pre-1967 borders? Had he forgotten that the Israelis were defending their lives against Arab aggression? And why was he advocating the establishment of a Palestinian state, a terrorist state on Israel's borders that would massacre women and children?

Rejecting self-determination for the Palestinians, Begin said that Kamel was a young man and was unaware that Hitler used self-determination to annex to Germany territories belonging to Czechoslovakia and other states. Had Kamel known Begin better he would have understood that this was not a hostile speech. It was the kind of speech that Begin delivered every day. He had said nothing which he had not stressed at Ismailia and in replying to Sadat's speech in the Knesset. The occasion required a different kind of speech but Begin was incapable of an after-dinner speech of witticisms and gentle humour which would have come so naturally to an Abba Eban. However, Kamel was also incapable of dealing calmly and diplomatically with such a situation, so great was his sense of outrage. Tearing up his prepared speech, Kamel proceeded, in effect, to rebuke Begin. They had hoped, he said, to while away a pleasant hour or two, free of tension after a long and difficult day's work but the Prime Minister of Israel had chosen otherwise. Kamel sat down without drinking a toast to peace or shaking Begin's hand. Kamel felt Begin's hands on his shoulders. Kamel saw surprise and concern on the Prime Minister's face. Begin told him that he had not intended any harm but Kamel did not answer and turned his head away.

Next day, exhausted, Kamel went to bed in the afternoon after negotiations with Cyrus Vance. He was woken up and given an urgent message from Sadat. Kamel and his delegation were to return immediately to Cairo. The reason for the recall, Kamel was instructed to say, was the attitude of the Israeli government, as shown by Dayan and Begin. A shaken Kamel felt that the recall was a mistake, as it played into the hands of the Israelis who might claim that the Egyptians were not serious about peace. He appealed to Cairo but was quickly told by Mubarak that the decision was irreversible.

Kamel was right to feel bewildered. The reason for the recall was hardly convincing. The probable reason was one that Sadat could not tell anyone. It was that he could not rely on his Foreign Minister, who had such a distaste for his peace policies, to carry them out effectively. It was even dangerous, from Sadat's point of view, for the Foreign Minister to deal separately with Begin and Dayan. It was time for Sadat himself to take centre stage and this could happen only in Washington. The road to peace, which seemed so smooth as he stood on the rostrum in the Knesset, was now proving to be filled with boulders and craters.

21 · *Bargaining for peace: vision and reality*

Looking at the situation after Kamel's Jerusalem débâcle, the Israeli plan to build dummy settlements in Sinai, President Jimmy Carter's persistence in demanding an unachievable comprehensive peace agreement, Anwar Sadat could have been forgiven for feeling that his dramatic Knesset gesture was proving a failure. Nor could he himself be absolved from having unrealistic expectations. It is doubtful that, despite giving assurances or impressions to the contrary, he was prepared at this moment to sign a full peace agreement, entailing the appointment of ambassadors, cultural and economic relations with Israel, in exchange only for Sinai.

However, Sadat was not even being offered the whole of Sinai. The Israelis wished to retain the two airfields and the settlements. Ezer Weizman used all his charm and friendship to persuade Sadat at their meeting in Aswan that he should make concessions. Sadat was gratified to hear that Weizman had described his journey to Jerusalem as the equivalent of man's first landing on the moon. But Weizman went on to say that the man on the moon also came down to earth.

Sadat's answer might be thought to have ruled out all doubts. 'I know my people and I believe in their devotion for peace. And you must understand that I am talking about full and genuine peace, with ambassadors, commercial relations, everything. You will receive genuine peace but first I must get back that part of the land that you took from us.' Nevertheless the argument by ex-Israeli Foreign Ministry director-general David Kimche that this was only the essential first basis of Sadat's demands at this time cannot be entirely ruled out.

Sadat's real feelings were revealed when he became furious at the changes Begin made in the West Bank autonomy plan. According to Weizman, Begin woke up to the perils of his plan which, like Sadat's visit to Jerusalem, was one man's initiative. What was meant to be the first steps to annexation could also be the forerunner of a Palestinian state. Consequently, Begin inserted fifteen modifications in his plan, some of them of a major nature. Sadat felt he had been made to look foolish. The autonomy plan sent to him by the White House bore little resemblance to the revised version. Israel seemed to be producing increasing numbers of obstacles to an accord.

Sadat could not be seen to be abandoning the Palestinians. To do so would confirm all the accusations made against him by the 'steadfastness front'. The campaign against him would have reached a new crescendo. So worried was Weizman by the mutual recriminations, so seriously did he take the anti-Jewish excesses in the Cairo press, that the Defence Minister summoned members of the General Staff and advised them to prepare for the worst. Incredibly, war had again become a possibility.

This was probably an overreaction by the very impressionable – and none the worse for that – Ezer Weizman. Even if his mind had turned again to war, Sadat did not have the means to conduct one. He had no partners and no adequate arms – and he could not have relied on surprise. But the mere fact that Weizman could even contemplate war as a possibility was a tragic confirmation of how the relationship between the two countries had suddenly deteriorated and was still deteriorating.

In this chilling situation, in February 1978, Sadat attached crucial importance to his visit to the United States. On the way to Washington, Sadat travelled to Morocco. This trip was psychologically vital for Sadat. King Hassan was a warm supporter of his peace initiative and was just the person to give Sadat encouragement. In the United States, Sadat, who was accompanied by the still doubt-ridden Kamel, was also warmly received by Carter, Cyrus Vance and Brzezinski. Perhaps the reception was too warm. Carter's entourage had become convinced that only Begin, intransigent, legalistic and pedantic, now stood between peace and continued discord that could lead to another conflagration. Begin had his valid critics, including Dayan and Weizman, but the American creation of a hate-figure was hardly productive. Begin did represent much of Israeli fears and hopes. There was too much at stake for the people of Israel for quick decisions to be made. The Brzezinski plan to turn American public opinion, including that of the formidable Jewish community, against Begin, while at the same time collude with Egypt against the Israeli government, was never likely to succeed. Paradoxically, the American failures were essential for the wider aims of peace.

Foreign Minister Kamel gave a revealing and instructive account – though he hardly saw it in such a light – of Sadat's methods of working. The Foreign Ministry had prepared a strongly worded memorandum on the position that Sadat should adopt during his talks with Carter. In essence, the memorandum proposed that Sadat insist that the US should put pressure on Israel to adopt a more positive attitude. Otherwise, Sadat would terminate the meetings of the Political and Military Committees and the situation would return to what it was before the Knesset speech. Kamel handed the memorandum to Sadat, who appeared to read it attentively and with approval. Sadat then handed the memorandum back to Kamel. In surprise Kamel suggested to Sadat that he should take it with him when meeting Carter. 'He looked at me in astonishment, saying that he had read it and absorbed its contents.' Sadat gave the memorandum to his private secretary and told him to hand it to him before the meeting with Carter.

When Sadat met Carter, Kamel was clearly pleased to note that the memorandum had apparently made a big impression. Carter informed his American officials and the accompanying Egyptian delegation that President Sadat had assured him that the Arabs, including Saudi Arabia, the Egyptian people and other friends of the US were indignant with the US. They were disappointed because they felt that Israel's intransigent attitude could not have been possible without US military and economic aid to Israel. Sadat had informed him that he could not pursue talks with Israel in the Military and Political Committees and would make an announcement to that effect at the International Press Club the following Monday.

This announcement by Carter caused consternation among his

aides. Cyrus Vance exclaimed that such a step by Sadat would be a catastrophe. Vice-President Mondale revealed the American thinking when he remarked that it was of the utmost importance that Sadat should retain the image of the prophet of peace if Israeli policy was to change. People, he said,

> should keep on asking Israel what it has accomplished in return. You should not allow the Israeli government the chance to exonerate itself from the people's accusations. You should not give Begin the chance to manoeuvre you into a position in which he would be able to say he no longer had to do anything. Pressure is mounting because Begin is not doing anything. The Jews here do not like settlements. They told me so. A day later [following the recall of the Egyptian delegation from Jerusalem] I heard differently. The best way to alter Israel's position is to exert pressure on Begin to move and show some progress. Were you to state that you would not engage in talks, they [the Israelis] will say that the Egyptians are not serious and use this as a pretext not to move.

Carter then intervened to make a very startling statement. Without Egypt and without popular support

> I cannot force Israel to change its position in the short or long term. With you I shall be able to exert pressure on them to modify their position. There is a growing feeling among American Jews that Begin and his government are obstructing the peace process by their insistence on the settlements. Were there to be a confrontation with Begin and myself, the American Jews would find it difficult not to stand by Begin. I am trying to win over leading figures in Congress and the Jewish leaders. I want them to put pressure on Begin to induce him to abandon his settlements plan and agree on a five-year transitional period for the West Bank. But if President Sadat decides to terminate the negotiations Begin will say 'we were willing but Sadat was not', and the argument that you want peace while they do not will sound rather hollow.

American strategy was fully revealed in these remarks but as if to make it even more plain, Carter went on to suggest to Sadat that they should work together to decide on the best means to obtain public support. 'We would consider what would be most likely to induce the Israelis to be more flexible.' At this point, Kamel intervened, rather courageously, suggesting a postponement of the negotiations with the Israelis to give the Americans time to persuade the Israelis to be more reasonable.

Sadat now picked up the mood of the meeting, saying that he did not really want to stop the talks with the Israelis but they were obstinate and it was now necessary for the Americans to state their position openly. Carter quickly agreed to this but, trained politician as he was, he insisted that he must also meet Begin. Otherwise it would look as if it was an American–Egyptian proposal and would be rejected out of hand.

Nevertheless, the two sides drew up a collusion plan in detail. Kamel describes the discussion without apparently appreciating the enormity of the plan, how far Sadat had won over Carter and how alarmed the Israelis would have been had they had an inkling of what was being prepared. 'In view of the fact that the United States was required to submit an American project, it would be appropriate that it should have before it an Egyptian project to counter the Israeli project. The American side requested that the Egyptian project on the West Bank and Gaza should include the maximum Arab demands, so that the Americans might be able to submit a compromise which would be closer to the Egyptian rather than the Israeli position.'

Only later did the Israelis learn of this American plan to trick them, with Sadat's help, as David Kimche alleged. But the bomb did not explode as intended. Kamel blamed both Carter and Sadat for this failure. Their strength, he complained bitterly, was more apparent than real. They spoke of noble principles but these were not ingrained in their souls.

Kamel, an Egyptian, had less excuse than the Americans to fall for Sadat's ploy. It is now certain that Sadat never intended to break off the talks with the Israelis but merely played along with his Foreign Minister, seeing a chance to obtain greater support from the Americans. No doubt, as Kamel claims, he felt satisfied with the outcome of his visit but, in view of his bitter experiences of negotiating with the Israelis, he could not have believed that they would so easily fall for the collusion plan.

Sadat's attitude to the Palestinians may well have been coloured by a humiliating incident shortly after his departure which affected him deeply. His friend, the writer Youssef El Sibai, was murdered by Palestinians in Cyprus. Shocked and furious, Sadat dispatched Egyptian commandos to punish the killers. Sadat probably had in

226

mind the celebrated commando rescue operation at Entebbe, Uganda, when Israeli and Jewish passengers of a French airliner were held hostage, with the connivance of the bloodthirsty General Idi Amin. In an operation that amazed the world, Israel sent highly trained and motivated commandos in US Hercules planes, which landed at Entebbe airport, killed the kidnappers and Amin's collaborators and brought the hostages back to Israel.

Alas, Sadat did not have such trained men and the Cyprus troops were somewhat different from Amin's motley, bedraggled army. The Cypriots, believing that their sovereignty was being challenged, fired on the Egyptian commandos and killed several of them.

When Kamel questioned the operation, Sadat exploded: 'Should we have allowed them to go on killing us while we looked on?' The insensitive Kamel asked for an investigation to discover who was responsible for the operation. Furious, Sadat replied: 'I ordered it!' The sense of national humiliation led to a violent campaign against the Palestinian Liberation Organisation and all Palestinians who were accused of ingratitude. For once Kamel was right in fearing that the tragedy would affect the strength of Sadat's attachment to the PLO cause, though he would never abandon it.

In a letter to Begin, clearly meant to bring about a resumption of talks, Sadat mildly rebuked the Israelis for their futile concepts. He approved Israel's need for security but it was not to be obtained at the expense of territory and sovereignty. Significantly, Sadat observed that the Steadfastness Front of states and the PLO, opposed to his peace policy, and the Soviet Union were actively attempting to abort the initiative but he had so far been able to resist this. However, Begin, by his inflexible attitude, supplied the rejectionists with ammunition with which to counter the peace initiative. Begin, while standing by his arguments, saw the real intention of Sadat's letter and proposed a renewal of the negotiations.

How much Sadat and his Foreign Minister were at odds was graphically shown when Israel staged a limited attack on Lebanon in March 1978. A group of Palestinian terrorists had landed on the Israeli coast near Haifa and seized a bus which they drove in the direction of Tel Aviv when they were stopped by Israeli troops. Thirty-five Israelis were killed and there was a national outcry. A major Israeli response was inevitable and the Egyptians, in fact, expected it but Kamel and his Foreign Ministry staff considered it out of proportion to the terrorist attack.

Kamel had tried throughout the morning of the attack to speak to Sadat but failed. Finally he issued a statement deploring the Israeli attack. At 1.30 pm, a still drowsy Sadat contacted him and asked why Kamel had called him several times. Kamel replied that the matter concerned the Israeli attack against Lebanon. Sadat laughingly inquired: 'Did they teach them a lesson?' Kamel could not believe that he had heard correctly, so he asked: 'What did you say?' Sadat replied by saying: 'Have they punished them yet?' Astonished and bewildered, Kamel responded: 'Quite the contrary, it is the Palestinians who have taught the Israelis a lesson.' Sadat did not argue but he could hardly have been convinced by the claim.

Kamel explained Sadat's reaction to his anger with the PLO for joining the rejectionist front. Sadat also felt that the bus attack was directed as much against him as against the Israelis. Nevertheless, Sadat wrote to Carter requesting an Israeli withdrawal from Lebanon. Sadat understood that a prolonged occupation could badly affect his peace initiative.

Other differences between Sadat and Kamel are also very revealing: the extent of Sadat's friendship with Ezer Weizman, the blocked vision of the Foreign Minister, the incomprehension of the Saudi Arabians regarding the peace initiative. While Kamel was working passionately to convince members of the Arab League Council, particularly the Saudi Arabian Foreign Minister Prince Saud el Faisal, who had assembled in Cairo on 27 March 1978, that Egypt was still totally loyal to the Arab cause, Sadat sprang a typical surprise. Casually he told Kamel on the telephone: 'Ezer Weizman cabled me asking if he could come to Cairo and I replied in the affirmative.'

A shocked and 'utterly amazed' Kamel blurted out: 'How could you agree, while the Arab Foreign Ministers are meeting here and the Israeli Army is spreading death and destruction in Lebanon?'

Sadat replied that Weizman 'must have some important message to convey'. The angry exchanges ended with Sadat saying 'You don't understand. Weizman is my friend', and he slammed the receiver down.

Later that day, when Sadat met the Saudi prince in the presence of Kamel, he told him that he would be receiving Weizman in Cairo. The prince stared at Kamel in utter astonishment but made no comment. He was voluble enough when he spoke later to Kamel.

While Sadat claimed that he had told Weizman that he was not seeking a separate or partial agreement but a comprehensive peace, Kamel wrote that Weizman's own account told a different story. Moreover, Weizman wrote that he had been invited by Sadat to visit Cairo and had not invited himself. The significance of Sadat's invitation, at a time when Arab Foreign Ministers were visiting Cairo, was fully appreciated by Begin and his Cabinet.

Kamel was profoundly shocked to read Weizman's revelations in *The Battle for Peace*.

> Summarising my conversation with Sadat put me in a better mood. Like us, the Egyptian President was not interested in a Palestinian State. He was willing to leave our West Bank settlements in place; he would substitute for Hussein should the king refuse to take part in the negotiations. I was gratified to have Aharon Barak [the Cabinet's legal adviser] listening in on our conversation. Without his testimony, no one in Israel would believe me.

However, on the following morning, Weizman was urgently summoned to see Sadat. Weizman noted that Sadat was extremely tense as he told him:

> After Carter's meeting with Begin, Carter asked me if I insisted on a Palestinian state. I gave the matter a great deal of thought, and my cogitation led me to make the far-reaching proposal I put forward yesterday. After meeting with you, I had a meeting last night with Palestinian representatives from Gaza. They did not accept my ideas. They want self-determination. At this juncture, Palestinian support is important for me. I cannot say that my plan of yesterday is in force.
>
> We have a problem. I know my limitations and I will not propose anything I am unable to carry out. But when I make an offer, I stick to it. Now, in view of the opposition of the Palestinians, I don't know if I can stick to it. Therefore I return to the position existing before yesterday. Begin must display flexibility. I don't demand a Palestinian state – only a link to Jordan. A link to Jordan implies that there is no Palestinian state. That was my view before the peace initiative. That is my view now. There will be a plebiscite.

Weizman responded by saying that a plebiscite would be unacceptable to Israel. 'Let us go back to our talk of yesterday and my proposal that we conclude a peace treaty at the first stage. You are a courageous man. You expelled the Russians, you launched the peace initiative and you should have the courage to bring it to a conclusion.'

Undoubtedly Ezer Weizman was disappointed, as Kamel pointed out, but by no means had he lost faith in Sadat. Kamel's partial account of Weizman's vivid and remarkably honest book gives a totally misleading impression. In the Israeli Cabinet there were strong divisions about Sadat's intentions. Weizman thought that Sadat asked for a fig-leaf to cover up his lack of interest in the Palestinians. Sadat, he thought, would have been satisfied with a declaration at the Ismailia summit of vague principles about the West Bank which would bind nobody. In contrast, Moshe Dayan insisted that Sadat desired something much more substantial, not a Palestinian state but a real homeland for the Palestinians, which Begin was not prepared to concede.

Moshe Dayan was to prove much more realistic on this point than Weizman. Sadat fought for the Palestinian cause not because he felt any obligation to the PLO – he detested their leaders, describing them as 'cabaret warriors' – but because as President of Egypt he could not sign a separate peace without any regard to the Palestinian people. Such a course, he told Weizman, would harm both Israel and Egypt. This was a thoroughly genuine feeling. Kamel's virtual accusation that Sadat was planning from the very beginning a separate peace, in which only Egypt's immediate benefits would be taken into account, is based on bitter bias not on facts.

Sadat's master plan was slowly developing. He would get back all of Sinai and would not allow any Jewish settlements to remain there. He would do his best to get a homeland for the Palestinians who would be joined by a corridor to their brethren in Jordan. In return, he would offer a peace pact to Israel. The full extent of it was still not totally clear in his mind. Sometimes he spoke about exchange of ambassadors and normal relations between neighbour states, such as tourism and trade. At other times, he said that such relations might have to wait for the next generation. The great test was to come soon at Camp David.

After his meetings with Carter, Sadat realised that the American President could provide the key for solving the problem with Israel. He had managed to charm Carter with his openness, smile and laugh, and apparent willingness to make great concessions for peace, in contrast to the 'obduracy' of Menachem Begin. Carter was, at that time, a novice in the intricacies of the Middle East and was an easy prey to his astute advisers. Sadat was very anxious to retain his lead over Begin in American public opinion.

Sadat made this clear to Kamel who protested at his President's acceptance, without previous discussion, of Carter's proposal of a tripartite meeting of the Foreign Ministers of the US, Israel and Egypt. 'You know how much importance I attach to a US role and how eager I am for the US to assume the role of a full partner in the negotiations. So I don't want to upset President Carter.'

Further evidence of the way Sadat's mind was working and how distant he was from the legalistic, traditional beliefs of his Foreign Ministry, was provided by his words after again meeting Ezer Weizman. Sadat told Kamel:

> I made it clear to Weizman that Begin's actions would result in the loss of the peace opportunity, since his behaviour shows that he is totally ignorant of politics. He could, for instance, have pulled back his forces from Sinai to the El Arish-Ram Mohammed line. His intransigence and covetousness have blinded him. I told Weizman that I could not engage eternally in futile negotiations and that if no radical transformation occurred in the Israeli position before October [when the mandate for the presence of the UN observers was due to expire] the situation would be very serious indeed. And I suggested that Weizman should try to convince Begin of the need to make some progress before that date, such as returning the city of El Arish to Egypt and flying the Egyptian flag. Then it would be possible to negotiate with the Israelis, and allow the Syrians and Jordanians to go there, should they decide to join the talks.
>
> He [Begin] could also restore to us Mount Sinai where I intend to build a religious compound for the Jewish, Muslim and Christian religions to stand as a symbol for the unity of religions as well as for love and peace.

These words did not bring any peace to Kamel. He walked away in intense anger and disgust. How, he asked himself, could the

President of Egypt lower himself to such a degree as to beg Begin to give him back El Arish, which would become an island in Israeli-controlled Egyptian territory? Was Sadat planning a pyramid for himself on top of Mount Sinai? Kamel was not the most perceptive or charitable of Foreign Ministers. His misconception of American thinking was almost as great.

Sadat showed considerable patience with his hot-tempered young Foreign Minister. However, when Kamel insisted on a meeting with Sadat before the Foreign Ministers' meeting at Leeds Castle, England, Sadat asked him: 'I have observed a change in you lately. Could you have discussed our plans with some member or other of the opposition and been influenced by them?' Kamel, of course, indignantly denied such an imputation. Then he thoroughly lost his temper, saying that he had not sought to become Foreign Minister but had done so because of their long association and because of national duty. He was duty-bound to give the President, the only one who could make decisions, outspoken and heartfelt advice.

Sadat was moved by these words and declared that he had chosen Kamel for his integrity. 'I do not want any assistant of mine to take my words at their face value without due discussion. There was no reason for you to flare up. I asked you a simple question, and I accept your answer. The matter is closed.' However, their differences were by no means ended, nor could they be.

Without the presence of Sadat, the Leeds Castle conference was bound to be arid. It was notable, however, for the emergence in the Egyptian diplomatic team of Dr Ossama Al Baz, who was to become both the President's chief adviser and a top Foreign Ministry official. Slightly built and deceptively easy-going, this Harvard graduate matched the Israelis in any argument. He had a masterly command of all the relevant facts. So effective was he at the Leeds Castle conference that the Israelis, particularly Moshe Dayan, their star negotiator, were both irritated and impressed by him. 'His strength lay in the sharpness of his tongue, his expert familiarity with every subject under discussion, the clarity of his formulation and his cutting replies in arguments, which at times verged on the offensive,' Dayan commented. Dr Ossama Al Baz was later to prove a doughty opponent at Camp David.

One answer to a question by Moshe Dayan given by Kamel made the outcome of the conference certain. Did the Egyptian proposals mean that the Palestinians should have the right to an independent state? 'Certainly', replied Kamel. Sadat had heard about divisions in the Israeli Cabinet but the revelation that the Egyptians were speaking with two contradictory voices must have been even more disturbing to Dayan.

Kamel's almost farcical bewilderment at the behaviour of Anwar Sadat was soon to reach a climax. There was a short period when he and the President appeared to be taking the same line – but this was deceptive. Following the abortive Leeds Castle conference, where Kamel became convinced that the Israeli and Egyptian positions were irreconcilable, Begin made a number of statements which angered Sadat. Addressing the Knesset, Begin said: 'Israel will not give away a grain of sand as a present but is ready to negotiate on the principle of reciprocal concessions.' According to Kamel, Sadat felt that his initiative was being undermined. Apparently reacting to Kamel's passionate prompting, Sadat rejected a proposal by Carter that yet another meeting of the three Foreign Ministers be held. Kamel was delighted to note the strong line taken by Sadat in rejecting the plea by Alfred Atherton, the US Under-Secretary of State for the Middle East, for such a meeting.

> I regretfully have to state that my attitude at present is that no further talks will be held at any level unless they [the Israelis] declare that territory forms no part of any compromise. In return we would go to the ends of the earth to give them the security arrangements they need. Land and sovereignty must remain outside the bargaining framework. We are not in a jungle where people seize other people's territory, although they in Israel, led by Begin, are trying to transform Israel into a great power in the area at the expense of our territory while obtaining security and peace at the same time.
>
> I do not insist that withdrawal should take place before negotiations are begun. They can state their acceptance of the principle with an American guarantee. Israel's aim is to exclude the United States from the negotiating table in one way or another, so they may have us to themselves!

When Kamel intervened and suggested that in their invitation to negotiate, the Americans should insist that the meeting be based on the implementation of withdrawal, as laid down in UN Resolution 242, Sadat responded sharply. 'No, no', he said. 'We have now reached the point of no return – either peace or no peace.'

This was a great performance by Sadat and left Atherton and the US Ambassador Eilts on the defensive and floundering. Sadat appeared to have gone back on his initiative but managed to put all the blame on Begin. As the two sad Americans left, Kamel went up to Sadat and kissed his forehead, saying: 'Bravo, Rais!' With a smile Sadat replied: 'What did you expect, Mohamed?'

Sadat's relations with Begin appeared to have plummeted disastrously. On Sadat's instructions, both General Gamasy and Kamel refused to receive messages sent by Begin to the President. The Americans now feared that Sadat was being influenced by the Saudi Arabians, who were worried about the effect of losing a similarly moderate leader, and were returning to the traditional Arab stance. However, Kamel's delight did not last long. He had not really understood the coded words that Sadat had used. It took some time for the Americans to realise that far from abandoning his peace initiative, Sadat wished to bring it to a climax. Meetings at foreign-minister level were a waste of time, especially as his own Foreign Minister was passionately and sincerely pursuing different goals. Before the conference, Sadat had told Ezer Weizman that it would fail.

Carter eventually took the hint. He decided in August 1978 to invite Sadat and Begin to Camp David, near Washington, and hammer out an agreement.

Cyrus Vance was dispatched to the Middle East to present the invitations. First he went to see Begin in Jerusalem, who accepted the proposal. Then Vance travelled to Alexandria, from where he went to the rest-house nearby where Sadat awaited him. With Sadat in the garden were several leading Egyptian figures. Sadat led Vance out of the garden and they were away for over two hours. The outcome was that Sadat agreed to meet Begin and Carter at the summit at Camp David.

Vance told Kamel that the summit conference had to be successful or it would mean the end of Carter's political career. Consequently, Carter intended to throw his whole weight behind bringing about the desired peace, with the United States taking an active and positive part in the talks.

Bargaining for peace

After hearing this startling news, Kamel rushed back to the rest-house to speak to Sadat although it was already one o'clock in the morning. He found Sadat having his pre-dawn meal of the Ramadan fast. When Kamel told him what Vance had said, Sadat replied: 'Yes, yes, this is what I have been working for from the very beginning. My idea is that America should act as a full partner and Vance informed me that he had been asked to convey Carter's assurance that this was precisely what he intended to do. Remember Carter has put his career on the line, and I feel sure we will succeed. Whether the conference succeeds or fails depends on us. It is about time that the United States pressurised Israel and cut Begin down to size! Have I not always told you that I was full of optimism and that my initiative would never fail?'

After a moment of silence, Sadat told Kamel: 'Do you remember when we were in prison? You will have a place in history with me, Mohamed.' Kamel could only mumble 'In Sha'allah' (God willing). So overawed was he by the projected mysterious and strange world of the tripartite summit that he asked a surprised Sadat for a short vacation. But Sadat himself was in his element. He believed he was on the road to achieving precisely what he wished – peace with honour.

22 · Breakthrough: anger and tears

As we have seen, Anwar Sadat's behaviour before departing for the Camp David summit with President Carter and Israeli Prime Minister Menachem Begin, bewildered and troubled his young Foreign Minister, Mohamed Kamel, who was frantically busy preparing position papers for the great conference. Long discussions were held by Kamel and a team of top Foreign Ministry officials which, of course, included Ossama Al Baz, the star of the Leeds Castle conference. Having had a short but invigorating holiday, Kamel was in a more optimistic mood and no longer feared a catastrophe at Camp David. Both possibilities that he and his team now envisaged were promising: either President Carter would succeed in overcoming Israel's stubborn resolve to hold on to the occupied Arab territories, thus inducing other Arab states to join the negotiating process later on, and ending Egyptian isolation, or the conference would fail to achieve any progress. In that event, Egypt would lose nothing, providing Israel's sins were made clear to the world. This in itself would be a gain for Egypt.

One thing troubled Kamel. In Israel, Begin was holding long discussions with his advisers about the conference. Kamel had been under the mistaken impression that Begin was keenly awaiting the summit as a means of gaining further successes for the Israelis. The truth was different. Begin and most of his ministers were very worried about the concessions they would have to make. Kamel was now less apprehensive. He noted that President Carter was also thoroughly preparing himself for the tough discussions. But what was Anwar Sadat doing? He was fasting and moving from one guest house to another in Maamoura, Ismailia, Suez and Port Said!

When Kamel spoke to him on the telephone, Sadat appeared to show little interest in the Foreign Ministry discussions, generally agreeing with Kamel's remarks and contenting himself with minor or even irrelevant observations.

Sadat, Kamel felt, was spending the days in listless indolence, fulfilling to the full the Ramadan fast. The evenings he spent on organising his newly formed National Democratic Party and receiving well-known national figures and delegations of men keen to join his party. He would make long, discursive speeches about Egypt's struggle for freedom and was vigorously applauded.

When Kamel's preparations reached the stage of requiring Sadat's approval, he asked to see the President. But Sadat requested a postponement of the meeting as he was fasting; work during Ramadan exhausted him. Kamel asked again and received the same answer. This caused great surprise and worry to Kamel, so much so that he rang Sadat to tell him that unless they could arrange a common strategy before the conference he, Kamel, would not go at all. Sadat responded by saying that he would meet Kamel a few days before the conference as he was convening the National Security Council at the Ismailia rest-house.

This was to prove a far from enjoyable occasion for Kamel. Highly impressionable as he was, his President's conduct shocked him and all his suppressed fears surfaced. He was 'dumbfounded' as Sadat asked a waiter to bring in Mrs Hummat Mustapha, director of the Television Authority, and Zaad Zagloul Nasser, press officer to the Presidency. Sadat, who had been watching a television show, asked that they be seated close to the conference table. As discussions of the National Security Council were highly confidential and no records were kept, Kamel was astonished to note the two media personalities with pencil and paper. Yet the meeting had been called to discuss the Egyptian approach to the Camp David conference.

Kamel felt resentful and his bewilderment grew as he listened to Sadat setting out the Egyptian stance. In his book *The Camp David Accords*, Kamel warns his readers not to be shocked at the President's 'contradictions, his truncated and unfinished sentences and his irritating habit of jumping from one subject to another. To be frank, I record his words with a feeling of shame and sorrow . . .'

What shocked Kamel particularly was Sadat's statement acknowledging that

> the 1967 borders dominate the thinking of the Israelis. Tel Aviv, for instance, is within shelling range of Jerusalem. Begin's preparations for Camp David are based on the assumption that I shall ask for a declaration of principles, and he will seek a separate or partial solution with us, such as withdrawal in Sinai to the Arish Ras Mohamed line. However, I did not go to all the trouble of launching my initiative just to come out with only a separate or partial solution.
>
> Begin's attitude will be that the restoration of the 1967 borders applies to Sinai and the Golan Heights but not to the West Bank and Gaza, for the latter constitute a threat to Israeli security. This is true because urban centres in Israel would be within range of gunfire from the West Bank and Gaza.
>
> My view of our strategy is that a declaration of principles is not a problem to be discussed at our level at Camp David. Camp David is the practical application of my peace initiative and it would be futile to discuss the question of a declaration of principles at the meeting of the three leaders, for to do so would give Begin a free hand. I have, accordingly, decided to discuss a 'framework of peace' rather than a declaration of principles. With this framework we shall prepare for peace, cutting short Begin's manoeuvres. The preamble to resolution 242 stipulates the inadmissibility of occupying territory. Well, this has to be implemented. As for the discussion of security in the West Bank, I approve of it although I did receive two cables, one from [King] Hussein and one from [King] Khaled. I say to them: 'Why are you foreclosing on us?'

As for a Palestinian state, Sadat said that his position was still that the Palestinians had the right to self-determination, with a tie to Jordan. 'I shall object to the PLO even if it is accepted by Israel!'

Were Hussein to refuse to join the negotiations, Sadat said he felt that Egypt had a right to speak on behalf of the Palestinians.

Asked by Sadat if he wanted to speak, Kamel replied heatedly: 'Yes, I do, there are quite a few things I wish to say!' Though warned by one of his aides to 'cool down', Kamel went on to tell Sadat that Egypt had no right to give up Palestinian territory to satisfy Israeli security. Sadat made no reply.

After the meeting broke up, Sadat told Kamel to prepare himself as they were leaving for Camp David in two days' time. Kamel replied that he was ready but he wanted to make a suggestion. Sadat should take a tougher stand than that envisaged in the Egyptian project, right at the beginning of the week-long conference so that the Egyptians would have elbow-room when the Americans put on the pressure later on. This provoked a dramatic outburst by Sadat. Laughing loudly, Sadat exclaimed with deep sarcasm: 'Do you imagine yourself to be a diplomat, Mr Mohamed? My God, Mohamed, you are no diplomat! What week are you talking about? As soon as I arrive there, I intend to spring my project on them, wreck the conference and return to Egypt within forty-eight hours!'

A highly embarrassed Kamel could only join in the laughter but managed to say: 'You are naturally free to do what you want, and, anyway, I have never claimed to be a polished diplomat.'

When Sadat arrived at Camp David he might have expected to achieve most, if not all, of his aims. He was at the peak of his powers; he knew precisely what he wished; he had the goodwill of President Carter. In contrast, both Carter and Begin were troubled men. Carter saw the Middle East as the place which would provide him with the golden opportunity to achieve a famous victory, bringing peace where only wars existed. The Middle East was also an area of vital importance to the United States. A difficult friendship had developed with Israel and the links could not easily be broken. But Arab oil was important. The oil embargo during the Yom Kippur War had shown how dangerous a split with the Arab world could be.

Carter had willingly accepted the recommendations of the Brookings Institute, prepared by Middle East experts, most of them members of the Democratic Party. It called for urgent efforts to achieve an overall settlement, as an interim settlement was incapable of solving the underlying problems. One of the key problems was seen as the Palestinian issue. The authors thought that the Palestinians' right to self-determination would ultimately find expression in either an independent state or a Palestinian entity with a federation link with Jordan. In return for a comprehensive peace agreement, which would include diplomatic and commercial relations, freedom of travel and an end to the Arab boycott, Israel would be required to withdraw to the pre-1967 war borders with only minor changes. Even those were conditional upon mutual consent. Equally unacceptable for Israel were the recommendations that the Soviet Union should be invited to take part in the peace process, and that each national group within Jerusalem should be entitled to political autonomy within its own neighbourhood. Fortunately for the prospect of an agreement, Carter painfully learned that he had to discard nearly all these recommendations.

Anybody watching Begin at Cabinet meetings must have worried whether he was in a condition to present Israel's case at Camp David. He often appeared to lose interest in what his ministers were discussing. He allowed his Finance Minister to conduct ruinous policies which led to one of the world's highest inflation rates. Weizman noted how the Prime Minister stared into space, as if under the wrong type of medication for his heart condition. Begin shared the pessimism of his Cabinet, with the sole exception of Weizman, that Sadat was prepared to accept terms that would not harm Israeli security. Yet a transformation took place in Begin's personality as soon as he arrived at Camp David. He became alert and showed much of his old fire. He was to prove a formidable opponent for Anwar Sadat. Disputes over wording and documents were precisely what Begin, the former lawyer, thrived on.

The Camp David retreat, with its trees and possibility for long walks, suited Sadat. He was used to long walks which, he believed, made him fit, kept his weight down and cleared his mind. The Camp had several huts with comfortable rooms and bicycles and electric cars were available for those who wanted them. Ezer Weizman, who was reminded of his youth in the woods of Mount Carmel, by the damp, musty scent of the trees and the rustling of their leaves, nevertheless felt restricted by Camp David. He thought of his days as a new recruit in the RAF. This feeling of isolation was to affect most delegates as the days passed. Both Weizman and Kamel noted the squirrels jumping from tree to tree but this did not induce a feeling of carefree freedom.

Weizman noticed that the Israelis and Egyptians could not telephone one another directly; they had to go through the American delegation. Only 100 yards separated the Israelis and the Egyptians, yet the gulf between them was as wide as if they were still in their own capitals. In fact Weizman recalled bitterly that whereas in Tel

Aviv he could telephone directly to the Egyptian War Minister in Cairo, he could not dial his opposite number at Camp David.

Even more disturbing was the almost total rupture in relations between Sadat and Begin. Sadat withdrew to his cabin and did not show his face. Begin also retreated into seclusion. Begin's aides tried to break the impasse by suggesting to him that he should go out and meet Sadat who had put on a blue training outfit and gone for a long walk. Surprisingly, Begin agreed and the two met on one of the paths. However, there was merely an exchange of polite greetings.

Begin had been the object of vicious personal attacks in the Egyptian media, while the Israeli attacks on Sadat were comparatively muted and were mostly political. Begin's willingness to greet Sadat was thus commendable. Unlike Sadat, Begin found it difficult to relax. Despite the heat, he insisted on wearing a suit and a tie, claiming that it would be disrespectful to President Carter if he did otherwise.

As Weizman cycled to Begin's Cabinet to find out how the meeting had gone, he encountered Sadat walking briskly, with Kamel vainly attempting to keep up with him. 'I am glad to see you', Weizman told Sadat as he embraced him. 'And I, you', replied Sadat. If ever two men voiced genuine feelings, this was certainly the occasion.

Weizman remarks that it was strange to see the Egyptian President perspiring with the physical effort. He had always seen him as the incarnation of masculine elegance, brushed and combed, carefully dressed in the most expensive of fashions, giving off the aroma of after-shave lotion. Sadat's sweaty tracksuit changed Weizman's view of him, making him less glamorous and more human. It is a pity that Mohammed Heikal, so sarcastic about Sadat's suits and uniforms, was not present to see his sweaty President.

In the dining room in the evening, the Israelis and the Egyptians sat coldly apart. Weizman tried to improve the atmosphere, reminiscent of the days before Sadat's visit to Jerusalem. He walked over to the Egyptian table, greeted the delegates and sat down for a minute or two. It was a brave effort but of little immediate value. It was President Carter and his wife who next tried to break the ice.

Rosalynn Carter proposed the text of an identical prayer for the success of the conference, a suggestion which was not taken seriously. Dayan told Begin: 'You will have to take your hat off for the Christians, and your shoes for the Muslims and then you will end up putting on a *yarmulke* (head cover) for the Jews!'

When Begin met Carter he was told that Sadat wanted Israel to accept the principle of the non-acquisition of territory by force. Weizman believed that this was Sadat's aim from the beginning, on the assumption that Israel's consent would automatically lead to Israeli withdrawal from all the territories occupied in the Six-Day war. If this was, indeed, Sadat's impression, it was an unrealistic one. It is doubtful that Sadat could ever have thought that he would gain such an easy victory. In any case, Begin was the last person to acquiesce in any such declaration.

'There are such things as defensive wars', Begin remarked, echoing words he had used, to Kamel's consternation, at Ismailia. 'If such a principle were accepted the whole map would have to be changed.' At a consultation with his ministers and aides, Begin remarked: 'We have a tough nut to crack. His name is Anwar Sadat.'

Before the fateful first joint meeting with Carter and Begin, Sadat had a discussion with Weizman. Warned that if there was not a concrete achievement at Camp David the situation would be grave, Sadat remarked: 'I shall do my best. I don't think that Camp David should conclude with a declaration of principles. Instead we should seek a framework for future discussions. We must make certain the peace process is maintained – that it never stops. No one will be able to blame me if it does.'

Sadat's full intentions were never more clearly revealed as when, in reply to a question by Weizman whether he wanted an agreement that would embrace Sinai and the West Bank and Gaza as well, the President said:

> Don't force me into the arms of the Soviets. If I insist only on the Sinai, the Soviets will gain control of the whole region. I look forward to peace. Here at Camp David we shall sign only a framework agreement, not the peace treaty itself. That can be signed later. I am willing to let Hussein join the negotiations but I will continue to negotiate even if he does not. I will be frank with you. I am fully entitled to conclude a separate agreement with you, particularly after attacks on me from various Arab

leaders. But we have a traditional saying that a father cannot neglect any of his children. If Jordan does not come to the negotiating table, then I will be prepared to continue the talks and take the responsibility.

When he met Carter and Begin, Sadat insisted that they should talk about the substance of an overall agreement. 'We must not turn Camp David into a television war, like the Geneva Conference where everyone was competing as if they were amateur singers seeking success so that they could go professional. We shall prepare a framework agreement and our aides will deal with the details later. I think that will need three months!' Then once again, Sadat did the unexpected. He did precisely what he told Kamel he was not going to do as he admonished him for being a poor diplomat. He read out the hard-line Egyptian view of an agreement which had been prepared by his derided Foreign Ministry officials. Very curiously, Kamel does not comment on Sadat's change of mind, nor on the fact that the conference did not break up as the President feared.

Undoubtedly the Israelis were shocked. Kamel displayed his deeply rooted prejudices when he attributed the Israeli reaction to the 'erroneous racist belief' of being the Chosen People. Weizman, for one, had no such feelings of superiority over the Egyptians and he was in despair. Sadat's change of mind could have been the result of finding Carter so desperate to achieve an agreement to rescue his faltering political reputation. Carter might thus be ready to put heavy pressure on the Israelis. But Carter was no longer the naive southern politician of his early days. 'The document is extremist', he told Begin. 'It seems designed to make an impression on the Arab world.' Begin himself feared that Sadat was deliberately trying to provoke Israel to break up the conference and incur international condemnation. 'We will not play the Egyptian game', he declared.

One demand in the Egyptian plan particularly enraged the Israelis – full compensation for all the damage caused by the Israeli forces and for exploitation of the natural resources of the occupied territories. Begin hissed: 'What chutzpah! What impertinence! That's the way to address a defeated nation required to pay for its aggression. We won't be addressed in such a way!' Dayan commented that 'Chutzpah is an understatement'.

To Weizman, the Egyptian document was both 'crazy' and 'bizarre'. Why should the Egyptians have come up with a demand that they had never made previously? What would happen if Israel responded with demands for payment for Jewish property in Arab lands confiscated by the rulers? It was, indeed, a bizarre situation but Weizman and the rest of the Israeli delegation did not realise that the extremist Egyptian paper had been prepared not under Sadat's guidance but by his Foreign Ministry whom he treated with such contempt.

The Israelis responded with a counter-paper setting out the Israeli position and adding, for good measure, that the Arab States should pay war damages. Weizman found this demand ridiculous, and he exclaimed: 'We don't have to ape them'. But the sole purpose of the Israeli document was to beat Egypt in the battle for world public opinion, should the conference break up, as now seemed likely. Although the Americans considered the Egyptian paper unacceptable, they took no action. This puzzled the Israelis. But the Americans were better informed about the divisions in the Egyptian camp. They ignored the paper and continued the discussions. Sadat, well aware of the move, did not protest. He knew that his ploy had failed.

The second meeting between Carter, Sadat and Begin was explosive. Begin believed that Sadat, with Carter's blessing, was now calling for a Palestinian state linked to Jordan. A verbal mis-understanding led to an angry outburst by Sadat. Begin complained that the Egyptian demand for damages was of a kind presented to a defeated enemy. Thinking that Begin was applying the term to Egypt, Sadat replied furiously: 'A defeated nation? We were but after October 1973 we are defeated no longer.' Although Carter intervened and cleared up the misunderstanding, Sadat remained angry. 'Sadat sounded very provocative', Begin later commented.

Another meeting led to further clashes. Carter suggested that if the Rafah settlements in Sinai were the sole and final obstacle to peace, the question of evacuation should be decided by the Knesset. Begin rejected the idea, claiming that there would be an absolute Knesset majority against it. But Weizman was not so certain – and he was to be proved right. 'We offer you peace and you want territory', Sadat exclaimed. 'If you don't consent to dismantle the

244

settlements, there will be no peace.' Begin retorted: 'We will not consent to dismantle them!'

Sadat demanded a freeze on building any further settlements. He was strongly backed by the Americans. Weizman was prepared to accept the idea but Begin reacted sharply: 'What shall we tell our young people? It would be madness, particularly for a government which claims sovereignty over the whole land of Israel. What kind of freeze can be imposed on the land of Israel?'

After a week of stalemate, when the atmosphere at Camp David was one of despondency, Weizman went to see Sadat. Both agreed that it was essential that progress be made and that much of the problem was psychological – 90 per cent, in Sadat's view. To Weizman's relief, Sadat declared: 'I won't go backwards. It is impossible to go backwards. I shall continue with my initiative.' But after listening to Weizman's plea about the settlements and airfields in Sinai, Sadat made it absolutely clear that not a single Israeli could remain in Sinai. How, he asked, could he show his face before the other Arab leaders if he agreed to less? His people would not allow him to cede even an inch of their territory. As for the West Bank, it did not belong either to Israel or to Jordan; it belonged to the population. In the interim period the Israeli forces could be in places assigned to them. Afterwards when the Palestinians decided on their future, it would be necessary once again for the Israeli forces to redeploy.

Despite all these demands, Weizman felt that there was still hope. Sadat's agreement to meet Dayan, whom he disliked and strenuously avoided, was a good sign.

After seeing Sadat, Dayan was convinced that no amount of pressure by the Americans would change the Egyptian position. Dayan had sought a compromise but Sadat had replied: 'Out of the question'. Dayan's comment was: 'This is the end of the road'. He knew Begin's inflexibility. When Weizman went into Dayan's room, he found him packing his suitcase. Carter had asked Dayan not to raise points of differences with Sadat but it was Sadat who insisted on discussing them.

As Dayan complained about the intransigent Arab attitude to Israel, he saw that 'opposite me sat an angry and troubled man. His Foreign Minister, Mohamed Ibrahim Kamel, he said, was anxious to follow his predecessor, Fahmy, and resign. His adviser, Al Baz, was strongly opposed to the peace treaty, was venomous in his outbursts among members of the delegation and strengthened their doubts. If there were no change in the negotiations in his favour, he would have to return to Egypt and admit he had failed'.

A different account of the meeting was given by Sadat to Ossama Al Baz. The two accounts are not necessarily contradictory, as Kamel thought. At one point, Sadat said to Dayan: 'Do you imagine that it is possible for me to conclude a peace treaty with you which did not include the removal of the settlements and airfields?' Dayan had replied that in that case 'we shall continue to occupy Sinai and pump oil'. Sadat then asked angrily why Dayan had not said so from the very beginning, instead of wasting everyone's time. Dayan said that the Israelis had done so but the Arabs did not want to listen.

One totally unexpected development came about as a result of an imaginative suggestion by General Abrasha Tamir, who was close to Weizman. He suggested contacting General Ariel Sharon, briefing him on the crisis and asking him to telephone Begin and urge him to consent to the evacuation of the settlements. Sharon was the driving spirit behind the settlements. Such a plea by him could have a tremendous effect on Begin. It seemed an altogether far-fetched idea but it worked. Begin told the delegation a few hours later that Sharon had phoned him, saying that he favoured the evacuation of the settlements if they were the last remaining obstacle to a peace agreement. Though Begin appeared unconvinced, Sharon's surprising intervention clearly had an effect.

Weizman now also became convinced that Israel would have to give up not only the settlements but the airfields. Dayan signalled to Carter that he, too, was changing his mind by telling him that the Sinai settlements could not be evacuated without the approval of the whole Israeli Cabinet and the Knesset. Begin was losing the support of the senior members of his delegation.

In the Egyptian camp, Sadat, too, was facing a crisis. Like Begin he was faced with an excruciating decision as the conference was drawing to a close. Only a couple of days remained. The tension he was experiencing was startlingly revealed at a meeting with his aides. Kamel was among members of the delegation who had come to Sadat's cabin. Suddenly Sadat shouted at the top of his voice: 'What can I do? My Foreign Minister thinks I am an idiot! Get out, all of you!' When Kamel strongly remonstrated, Sadat said to him: 'What's the matter with you, Mohamed? Don't you know what I am going through? If you don't bear with me, who will?' It was a cry from the heart.

Next day, Kamel heard that Sadat had ordered his delegation to leave. Sadat telephoned his wife, Jihan, who was in Paris with their children, and told her of his decision. She begged him to show more patience but he insisted that he had no option but to leave.

When Kamel went to see Sadat he found him in a state of great agitation. Sadat asked that Cyrus Vance should come over and see him immediately. 'I have decided to withdraw from the conference and appear on TV to explain exactly what has happened, after which I shall return to Cairo.' Asked what event had occurred to make him take this drastic step, Sadat exclaimed: 'It's quite impossible to reach any understanding with Begin. He is simply playing with poor, naive Carter. He wants us to sign only what he feels like signing and leave everything else in the air.' When Vance told Sadat that his departure would greatly disappoint and embarrass President Carter and that only Israel would benefit, the President appeared disturbed and somewhat hesitant, according to Kamel.

As Sadat began to explain his attitude, one sentence particularly shocked Kamel – he would never have agreed to concessions were it not for the desire to help Carter. Carter arrived, Sadat took him by the hand and led him to another room. Half an hour later Sadat sent for the Egyptian team. He appeared pleased.

> President Carter is a great man and extremely intelligent. He solved the problem with the greatest of ease and I am completely satisfied. He told me I could make any agreement we signed dependent on the approval of the constitutional institutions of Egypt and Israel – that is the People's Assembly in Egypt and Knesset in Israel. Were either or both to reject the agreement, any commitments entered into by the two sides would be cancelled.

There now occurred the inevitable confrontation between Sadat and Kamel. Unfortunately, we have only Kamel's version and it would be strange if he did not want to show himself in the better light.

When Kamel remarked that what really mattered was the kind of agreement Egypt signed, Sadat replied: 'I shall sign anything proposed by President Carter without reading it.' Kamel again displayed his naïveté when he responded by asking why Sadat should sign anything without reading it. Not surprisingly, Sadat rose to his feet and repeated: 'No, I shall sign without reading it!'

Sadat had shown a great deal of patience with his young, impressionable Foreign Minister. For Kamel even to believe that Sadat, who had rejected so many texts presented by Carter, really meant what he had said was surprising. Even when writing his memoirs, Kamel did not realise what a simplistic figure he shows himself to be in this exchange, though his honesty and hot-blooded courage cannot be denied.

Later that day Sadat summoned Kamel and Ossama Al Baz to his bungalow. As he was waiting, Kamel overheard Sadat speaking in a loud voice on the telephone to Jihan in Paris and telling her that there was a possibility that they would reach an honourable agreement in a day or two. Sadat then asked Jihan to bring their grandson, Sherif, to the telephone. Sadat could be heard saying several times 'Sherif, you bad boy!', then laughing uproariously. Why Kamel should have found this delightful incident not to his liking is very curious and, is, perhaps, characteristic of the man.

Sadat showed the document that had been prepared for the signature of the three leaders. It bore Carter's initials and stated that he intended to close the conference the following Sunday, 17 September. He invited both sides to submit their final comments by next day on the US project. President Carter would then present his framework for peace for signature by President Sadat, Prime Minister Begin and himself. Apparently Sadat expected a warmer reaction from Kamel but he was unimpressed. 'Your only flaw, Mohamed, is your Turkish blockheadedness', Sadat told him. 'You don't want to understand.' Kamel responded by saying: 'I understand only too well'. Sadat patted his knee and said: 'Please, have faith in me, don't you have confidence in me?' Kamel replied that the paper 'deals with matters of procedure and is completely worthless'. Sadat snatched the paper out of Kamel's hands, exclaiming: 'No, it's a very important document and in Carter's handwriting, too.'

Next day, Kamel went to see Sadat, ready to resign. Astonishingly, Kamel does not mention that the projected accord would entail Israel giving up all the Sinai settlements and airfields. His concern was that Israel would remain in control of the West Bank and Gaza in the transitionary five-year period, as well as of the Golan Heights. He argued that the Arab world would see the deal as a separate peace between Israel and Egypt.

At one point in an acrimonious discussion, Sadat told him:

> You know nothing of the Arabs. I know them only too well. If they are left to themselves, they will never solve the problems, and Israeli occupation will be perpetuated. Israel will end up engulfing the occupied Arab territories, with the Arabs not lifting a finger to stop them, contenting themselves with bluster and empty slogans, as they have done from the very beginning. They will never agree on anything.

When Kamel offered his resignation, Sadat immediately accepted it.

An even sharper encounter occurred when Ambassador Nabil El Araby, director of the Foreign Ministry legal department, went to see Sadat to tell him that the letters exchanged between the leaders about Jerusalem were of no legal or political value. After Araby had explained his objections, Sadat said to him quietly:

> I have heard you without interrupting you, so nobody can claim that, as is rumoured of me, I neither listen nor read. I would like you to know, though, that what you have just been saying has gone into one ear and out of the other. You people in the Foreign Ministry are under the impression that you understand politics. In reality, however, you understand absolutely nothing. Henceforth I shall not pay the least attention to either your words or your memos. I am a man whose actions are governed by a higher strategy which you are incapable of either perceiving or understanding. I do not need your misleading and insignificant reports. And now your Minister, Mohamed Kamel, insults President Carter in my very presence! Does he not realise that President Carter is my trump card for the establishment of a comprehensive peace?

After being silent for a minute, Sadat added (according to Kamel): 'Are you not aware that your relative, Mohamed Heikal, attacks me in all places and is plotting to topple the regime? I lend not the slightest importance to all his lies and absurdities which are motivated by sheer malice and black rancour.'

Although some of Kamel's worst fears -- from his extremist point of view – were not altogether misplaced, he had no conception whatever of the agonies that Menachem Begin was going through. Weizman had felt before the conference that Begin did not want any discussion with Sadat which would inevitably lead to concessions. The autonomy plan for the West Bank and Gaza, so derided by Kamel, marked a sacrifice by Begin, for which he was strongly criticised by a few of the more independent members of his Herut party. There was astonishment that Begin accepted the 'legitimate rights of the Palestinian people'. For a leader of a party which saw the West Bank as the eternal portion of Israel, these were extraordinary concessions. Now Begin was faced with a stupendous dilemma: to give up the Sinai settlements and airfields which he had often described as vital for Israel's security or abort the Camp David conference and face a bitter row with the United States.

Strangely, changing a few words brought about the seemingly impossible breakthrough. To Begin and Sadat the words 'the non-acquisition of territory by force' were all-important – one wanted them deleted, the other wanted them included. In a passionate appeal to Sadat, Carter stressed that the impasse was endangering his political standing. Sadat, wishing to help his friend, finally agreed, contenting himself with a reference to UN resolution 242.

Armed with this concession, Carter met Begin in a last desperate bid to break the deadlock. Appreciating the concession, to which he attached great symbolic importance – though not of any practical value – and faced with unprecedented pressure by the Americans, Begin totally reversed his stand with a dramatic declaration. 'If what is holding up peace are the Sinai settlements', he told Carter, 'I shall submit the matter to the decision of the Knesset and honour whatever the Knesset decides. I shall even recommend that on this important and sensitive issue, party discipline shall not be enforced in the voting. This is all I can do. Nothing more.'

As the opposition Labour Party would certainly vote for such an agreement and as Begin's Herut party would support him, the outcome was certain. However, there was still one unexpected hurdle that had to be cleared. It emerged that Carter had promised Sadat a letter in which the United States would declare that it viewed East Jerusalem as occupied territory, just like the rest of the territory that Israel had occupied in the 1967 war. On hearing this, Begin remarked grimly: 'If that is the case we can pack our bags and go home without another word.'

The crisis was overcome by a letter stating that the American position on Jerusalem remained as defined at the UN General Assembly in June 1967 when the US called for international supervision of the holy places and refused to recognise Israel's annexation of East Jerusalem.

The Camp David Accords did not produce a complete agreement. There were, in fact, two framework agreements, one between Israel and Egypt, which entailed Israel's total withdrawal from the area, and one for the West Bank and Gaza.

The United States promised to construct two airfields inside Israel to replace those in Sinai. Israel wished to have the whole area demilitarised but failed. Instead, it was agreed that a wide buffer zone would be created between the Israeli and Egyptian forces. The second agreement, while concentrating on the West Bank and Gaza, was also intended to be a framework for an overall Middle East settlement – and this was the reason why Sadat signed it. Egypt recognised Israel's need for security on the West Bank and Gaza, while Israel undertook to grant full autonomy to the inhabitants.

Sadat could point to real achievements. For the first time Israel consented to include Palestinian representatives from outside the areas in the negotiations and a solution of the Palestinian problem 'in all its aspects'. An agreement had to acknowledge the legitimate rights of the Palestinian people and their just demands. Both sides agreed that autonomy would apply for no more than a five-year interim period. Israel, however, had a right to demand full sovereignty – as did the Palestinians – at the end of this period.

Inevitably, some of the details of the second agreement were left vague. But for this Yasser Arafat's PLO was as much to blame as anyone. Had they not refused to participate in the talks, they might have obtained much clearer concessions. They were prepared to accept worse conditions for negotiations in Madrid in 1991.

There were doubts not merely in the Egyptian camp. Some members of the Israeli delegation were also worried. Weizman, as ever, came up with a typical remark: 'An agreement is like a Jewish marriage contract. You don't look at it, you put it away in the closet.

If things go wrong with the marriage you get it out and study it – but by then it is too late and heaven help you if you need it!'

A storm was raging as the final agreement was reached. Weizman suggested to Begin that they should pay a visit to Sadat. Begin telephoned to Sadat and after congratulating him on the agreement, asked if he could come and see him. 'With great pleasure', Sadat answered. When Begin entered Sadat's cabin, he shook the President's hand with great warmth. Later, Sadat paid a return visit to Begin's cabin. Weizman filled glasses with wine for everyone, including Sadat, forgetting that the President, a devout Muslim, did not drink alcohol. 'I am not a heathen like you', he playfully rebuked Weizman. Holding their glasses of wine or, in Sadat's case, fruit juice, they all drank a toast to life 'L'chaim!'

Afterwards the delegation flew by helicopter to Washington for the signing ceremony at the White House. Sadat expressed his thanks and gratitude to President Carter. 'You made a commitment to be a full partner in the peace process. I am happy to say you have honoured your commitment.' He called upon Carter to continue his efforts so that the peace process might be completed and thereby strengthen the belief of the Palestinian people in the reality of peace.

After the three leaders had spoken, Carter announced that it was time to sign the agreements. When the signing was completed, the three leaders embraced one another. However, transforming the agreement into a viable peace treaty between Israel and Egypt was to prove exceptionally difficult. Week after week, the negotiators wrestled with new and largely unforeseen problems. Disagreements included the target date for self-rule on the West Bank and Gaza; guaranteeing the primacy of the Israeli–Egyptian treaty over any other international obligations by either side, Israel particularly fearing Egyptian continued loyalty to Arab states in case of war; and Israel's rights to the oil fields that Israelis had discovered in Sinai. Both Dayan and Weizman (who was now negotiating not with Gamasy, who had been replaced by Sadat, but with Kamal Hassan Ali, as Defence Minister) felt that they were losing the confidence of the ministers back home.

As at Camp David, it was Jimmy Carter's personal intervention that saved the situation. He came to the Middle East and subjected both Begin and Sadat to intense pressure. He was even reported to have gone so far as to threaten them – though it is very doubtful that Sadat needed much persuading. After a nerve-racking tour, Jimmy Carter achieved his aim: an Israeli–Egyptian peace agreement was reached.

In Washington on 26 March 1979, Jimmy Carter, Anwar Sadat and Menachem Begin, in a ceremony lasting only five minutes, affixed their signatures to a peace treaty to end 30 years of war and bring about a period of prolonged peace. For the first time an Arab leader pledged never to wage war on Israel. For Sadat the moment signified the realisation of a dream.

23 · Unfulfilled hopes: the road to tragedy

Anwar Sadat returned to Cairo elated, feeling that he had broken the back of the conflict with Israel, was bringing peace to the whole Arab world and establishing a special warm relationship with Jimmy Carter and, through him, with the American people.

Though at times, he had been angered by Begin's 'intransigence', Sadat appeared not to bear any grudges. He still saw Begin as a strong and honest man who was concerned for his small country's security but was yet prepared to make peace with the largest Arab state.

Among the ordinary people in Cairo there was a momentary return to euphoria and wonder that had characterised their behaviour immediately after Sadat's departure for Jerusalem. There were well-authenticated reports of enthusiastic taxi-drivers offering free rides to Israeli visitors, as a gesture of the new-found friendship. These offers were rarely accepted, as even a cursory look at the old and appallingly maintained taxis revealed that the drivers were in no position to lose any of their earnings. However, the gestures were appreciated.

Equally, if not more, remarkable, was the incident outside the impressive synagogue in Adly Pasha Street in Cairo, witnessed by the present writer. As members of an Israeli delegation for talks with the Egyptians were attending a service at the synagogue a large crowd assembled outside. Those in the synagogue were startled to hear a loud noise. They exchanged startled looks. Was the crowd becoming hostile and was this noise the beginning of a pogrom? The Israeli delegates and their Egyptian–Jewish hosts went outside to find out exactly what was happening. To their utter astonishment they heard the words 'Begin! Begin!' chanted in

254

unison. The crowd, believing that the Israeli Premier was in the synagogue, were trying to greet him. So enthusiastic did the crowd become, clapping and laughing, that the police, fearing an incident, dispersed them without using any force.

If there had not been so many witnesses to this scene, it could never have been believed and written about. After all, only a few months before, Begin had been vilified in the Egyptian press and on the radio and television as worse than Shylock and the very personification of evil. Sceptics will say that this was yet another example of the Egyptian authorities marshalling crowds for political purposes. However, this did appear to be a genuine demonstration.

Public opinion swung wildly as the peace hopes rose and fell and rose again. Hopes of a tremendous change in the lives of ordinary people as the result of peace with Israel and the patronage of the super-rich United States rose to great, unrealistic heights. Like investors in a gold mine found to possess immense deposits, the Egyptian people waited for fortunes or, at the very least, better economic conditions to descend on them. Anwar Sadat was delighted to notice that once again he was the 'hero of peace', the man responsible for bringing about this dramatic transformation. Long forgotten were the bitter feelings which led to the food riots two years earlier.

Even as it became apparent that the detailed negotiations about West Bank autonomy were running into difficulties, Sadat retained his serenity, puffing away at his pipe as he spoke of his hopes of building a new Middle East, based on harmony and co-operation between Jews and Arabs. Frequently he would refer to his plan to build a religious complex in Sinai, with a mosque, a church and a synagogue as the central points. In his mind he saw meetings of the leaders of the three sister religions, as well as masses of ordinary Muslims, Christians and Jews congregating there and having fruitful discussions. Fantastic though such an idea appeared to sceptical foreign observers, Sadat was convinced that it was practical and a natural extension of his peace with Israel.

Sadat refused to lose hope about reaching a reasonable agreement with Israel about the West Bank and Gaza even when the signs were not at all propitious. Sadat could still speak with emotion about his hopes for peace and harmony. Doubts about a West Bank agreement were not confined to critics in Egypt. In Israel, too, Moshe Dayan and Ezer Weizman began to be increasingly concerned about Menachem Begin's real intentions.

According to his Israeli critics, Begin had revealed what was in his mind when he chose the wily veteran National Religious Party leader, Yosef Burg, the Interior Minister, not an expert on foreign affairs and not one likely to take an independent stand, instead of Moshe Dayan as the head of the negotiating team about West Bank and Gaza autonomy. Weizman and Dayan drew the conclusion that Begin had had second thoughts about giving the Palestinian Arabs real autonomy and an opportunity to claim their 'legitimate rights'. Although in the Knesset vote, members of Begin's party dutifully joined with Labour in voting in favour of the Camp David Accords, there was no unanimity. Important voices within Likud expressed deep concern and even astonishment that the heir of Jabotinsky could ever risk endangering Israel's possession of treasured parts of Eretz Israel. Two leading figures in the party, Yitzhak Shamir, who was to succeed Begin as Prime Minister, and Moshe Arens, who was to become Foreign and Defence Minister, were among 17 abstainers, while a prolific writer, Shmuel Katz, once close to Begin, opened a vitriolic campaign against him. The fiery right-wing Geula Cohen, famous as a radio announcer for the underground groups against the British, called for Begin's resignation.

Moshe Dayan realised that Begin was deliberately bypassing him regarding policy towards the Arabs. Ministers began to inform their favourite press contacts that they and, by inference, Begin, were unhappy about Dayan's meetings with leading Palestinian Arabs, like Dr Haider Abdel-Shafi who was later to be prominent in nego-tiations with a Labour Government. It was being suggested that Dayan was too liberal, too willing to make concessions to the Arabs. Had Dayan's health been better he might have remained in the Cabinet, as he did when his position was even more difficult after the Yom Kippur War. But cancer and fears that he was losing the sight of his one eye persuaded him that it was time to leave.

In his resignation letter, Dayan told Begin:

It is not possible for a foreign minister to perform his functions properly without him being personally engaged, involved and being among the formulators of Israel's policy on this question [Israel's relations with the Palestinian Arabs]. It is no secret to you that I differ over the manner and the substance whereby the autonomy negotiations are being conducted, and this applies, too, to a number of actions performed by us on the ground.

Weizman held out a few months more but his disagreements with Begin were as wide as Dayan's. Weizman's rather unwise step in establishing contacts with PLO figures added to the tension between him and Begin and the parting of the ways became inevitable. In May 1980 Weizman said farewell to his defence establishment. Like Dayan, he felt alarmed about the peace treaty that they had signed with Anwar Sadat. Begin and his supporters had eroded their achievement 'by provocative settlement programs and unnecessary land confiscations, trumpeting verbal challenges to the world as they withdrew into their mental ghetto'.

Sadat refused for months to give up hope that an agreement would be reached. In a characteristic gesture, showing him at his spectacular best, Sadat, accompanied by Jihan, sailed into Haifa harbour on ex-King Farouk's royal yacht. They were deeply touched by the cheers of an enthusiastic Israeli welcoming crowd, which contrasted so starkly with the bitter hostility from the Arab camp. Sadat announced that he would sell every year to Israel two million tons of Sinai oil. In a further gesture, he gave his approval for the twinning of Alexandria with Haifa. Emotionally he spoke of his vision of the Nile waters irrigating not only the huge empty barren spaces of the Sinai Peninsula but also Israel's Negev desert. If the soul of David Ben-Gurion, whose body lies in a simple grave in the Negev settlement of Sde Boker, hovered above the Egyptian President, it must have worn a wistful or bemused smile.

In mid-1979, in the immediate months after the signing of the Camp David Accords, Anwar Sadat was still in a serene mood as he introduced the 'Era of Peace'. To give a spur to the negotiations with the Israelis about Palestinian autonomy, Sadat appointed the Western-educated, softly spoken Mustafa Khalil as head of the Egyptian delegation. But despite meetings in Alexandria and Herzlia there were no signs of coming nearer an understanding. The differences remained solid and apparently unbreakable. Israel insisted that Jerusalem should remain united under Israeli rule.

Egypt argued that a special status should be given to east Jerusalem. While Israel wanted merely an administrative council for the West Bank and Gaza, Egypt called for a council with full legislative powers, which came close to statehood. Begin insisted that new settlements be built and the existing ones enlarged. Sadat declared that such a course contravened the Camp David Accords. With the support of the Americans, Sadat wished to provide the Palestinians with an infrastructure, both legislative and administrative, that would enable them to take over power effectively when the three-year interim period was completed. Begin was greatly alarmed by a Palestinian take-over, fearful that it might lead to the establishment of a state that would herald the end of Israeli sovereignty over the area, a devastating possibility that ran totally against his ideological and patriotic convictions.

Sadat began gradually to despair of reaching any agreement with Begin. The President's low opinion of PLO leader Yasser Arafat and his followers was strengthened as he noticed as they, in his view, played into Begin's hands by refusing to express a wish to participate in the negotiations, accept Israel's right to exist and renounce terrorism. Begin did attempt to establish an alternative Palestinian leadership, free of PLO influence, by forming Village Leagues led by men from the villages, but these proved ineffective and were constantly in danger of assassination. Even the lifting of military government and its substitution by a civilian administration, of a limited kind, confirmed Israel's intention to retain the territories.

Angered and exasperated by the Israelis, the Palestinians, who showed no appreciation of his strenuous efforts on their behalf, and King Hussein, who showed no desire to join in the talks, Sadat spoke bitterly about those he felt were sabotaging his peace initiative. In August 1980, Sadat wrote to Begin that the failure to produuce a plan for co-existence and reconciliation between Israel and the Palestinians might backfire on Israel and on the peace accords. Sadat stressed that he had been hoping to complete the autonomy talks by 26 May 1980, one year after they had started, but he was appalled by the wave of Israeli settlements and by Israeli 'acts of oppression' against the Palestinians.

Israel's decision to transfer to Jerusalem some government offices, including that of the Prime Minister, particularly incensed

Sadat. He saw this action as an 'insult to the 800 million Muslims' who had as much right to Jerusalem as the 'eighteen million Jews'.

Sadat also saw the Israeli move as a 'breach of confidence', basing himself on the talks with Begin in Haifa, Alexandria and in Aswan. The President spoke frankly and, at times, passionately to Begin, stressing the significance of Jerusalem to the Arabs. He believed that, without dividing Jerusalem, a way could be found to ensure peaceful co-existence between Muslims, Christians annd Jews through 'the restitution of the Arabs' historical and legal rights to the city'.

Though rebuffed by Begin who argued that Israel's stand was in accordance with the Accords, Sadat wrote again to him in moving and prophetic terms. His ideas, he stated, had occurred to him while he was praying and reading the holy Koran on the summit of Mount Sinai. He realised during his meditation that his peace initiative was a 'sacred mission and divinely inspired. The Almighty would bring to a full circle the history of the Hebrews, which had begun on Egyptian soil'.

At the same time, Sadat begged Begin to realise that unless the Jerusalem problem was resolved in a manner which took into account the national aspirations of the Palestinian Arabs, a great oportunity would be irretrievably lost. He pledged that if the Israeli settlers were evacuated from the West Bank, he would supply water from the Nile to help resettle them in the Negev. But as there was no response from Begin, Sadat saw no point in continuing the negotiations, as they would only make the situation worse.

Much of Sadat's increasing bitterness was evident in his interview with the Israeli national newspaper *Maariv*, on 22 August 1980. For the first time he admitted that in May 1971, during the Rogers initiative, he was prepared to sign a cease-fire rather than a peace agreement. However, all the steps he had since taken towards strengthening the peace and normalisation had not met with the right response. Even his invitation to Israeli President Navon to visit Egypt, as part of the normalisation process, had been misunderstand as an attempt to undermine Begin's authority.

Sadat claimed that his efforts to strengthen peace between Israel and Egypt went well beyond his obligations under the Camp David Accords and that he had taken 'ten steps forward for each single step that the Israelis have made'. Nevertheless, Sadat praised Israel's unilateral decision to advance ahead of schedule the withdrawal from parts of Sinai. He emphasised that no more wars would ever mar the relations between Israel and Egypt and that their differences would be resolved by negotiations. The voice was already muted. There was not going to be a hot war but the peace would be cold.

Sadat, with his keen sensibility, could already feel the creeping disappointment among his people. Sadat's initiative had brought them neither plenty, nor an end to their problems, nor even a stoppage to the squabbling with Israel. At the same time, the Arab nations were stepping up the campaign against him, describing him as a traitor to the Arab cause.

His people had such high expectations! When he visited El Arish exuberant Egyptians waved flags with the slogan 'peace and prosperity'. Were all these high hopes, this euphoria, to be succeeded once again by apathy, helplessness and cynicism? Sadat's mood and behaviour changed.

His friends noticed with alarm that he was becoming withdrawn, irritable and even slightly paranoid. He spoke increasingly in mystical terms as he appeared to be finding solace in religious reflections. He had a number of times told Jihan that once he achieved peace with Israel he would seek peace with himself. Jihan believed that he was sincere in his wish to retire from office and public life late in 1982 when all of Sinai would have been returned to Egypt.

Bitterly contemptuous of the Arab leaders, seeing them as weak, puny, and narrow-minded, leading simple populations who lacked the history and maturity of the Egyptians and owing their status to the mere fortuitous discovery of oil on their lands, Sadat was angered by their barbs. He looked with disdain on their followers in Egypt.

Yet these Arab leaders still had the power to turn most of the Arab world against him, at least formally. These men with their tiny minds and the outlook of corrupt tyrants, as he saw them, could assemble summit conferences, denounce Sadat and attempt to isolate Egypt, which by itself was half the Arab world. At the Baghdad summit, Egypt was expelled from the Arab League and its headquarters was transferred from Cairo to Tunis. All Arab countries were ordered to cease giving financial aid to Egypt and to cut off diplomatic relations. At one stroke, Egypt found itself economically and culturally boycotted by the rest of the Arab world.

These measures had a catastrophic effect on large numbers of Egyptians – some estimates put the total at over two million – who worked as doctors, engineers and teachers in Arab countries. Many had families in Egypt who relied on their earnings for their daily sustenance. In their anger with Sadat – in some cases more public than private – Arab leaders expelled these hapless Egyptians whose services were so much needed. It was the kind of vengeful, primitive act that particularly enraged Sadat and confirmed him in his view that he was dealing with 'pygmies' and nonentities.

At home, too, Anwar Sadat noted an increase of organised opposition to him and his policies. His opponents did not come from one group, they encompassed those who disliked his open-door economic policy annd those who bitterly joined in attacking his peace with Israel. A particularly dangerous development was that his critics now included the Muslim fundamentalists. They were, at first, bemused by Sadat's genuine Muslim faith and his characteristically open displays of his beliefs in the message of Islam. But as Sadat refused, despite provocation from Begin, as they saw the Israeli moves, to abandon the path of peace for the traditional Muslim conflict with the Jews, the fundamentalists turned away from him. The anger against him was further fuelled by his refusal to adopt all the aspects of an Islamic republic, as had happened in Iran under Ayatollah Khomeini. They began to see him as a heretic who deserved punishment and death.

The most fanatical among them began to plot his assassination. His attitude to them was equivocal. No one within his own government knew as much as he about the Muslim Brotherhood and its various offshoots. He had befriended the founder and leader of the movement and there are indications that he was near to joining them in his earlier years when he was still seeking an identity for himself. What prevented him from joining their ranks and identifying himself with them was his constant search for new experiences and new truths, his refusal to be hemmed in by a narrow ideology. He was fascinated by the achievements of modern science and technology, of which the powerful United States was a prime example.

However, Sadat did not appear to have realised the extent of the disillusionment among the Arab masses and the effect of the Khomeini revolution in Iran, which was to go on growing to frightening proportions. Great wealth was being amassed by the princes and sheikhs of the Arab world from the rich oil deposits but only a tiny part filtered down to the mass of the population. Egypt, not blessed with great oil reserves, had to deal with even greater problems of a population increasing at the rate of over a million every year.

The country was undergoing a dramatic change. Sadat could speak with love and nostalgia of his village and keep on describing himself as a proud peasant but the real peasants were rather less rhapsodical. Sadat's own village life was, after all, privileged and he never suffered the pangs of hunger. Grinding poverty with no possibility of ever breaking out from the treadmill of bone-breaking labour for a pittance, prompted great masses of people to seek an illusory salvation in the big towns. While the countryside was being emptied, the big towns grew to monstrous proportions. Within a decade the population of Cairo more than doubled – from four million to over eight million – and continued to expand at a terrifying rate. In the next decade the eight million doubled to 16 million, as the country's population grew from 40 million to 60 million.

These masses provided rich soil for extremism, despair and the desperate search for certainties. Only Islam would be able to solve all the religious, political and economic problems, the devotees believed, because from its birth Islam had been a political as well as a religious movement, with social and cultural aspects. Had not the Prophet Mohammed fought on behalf of the poor and the weak against the powerful and the rich in Mecca? Did not these very rich and corrupt men fear the effect of the Koran which would undermine their power? And was there a country more corrupt and evil than the United States, controlled by rich Zionists on behalf of Israel?

Long before Israel was established, there had been attempts to bring a purified form of Islam into everyday life. There was the Wahhabi movement, which originated in the Najid region of Arabia in the eighteenth century and became the official Saudi sect. It is still today the ruling group in Saudi Arabia. The fervent desire to return to the original purity, rejecting all innovations, affects powerfully the daily life of the people. Other revivalist movements in Sudan and Libya sought similar aims with less lasting success.

Significantly, it was in Egypt that the Salafi movement, with its blend of the principles of Islam and modern ideas, arose and took root. Sheikh Mohamed Abdu, an outstanding nineteenth- and early twentieth-century thinker, argued that there was no contradiction between the ideas of modernisation and Islam. If any Arab thinker influenced Anwar Sadat's political as well as religious outlook, it was Sheikh Mohamed Abdu. However, the Muslim Brotherhood, founded in Egypt in 1928 by a follower of the Salafi movement, broke with Sheikh Abdu's pacific ideas and advocated force and violence to achieve Islam's victory. Such militant ideas, which projected Islam as a fighting force which would tolerate no hindrance and which saw Muslim opponents as heretics worthy of elimination, found an objective in British troops. Britain agreed in 1936 to withdraw its troops from Egypt but retained a garrison to guard the Suez Canal, which was seen as vital to Britain's imperial interests. The Muslim Brotherhood's military wing attacked not only British troops but all targets seen as symbolic of Western imperialism and Western decadence. Cinemas and clubs were attacked and burnt down. King Farouk tried to use the Brotherhood as an aide to retaining power but quickly realised his mistake and attempted – unsuccessfully – to suppress it. Nasser, too, saw some benefits in having the Brotherhood on his side but, on realising its true purpose, decided to ban it, equally unsuccessfully.

In Syria, a branch of the Brotherhood came into direct conflict with President Hafez Assad's regime. The Brotherhood took over an entire town, Hama. Assad sent in his heavily armed troops, with tanks and aircraft. Slowly and systematically the Brotherhood and the townspeople, who were forced to back them, were killed and their homes destroyed. As many as 30,000 died in the rubble. After this slaughter, which caused no great revulsion in the Arab world, the Brotherhood's influence waned in Syria.

Islam had been exported to the Indian sub-continent and returned to the Arab world in a much more militant form. The Muslims

263

facing the Indians were involved in mortal conflicts where the massacre of whole communities was a frequent occurrence. Islam in Pakistan became a militant force, mixing intense nationalism with even deeper religious faith. Pakistanis read avidly the books of the preacher and agitator Abul el A'ala El Madudi which advocated militancy in facing the more powerful enemy. His books were translated into Arabic in the 1950s and 1960s. They influenced the Mulsim Brotherhood. His ideas were also skilfully propagated by Sayed Kotb, a member of the Brotherhood, whose book, *In the Shades of the Koran*, became a bestseller.

Sadat had at one time spoken with a measure of contempt about the docility of the Egyptian people, prepared to accept and pay tribute to firm rule, provided it was considered fair and satisfied the stomachs of the masses. But he and his comrades had already, by their own conduct, shown a more steely constitution. A section of the Muslim Brotherhood adopted violence as an integral part of their policy. The harsher view of Islam that came from Pakistan and the Far East found many adherents in Beirut and in the rat-infested streets of Cairo's shanty towns. This fanaticism was further fuelled by the downfall of the Shah, despite American support, and the triumph of Ayatollah Khomeini. The manner in which the Shah was abandoned by the West, which so much disgusted Anwar Sadat, added to the extremists' feeling of victory and contempt for Western values.

Affected by the militancy of Teheran and Islamabad, the Cairo fundamentalists were not discouraged by the fact that, as Sunnis, they belonged to a part of the historic divide not associated with revolt and violence. This schism in Islam originated in a dispute some 25 years after Mohammed's death in the year 632. He was succeeded by Abu Bakr, his father-in-law, followed by Umar and then Uthman, all of whom had the title of Caliph. Ali, Mohammed's son-in-law, became Caliph after Uthman's death but was opposed by the powerful Ummayad clan of Mecca. When the dispute was put to arbitration, the winner was not Ali but Mu'awiya, a candidate of the rich merchants, who became the fifth Caliph and founded the Ummayad dynasty. Ali was murdered two years later but became a vibrant symbol of the revolt of the poor against the rich and power- ful. His followers became known as Shias, partisans, as opposed to the Sunnis, traditionalists.

How strong the influence of the Teheran revolution had become was revealed a year later when a radical group in Mecca seized control of one of Islam's holiest places, the Holy Shrine. The rebels proclaimed that they had come with a new message warning against decadence and corruption in the servants of the oil companies. The rebels demanded the creation of an Islamic state of Saudi Arabia and breaking ties with the Western world. The Saudi leaders were shocked and appeared impotent to crush the revolt, as the rebels had a plentiful supply of guns and ammunition. Moreover, a section of the local garrison backed them. In desperation, King Khaled privately approached President Giscard d'Estaing. He sent well-trained French anti-terrorist forces which quickly crushed the rebellion.

In Egypt this hard trend in Islam was to claim Anwar Sadat's life.

24 · Death on Victory Parade

Anwar Sadat hesitated for a considerable time before taking action against the extremist Muslim groups. Unlike Nasser, he agonised over whether strong measures against highly motivated Muslims were justified. In some respects he felt a kinship with fervent Muslims and understood their passion. He prayed with a passion and commitment which impressed even the fundamentalists. They were, at first, somewhat bewildered by the division between his religious and political beliefs, his regular daily prayers which made a permanent mark on his forehead – so it was claimed – and his insistence on making peace with the infidel, Israel, the Jewish 'robber state', pawn of the 'American devil'.

Sadat's hesitation was probably also influenced by his increasing political and economic problems. He may well have considered harnessing the power of the Muslim Brotherhood and fringe Muslim groups as a force against his secular opponents. However, to Sadat's fury, the Muslim fundamentalists themselves joined his critics. Moreover, communal conflicts between Muslims and the Christian Copts erupted, leading to murderous clashes. The endemic economic problems became even more acute, enabling Sadat's critics to deride his claim of introducing 'the age of prosperity'.

A motley group of parties, opposed to Sadat's home and foreign policies, was able to organise itself into an opposition. Sadat could not prevent this happening as, ironically, they were using the very freedom which he had granted the country in 1976. The right-wing Liberal Socialists believed in Sadat's open-door policy and free enterprise. They thus did not challenge the President but, to the left, the Marxist and Nasserist groups, though a minority in the Assembly, were a

266

thorn in Sadat's side. Sadat encouraged the establishment of his own National Democratic Party which, inevitably, became by far the largest in the Assembly. Even the old Wafd Party, which Sadat so detested in his younger days, re-emerged as the New Wafd.

Yet hardly anyone was happy. Most parties felt that their true strength was not represented in the Assembly and that they were being illegally harassed by Sadat's police. Sadat believed that the Nasserists and Marxists were plotting against him and the State. He began to understand the personal threat that he faced from the Muslim fundamentalists though he was still not aware of the extent to which they had penetrated into the army.

Sadat acted decisively in May 1978 but aroused an even greater enmity among his critics. He put before a national referendum the question of the political rights of the individuals who were corrupt. Having obtained a massive mandate to act, Sadat was able to remove from the Assembly all those whom he considered objectionable. The New Wafd party voluntarily dissolved itself. It protested that Sadat's limited democracy could not stand the test of criticism and independent opposition.

In launching his new National Democratic Party, Sadat tried to achieve the impossible. He advocated a 'modern state based on science and faith' but the adoption of Shari'a (Holy Muslim Law) as the main source of legislation. This move did not greatly impress the fundamentalists. Although his party won a landslide victory in the general election, Sadat was unhappy at the continued sniping by small groups in the Assembly. In May 1980, Sadat arranged a new referendum which gave him exceptional powers and led to major constitutional changes.

Sadat could now seek re-election as many times as he wished. Thoughts of retiring in 1982, when the last stretch of Sinai was due to be returned by Israel, were abandoned. A proud man, he could not consider leaving the scene when the country was in such turmoil and when his opponents were so vocal. Above all, he worried about the peace with Israel which he had achieved. To him the peace initiative was his greatest achievement which one day all the Arabs would recognise and applaud. The more the Arab leaders condemned his peace with Israel, the more he castigated his Egyptian critics. How could they be so blind and simplistic; they who, unlike the Arabs elsewhere, enjoyed the benefit of a long history and civilisation?

In truncating the democratic system in Egypt, and in establishing a more just and paternal system, as he saw it, Sadat had before him the sad example of his beloved friend, the Shah of Iran, who had succumbed to so-called democratic pressure and found himself exiled and humiliated. Sadat resolved never to give in to his bitter critics and not to rely on their justice. He would fight them to the end. He would not leave the country to their machinations.

Aware of the criticism by the fundamentalists that the Shari'a concession was not sufficient, Sadat proposed that the Holy Law would become the sole and not merely the main source of legislation. In a further move to weaken the Assembly's powers, Sadat won the right to create a legislative council where, he hoped, there would be no trace of opposition to him. In addition, Sadat passed the Law of Shame, enshrining in law the spiritual and ethical values that he had presented in his National Democratic Party.

All these complicated and seemingly decisive steps did not arrest the criticism or reduce the number of opponents. On the contrary, they provoked new outcries. Particularly resented was the Law of Shame. His new style of rule by referendum and decree led to protests and a petition, signed by many notables.

Ignoring these attacks with total disdain, Sadat took over the premiership from Mustafa Khalil, the more effectively to carry through the changes. Sadat took comfort from the various referenda which gave him a popularity rating of over 90 per cent. But his critics derided these figures, as of all the elections, claiming that the government rigged them. The opposition press claimed that one significant exception occurred in Assyut in Upper Egypt, a centre of the Muslim fundamentalists, where the armed local population confronted the pro-Sadat officials who had come to collect the ballot boxes and demanded that they be opened in the presence of the townspeople. The local anti-government hero, Mumtaz Nasser, was found to be the overwhelming victor.

Critics also alleged that the open-door policy had led to widespread corruption, with the rich becoming enormously rich while the poor became more exploited than ever. Huge amounts of consumer and luxury goods were pouring into the country which benefited the few able to buy and sell them at huge profits. Sadat hoped for large-scale foreign investments but European and American investors were chary of investing in a country which appeared so unstable, so riddled with corruption and inefficiency, so lacking the powerful infrastructure needed for the creation of a modern industrial state.

Anwar Sadat was also hurt personally by allegations of corruption which came close to his own family. His own brother, Esmat, was accused of making a fortune through criminal means during his presidency. After Sadat's death, Esmat was convicted and imprisoned. It became the fashion in Egypt to attribute all the corruption to Sadat's laxity, although he personally was not accused of the crime. Yet there were a few Egyptians who saw the injustice of this outlook. Sadat was horrified by the corruption around him. His leniency to his brother was partly due to his mistaken belief that his enemies were deliberately using his brother's conduct to beat him with and denigrate the regime.

Sadat was infuriated by the criticism which began to appear in the Western press, where his commitment to democracy was now being doubted. During a press conference for foreign correspondents which he convened in Mit Abul-Kum, Sadat became agitated and aggressive. Turning on the correspondents he exclaimed in a loud and indignant voice: 'How can you write these lies about me?' Quoting passages from *The Times* of London and other prominent Western newspapers, which questioned aspects of his rule, he shouted: 'These are vicious lies! How can you write these things?' Brandishing a tape, he told the correspondents: 'I am going to make you listen to this tape, to make you hear the truth about the vicious lies that are being spread about me and about Egypt.' The tape was an interview with a British correspondent, David Hirst, who had been expelled by Sadat in 1977. The original recording had been secretly monitored by the Egyptian security authorities. This fact shocked the correspondents.

A question by a correspondent whether Sadat had received implied or explicit approval from the US government, when he recently visited Washington, for the large-scale arrests of Egyptian dissidents, threw him into a fury. 'I have the right to shoot you for asking such a question but this is a democracy.'

Retreating to his beloved village, Sadat could not find inner peace. When his daughter, Camellia, visited him in August 1981, before she went on a study trip to the United States, she was alarmed by his appearance and by his manner. He appeared to be despondent, very irritable and was clearly losing weight. He would not answer her questions about his health but remarked, mysteriously, that this situation could not go on much longer. As he bade farewell to his daughter and granddaughter, Eqbal, Sadat remarked that he might not live to see them again.

Mass arrests of critics from all sections gave the impression that Sadat was losing control of the situation rather than strengthening his grip. His decision to arrest the Coptic Pope Shenouda came as a particular surprise. The Copts were angered by Sadat's apparent reluctance to take strong action against Muslim fundamentalists who attacked them. Shenouda disliked Sadat's enactment making the Muslim Holy Law the basis of legislation in Egypt. The rift reached an explosive stage when the Copts placed advertisements in North American newspapers protesting against Muslim fundamentalism and the Sadat regime. Murderous clashes between Copts and Muslims followed the charges and counter-charges made by the Copt and fundamentalist leaders. The government-inspired campaign against Shenouda added fuel to the crisis. Sadat's decision to exile Shenouda to the Libyan desert merely added to the Copt resentment.

So great was Sadat's contempt for his internal and external denigrators, especially in regard to his peace treaty with Israel, that he appeared on occasions to provoke their outcries. He meekly accepted the July 1981 Knesset's 'Jerusalem Law' stipulating that the city was for ever Israel's capital and could not be a subject for bargaining with the Arabs. There was uproar throughout the Islamic world but Sadat, to the consternation of many Egyptians, reacted calmly. Coming from someone who spoke in such passionate terms about his love of Islam, his reaction was puzzling.

Sadat caused concern among Israel's Labour Party when he agreed to meet Menachem Begin at Sharm al Sheikh. The timing was significant. The meeting was taking place just before Israel's June 1981 general election. It was inconceivable that Begin, a consummate politician and veteran parliamentarian, did not realise the

270

benefit he would gain from the publicity. Sadat, too, would have known that he was making a gesture calculated to help his peace partner and powerful adversary. Labour leaders, who were to lose the election, were left wondering what precisely were the Egyptian President's motives.

The timing of the Sadat–Begin meeting became an even greater subject for speculation and suspicion when only a few days later Israeli warplanes bombed and destroyed Iraq's nuclear reactor near Baghdad. Many Egyptians and most Arabs alleged that Sadat was told by Begin of the impending attack and gave his approval, or gave an assurance that there would be a mild Egyptian reaction. How otherwise would Begin have dared to attack a highly important and prestigious nuclear plant so near the heart of an Arab capital?

Even some Israelis wondered what precisely Begin told and did not tell Sadat. Many Israelis, including a number of Labour Party leaders, came to believe that the daring and devastating attack on the Iraqi reactor was a major factor in Begin's electoral victory. Though most probably true, Sadat's denial that he knew anything about the attack was not believed by his critics.

Sadat's inaction when Israel bombed the PLO headquarters in Beirut, following fierce exchanges in south Lebanon, was seen by the fundamentalists as a further provocation. So was Sadat's meeting with Begin after the victorious election and the decision to renew the autonomy negotiations. To the critics, all this seemed to confirm Sadat's guilt. However, Sadat disdainfully ignored the vituperation. He chose instead to concentrate on an issue which was calculated to inflame further the Muslim fundamentalists by widely publicising his plan to erect a religious complex in Sinai, consisting of a mosque, synagogue and church. He had first mentioned the project in an interview with the foreign editor of the London *Jewish Chronicle*. He attached great importance to the plan, which he saw as encompassing all his ideals. But to the fundamentalists the plan was one more proof of the President's perfidy and abandonment of Islam. The plot to assassinate the President and 'safeguard Islam' became, in their eyes, an urgent necessity.

To the blind Sheikh Omar Abdul Rahman, scholar of Cairo's Al-Azhar University and lecturer in theology at Assyut University, Anwar Sadat and his Vice-President Hosni Mubarak represented the messengers of Western evil. Later Rahman was to leave for New York from where he fuelled the campaign against foreign tourists to Egypt, many of whom were consequently shot and injured. 'They spread corruption and unlawful sexual activities, transmitting disease and Aids across our country and trying to destroy Islamic values', he explained.

In Cairo his fiery sermons to the faithful made him the spiritual mentor of the Gama'a al Islamiyya, the most militant of all the fundamentalist splinter groups. He had already shown his passionate extremism in 1970 when he urged his followers not to pray for the dying President Nasser. His sermons won him an eight-month jail sentence. This merely encouraged him to pursue his campaign 'to confront Islam's enemies and overcome them'.

Sheikh Rahman and his fanatical followers saw Sadat as an even more objectionable figure than Nasser. The late President had made no secret of his hatred of the fundamentalists and suppressed them. President Sadat was trying to deceive them, arresting and releasing them, pretending to bring in Muslim Holy Law but actually seeking to overthrow it and all the time scheming with Islam's greatest enemy, Israel. A swift elimination of President Sadat, execution of his closest associates, and a proclamation that Egypt was becoming a true Islamic country would bring the Egyptian masses onto the streets in joy and dedication. All the evil of the Western world would be swept away in blood and jubilation.

In their eyes, President Sadat was creating the conditions for his own downfall. He arrested 3,000 students, leading politicians, top journalists, prominent religious leaders, as well as fundamentalists. They accused him of wanting to destroy all opposition to his rule, to become a new tyrant, beholden to no one except the Americans. Stories were spread that Sadat had become a recluse and mentally unstable, shouting and screaming at the slightest provocation.

In his last book *My Legacy*, or *My Last Will*, published post-humously, Sadat did not give the impression of a man who was at war with himself and had given up all hope. There was, on the contrary, a serenity in his message which suggested that he felt that he had fulfilled his mission for the Egyptian people. His wife, Jihan, was convinced that he was sincere in his wish to retire but was held back by the desire to see all Sinai returned by 1982.

The picture given of a man who had lost control of the State and the confidence of his immediate associates in government and outside, is not borne out by events. The Egyptian people did not rise up to overthrow the regime, nor was it necessary to call out the armed forces to suppress any great rebellions. The whole apparatus of state, from Hosni Mubarak downward, did not abandon Anwar Sadat's policies, nor break the peace accord with Israel. Even when Israel launched a war against a neighbouring Arab country, Sadat's associates did not have to vilify his name to save their skins.

A famous Egyptian psychiatrist from Al-Azhar Unviersity, Dr Muhammed Sha'alan, suggested that Anwar Sadat sought martyrdom because he disliked the harsh personality he had become, so different from the original idealistic one which he developed in prison. 'He constantly ignored security measures despite warnings of plots by Muslim fundamentalists to assassinate him. He refused to wear his bullet-proof vest on 6 October and even dismissed the guards surrounding him.' So wrote Dr Sha'alan to prove his point. Yet such an estimate does not take fully into account Sadat's true character, his pride in his achievements and his conviction that no one had such an understanding of the Egyptian people nor had such a uniquely warm relationship with the ordinary man and woman. Ossama Al Baz recalls the many warnings given to Sadat about the danger of riding in an open car or standing exposed on a lorry. Sadat invariably replied: 'I am not going to allow these few fanatics to stop my people from seeing me!' By not wearing a bullet-proof vest and dismissing his guards, what Sadat was intimating was not that he wished to be shot but that on such a great anniversary, the October War, which brought honour back to the Egyptian people and army, no one would dare to harm the Hero of the Crossing who brought about this transformation.

Jihan Sadat was to write later that 6 October 1981 was one of the few days out of thousands that she did not fear for her husband's life because of the huge significance of the day to the Egyptian people. So certain was she that on this day he faced no danger that she almost did not attend the anniversary military review in Nasr City on the outskirts of Cairo. In her eyes Anwar looked particularly handsome that morning, wearing the new uniform which he had designed specially for the occasion. 'In other years, my daughters

273

and I would tease him about his vanity as we tugged and tugged at his boots, helping him to pull them up over his long breeches. "Don't you think the uniform should be a little looser?" I chided him as he struggled into it. "Oh, Jihan, don't say that", he would say with pretended impatience, "You know nothing about the military".'

Anwar Sadat cared very much about his appearance that day. To stress his pride in being an Egyptian officer, he used to carry a Field-Marshal's baton under his arm, an affectation which Jihan did not like. 'People will think you are showing off and you are not a show-off', she would tell him. Sadat answered that the stick represented 'the true style of military life'. Curiously, on this 6 October he did not take the stick. Had he forgotten it, or did he deliberately leave it behind to please Jihan? She was never to know. However, he did not forget to tell Jihan to bring his five-year-old grandson Sherif 'in his uniform' to the parade. 'He is grown-up now. I want him to watch the parade.' Jihan assured Anwar that she would indeed take Sherif with her. But as the little boy suffered from asthma, Jihan decided not to dress him in the heavy uniform which Sadat had had copied from his own. The boy wore light clothes more suitable for a warm day.

When Anwar Sadat entered the reviewing stands, his wife saw a very happy man, certainly not one who had any premonition of imminent death. 'Never will I forget the smile on his face when he entered the reviewing stands amidst a swell of applause and looked to see his four grandchildren standing there with me. His face, usually quiet and thoughtful, was suddenly filled with the warmth of the sun as he waved at us. Always now in my mind, I see the beauty of that smile, remember the happiness his face was radiating.'

There were some inexplicable delays in the parade but then the Egyptian Air Force planes came in formation to be greeted by applause. Then Jihan noticed with surprise and concern an army truck pulling out of the line of artillery vehicles and stopping in front of the reviewing stands. She saw army men with machine guns running towards the stands. The sound of an exploding grenade was almost drowned by the roar of the aircraft above. The glass through which Jihan and her grandchildren were watching the parade was smashed by bullets. As she looked down she saw Anwar Sadat standing up and pointing at the guards, as if to instruct them to put a stop to the outrage. This was the last time that she saw her husband alive. As he stood astonished and bewildered, bullets ripped into him and he fell to the ground. 'This is inconceivable,' he said to Hosni Mubarak as he died.

When later she visited the hospital she noted that 'his body had not been torn apart by the bullets. On the contrary, when the sheet was removed I could see only three tiny holes, one in his leg and two in the chest, just above the heart. They looked more like little bruises than mortal wounds, far too insignificant to have felled such a man. I reached out to touch him because he looked so alive. But where my hand felt his body, it was freezing. There was no life.'

Leaders of the Gama'a al-Islamiyya had prepared their plan well. Lieutenant al-Islambouli, a young artillery officer and a fervent adherent of the group, and his fellow conspirators planned meticulously. Although troops on parade were not permitted to carry live ammunition, they obtained some. Since the beginning of the year they had planned to remove Sadat as part of an ambitious plot for an Islamic take-over. The 6 October parade presented an ideal opportunity to remove in one stroke not only Sadat but every one of his leading associates. After the assassination of Sadat and his entourage, an announcement was to be made by the radio station at Assyut that the Islamic era had dawned in Egypt after the removal of the 'tyrant'.

However, most of Sadat's associates, notably the Vice-President, Hosni Mubarak, were not killed. Mubarak, of whom Sadat had always spoken highly, had escaped any injury. The conspirators were pursued and caught. They were put on trial, convicted and hanged. Sheikh Rahman was charged with complicity in the murder and plotting to overthrow the government but he escaped their fate and was acquitted.

Conclusion: reflections on a tragedy

'Negligence killed my husband. Carelessness killed my husband.'
This was Jihan Sadat's verdict on the tragedy. She added that
Anwar Sadat's own affection for the armed forces, his belief that
they could not be infiltrated by the Muslim fanatics had helped to
kill him.

Jihan's bitterness is totally understandable and reflects her deep
love for Anwar Sadat. Most of her criticism is fully justified. True, as
she herself wrote, Sadat had asked his personal bodyguard not to
stand between him and the armed forces, believing not only that he
did not need protection from his own army but that such a show of
security would signal vulnerability. Even the President's special
security force stood on the far side of the reviewing stands, out of
sight. They did so because that was what Sadat wanted.

Yet, as Jihan Sadat rightly pointed out, there were a number of
inexplicable lapses. On previous occasions a regiment of guerrilla
fighters led the parade and then taken up a position between the
President and the rest of the troops. This year they had not done so.
Previously there had been government marksmen on the roofs of
the surrounding buildings to watch out for potential saboteurs.
This time there was none. Each army vehicle and each gun was
supposed to have been checked several times at various checkpoints
before reaching the reviewing stand to ensure that no one carried
live ammunition. But somehow an officer and two men had evaded
all inspections, if indeed there were any, and had arrived with live
ammunition in front of the President.

A question has also to be asked about the conduct of the security
chiefs. Even though President Sadat had asked for the removal

276

of the guards, a purely personal and political gesture, should they not have taken discreet precautions? They had detailed information about the various plots to kill the President. They even had a cassette in which a would-be assassin described how he planned to carry out his deed. How could they leave the President totally exposed to the antics of any lunatic, as well as the criminal designs of fanatical killers? No satisfactory answer has yet been given.

The suggestion that Anwar Sadat deliberately sought martyrdom on the most honoured day of his life, as an acknowledgement of his failure as a man and as a President, can be dismissed as intrinsically preposterous. Anwar Sadat did not see himself as a failed President, or as a man who had lost his ideals and had changed his personality. He was, at times, overcome by a feeling of despair at the seeming impossibility of providing a better life for the Egyptian people, the apparently insuperable difficulty of introducing a modern infrastructure into the country's economy, and the apparent impossibility of reaching an agreement with the Israelis about the Palestinians. But he was immensely proud of his achievements. He had brought honour back to the Egyptian people and army through the October War. Above all, he had ended an era of war with Israel at Camp David while regaining Egyptian land, making it possible to reopen the Suez Canal to world shipping – a glorious event. Moreover, Anwar Sadat would never have planned his own death by fanatics, whom he despised, in front of his wife and grandchildren. It is a totally untenable concept. He did speak of death to his wife, feeling that he had accomplished great things for the Egyptian people and was declining in physical strength as a result of his herculean efforts. Anwar Sadat loved to dramatise his life, to see it in the colours of his childhood heroes. His was a theatrical rather than a real death. It was because Jihan realised this that she could discuss his death and burial with a smile on her lips and a twinkle in her eyes.

There have been suggestions – some from within the Egyptian government – that a foreign hand was involved in the assassination. Inevitably the name of the Libyan President Muammar Gadaffi has been mentioned. He hated Sadat and wished to see him removed from power. But no evidence whatsoever has been produced that Gadaffi was directly involved in the assassination.

Anwar Sadat was buried in a tomb shaped like a small pyramid right across the parade ground where he was murdered. This was not his decision. According to Jihan, in the last months of his life, when he felt his death approaching, he had expressed a desire to be buried in his village of Mit Abul-Kum in the Nile Delta. She had tried to deter him from mentioning the subject by remarking jokingly, 'Oh, Anwar, it will take the children and me an hour and a half to go and visit you there!' However, Sadat would not be diverted. 'If not Mit Abul-Kum, then at the foot of Mount Sinai by St Catherine Monastery where we will be building a mosque and a synagogue. If I am buried there, it will tell people that all religions are the same, that God is one for all of us.'

To be buried in Sinai was also symbolically important for Anwar Sadat, Jihan remarked, because he had dedicated himself to regaining the land taken by the Israelis in Nasser's time. Jihan had, teasingly, tried to persuade her husband not to choose his own tomb. If Mit Abul-Kum was inconvenient to visit, Mount Sinai would be a hardship. 'It will take a plane and a car to get there, Anwar', she told him. 'I could visit you only once or twice a year. Better to be buried in Mit Abul-Kum!'

When President Mubarak asked Jihan where her husband should be buried, she decided, however, to ignore Sadat's wishes. This was a great, not an ordinary, man, she reflected. Why bury him in a place where it would be difficult for people to visit him? Why not bury him where he died, a military place of which he was very proud? Sadat had enjoyed every year his visits to the Tomb of the Unknown Soldier, listening to the music that was played on 6 October, and reviewing the troops who had so bravely served Egypt. Burying him there would remind everyone of all he had done for the country. Each year at the Sixth of October parade, every soldier and every officer would pass by his tomb and know that Sadat was there and salute him.

Few people were on the streets of Cairo as Sadat's funeral procession passed. A state of emergency ensured that there would be no groups larger than five people. The Egyptian people watched on television the funeral of their murdered President. A documentary of notable events of Sadat's life was shown – going to the front in the October War, praying at the Al Aqsa Mosque in Jerusalem in 1977,

278

addressing the Knesset. 'My husband', Jihan wrote perceptively, 'was not a victim of war. He was a victim of peace.'

In accordance with Egyptian tradition, only men marched in the funeral procession – and they were leaders of several countries: Jimmy Carter, Richard Nixon and Gerald Ford, all former US Presidents; Prince Charles of Britain; King Baudouin of Belgium; Chancellor Helmut Schmidt of West Germany; President Mitterrand of France; leaders from the Soviet Union and Africa, and most significantly, Prime Minister Menachem Begin of Israel.

No Arab leaders, apart from President Numeiri of Sudan and President Siad-el-Berry of Somalia, came to the funeral. No wonder Jihan Sadat was shocked and saddened.

When Sheikh Omar Abdul-Rahman, spiritual mentor of Sadat's assassin, Khaled al-Islambouli, was asked if he had issued a fatwa for the murder he did not give a direct answer. Sadat's 'execution did not need any fatwa. Sadat's crimes and his infernal behaviour provided more reasons for his fate than any fatwa. Islam will prevail in Egypt. The future of Egypt will be in the hands of the Muslims who will take the power of the government from the aggressors who hold it now.'

President Hosni Mubarak, said the sheikh, should meet the same fate as President Sadat. 'The government [of Mubarak] is against Islam and is repressing religion. We will ensure that our religion prevails.' The sheikh was speaking in New York, having managed to obtain an American visa in Sudan after fleeing from Cairo where he was wanted in connection with the attempted murder of two policemen and of inciting violence outside an Egyptian mosque in 1989. American police questioned him in connection with recent terrorist activities, particularly the bombing of the World Trade Center in New York when several people died and a thousand were injured.

Although Anwar Sadat was severely condemned by critics at home and the media abroad for the mass arrests in the last months of his life, Jihan Sadat argued that these arrests saved the country from a possible fundamentalist takeover after the assassination. Sadat, she said, realised that many fundamentalist agitators had infiltrated into the heart of the government and provided a threat even in his lifetime. He feared that their conduct would, by alarming the Israelis, somehow prevent the return of the last part of Sinai to Egypt, thus spoiling his crowning achievement. Aware of their fanaticism, Sadat saw the fundamentalists as powerful rivals who had to be challenged and defeated.

Events after Sadat's death suggested that he may have over-estimated their strength. Only a tiny fraction of the armed forces had been won over by fanatics and only a small section of the vast population had sworn allegiance to their aims. Yet fundamentalists occupied many strategic positions within the government and local administration. The town of Assyut, with which most of the plotters were associated, was a hotbed of fanaticism and militancy. Had all the fundamentalist leaders been free to act after the assassination they might not have been able to take over power entirely and over-throw Hosni Mubarak but they might have inflicted huge wounds on the country. Bloodshed on an unparalleled scale might well have engulfed Assyut and Cairo.

Sadat had solid evidence for his anxieties. He could never forget that an attempt had been made on his life, as long ago as 1974, by a young doctor of philosophy, Saleh Sarrieh, head of a fundamentalist group, the Islamic Liberation Army. Sadat noticed that in the universities and colleges, many young girls began wearing Muslim dress, the zay shar'i, covering their bodies and faces. Demands were increasingly made for male and female students to sit apart. Student groups became increasingly belligerent. This attitude particularly infuriated Sadat who felt that the students were spoiled as well as immature. He had no objection to the students being religious but found it intolerable that they should mix fanaticism with education.

Anwar Sadat's death did not stem the tide of fanaticism, though the man who made peace with the infidel Israel was no longer a living target. For a time the worst excesses of extremism were force-fully suppressed by Hosni Mubarak's police and army but inevitably, it burst out again.

Militant Islam, violent and intolerant, fuelled by Far Eastern agitators, soon made widespread advances. It affected Muslims not only in lands stricken by poverty and overcrowding but in comparatively prosperous Western countries such as Britain. British Muslims were the first to draw Ayatollah Khomeini's attention to

Salman Rushdie's novel, *The Satanic Verses*, and to press for a ruling, leading eventually to a fatwa demanding the author's execution for insulting Islam.

Violence and cultural infiltration are the methods now being used by the fundamentalists to destroy the present regime and establish a fully-fledged Islamic republic similar to that existing in Iran. They are seeking the complete destruction of the present government system in Egypt and not merely changes. The state institutions, corrupt, degenerate, weakened by corruption and bribery, were, according to them, incapable of remedying the present malaise. Western methods and thinking were destroying the moral fibre of the population and attempting to eliminate Islam while education was being used as a tool for destroying Islam.

A murderous campaign has been launched against foreign tourists, who are described as the messengers of evil and disease. A number of foreign tourists have been killed and many more injured. As a result, tourists who came eagerly to visit the pyramids near Cairo and the Valley of the Kings, the burial place of Egypt's pharaohs at Luxor, have dwindled. The vast annual revenue of a billion dollars that the Egyptian government and people earned from tourism has consequently been drastically reduced almost to insignificance.

Cabinet ministers and government officials have also become targets of the Islamic terrorists in an effort to overthrow the Mubarak administration. They attempted to assassinate Interior Minister Hassa al-Alfi, seriously injuring him and killing four of his body-guards. Mr al-Alfi, who had only recently returned to his office after an operation in London, went on television after recovering consciousness. Speaking from his hospital bed, in bandages and plaster, the minister said: 'What was it for? What religion or value system is based on attempting to kill innocent people? Those people [the attackers] should get what they deserve. God willing we shall keep the peace of Egypt. This should be a sign to the whole world that the terrorists are butchers with no religion.' These words echoed Anwar Sadat's condemnation of the bloodshed of Ayatollah Khomeini's Iranian Islamic revolution.

When the attack on the minister was taking place, President

Mubarak was in Tripoli, trying to persuade Colonel Gadaffi to hand over to Britain and the United States two men accused of putting a bomb on the Pan-Am plane which crashed at Lockerbie killing 270 people. This action was said to be in retaliation for the American bombing of Tripoli following Libyan terrorist attacks.

Such Libyan actions would not have surprised Anwar Sadat. He held Colonel Gadaffi responsible for many irrational and dangerous acts. Sadat accepted the Israeli Mossad warning that Gadaffi was planning to assassinate him.

From the beginning of the terrorist attacks ordinary Egyptians have felt frustration at the inability of the security forces to crush the militant groups, despite ruthless police raids. Anger and scorn have been directed at Saddam Hussein's Iraq which has gloated over Egyptian police failures. Egypt joined in the American-sponsored Western–Arab alliance which defeated Iraq following Saddam Hussein's invasion of Kuwait. Saddam Hussein's revelling in President Mubarak's discomfiture at home is thus understandable but none the less offensive to Egyptian officials and press.

Hundreds of militants have been killed by the police and security organisations. A shoot-to-kill policy has been adopted by the police when confronting armed militants but still the attacks on foreigners and officials continue. The threats have widened and all foreigners and not merely tourists have been told to leave the country. 'We implore tourists and investors to leave the country because the next operation will be extremely ferocious and strong', a spokesman of Gamaa al-Islamiyya said after a police raid in al-Zawya al-Hamra, a slum district of Cairo, during which seven of its members were killed. Many militants have also been tried by military courts and a considerable number have been hanged after being convicted of murder.

Equally if not more dangerous has been the attempt by the militants to infiltrate the state and religious institutions, universities, and cultural centres. Egyptian intellectuals who had managed to display a measure of independence now fear that militant and political Islam is infiltrating the country's culture through a process of intimidation.

A committee associated with Cairo's Al Azhar theological centre, the leading religious institution, has condemned books by one of the leading opponents of political Islam. Judge Said Ashmawy, who already has 24-hour police protection because of previous threats to his life, is now accused of twisting Islamic history to give offence to the Koran, the Prophet Mohammed and the Caliphs. The militants were infuriated by his use of Islamic sources to undermine their basic beliefs that Islam contains a complete political and judicial system.

A revelation that a branch of the Egyptian judiciary has endorsed Al-Azhar's role as censor over music, songs, films and videos has increased fears about the trend in Egypt's cultural life. Sadat's influential critic, the journalist and author, Mohamed Heikal, has bravely – in the present circumstances – ridiculed some of the militants' claims, asking what precisely is Islamic foreign policy, but is unlikely to stem the tide. President Mubarak has set up a much-publicised higher council of culture composed of writers, critics and journalists, with the laudable aim of holding back the political Islamists but it faces an uphill struggle.

With much justification President Mubarak and his ministers are accusing the Islamic fundamentalists, now in power in Iran and the Sudan, of fomenting insurrection in Egypt. It is certain that funds and arms are being sent to the militants from these countries. There are serious suggestions that toughened former fighters against the Soviet occupation in Afghanistan are among the militants launching terrorist attacks in Egypt.

Concern is now being felt in the Western world at the position of President Hosni Mubarak and his pro-Western administration. A US intelligence report, quoted in the London *Sunday Times*, stated that Egypt was on the verge of civil war and economic chaos. The report is said to have warned that if Egypt were taken over by Iranian-style fundamentalists the consequences for the Middle East peace process would be catastrophic. President Mubarak's tough line against the extremists is allegedly criticised in the report which warns that these tactics would fail. An alternative policy of political and economic reforms is advocated.

The contents of the report, as quoted in the *Sunday Times*, were taken very seriously by Western and Israeli diplomats who moved quickly to dampen its effect. They voiced confidence in President Mubarak's ability to crush the extremists whose terrorism had led to over 1,000 people being killed in the first two months of 1994. Israel's Foreign Minister Shimon Peres remarked: 'Throughout history there have been violent episodes such as this and I believe the Egyptian Government is well able to deal with it.'

The British Foreign Office, which is well informed, also rejected the notion that the Mubarak government is close to being overthrown. The US report was described in Western capitals and in Jerusalem as 'highly exaggerated'. Certainly one cannot take seriously the report's suggestion that the militants can be won over by political and economic reforms. Some American agencies do not appear to learn from history. It was precisely this kind of advice, strongly backed by the naive President Jimmy Carter, that led to the downfall of the Shah of Iran and the consequent triumph of the Islamic fundamentalists.

Sadat knew the power of the fundamentalists and appreciated their single-mindedness. He had a fatalistic approach to them. When Jihan warned him about the dangers he was facing because of his refusal to take precautions against some lunatic gunman, Sadat replied: 'I will never be killed except by the fundamentalists because they are the ones who believe in what they are doing.' And when Jihan asked him, only a few days before the murder, why he drove about in an open car, he replied: 'Jihan, when it comes, it will come. Nothing will be added to me and nothing taken away.'

Sadat worried, though, about Jihan. He had heard that a dangerous fundamentalist was free again and told Jihan to reduce her public activities. With such an approach, Sadat would have understood well the problems facing his successor and would undoubtedly have taken similar measures to suppress the terrorism. Anwar Sadat was worried by the spread of Iranian-type Islamic ideas. He could not understand how violence and blood could be reconciled with Islam. His fears have been fully justified. Muslim fundamentalism now reigns supreme in Libya, the Sudan and Iran. This violent outlook has spawned terrorist movements, like the Hezbollah in Lebanon and Hamas in the West Bank and Gaza.

The great danger now is that fundamentalism will gain power throughout the Middle East. Should this occur, all Anwar Sadat's work would be undone. Wars between Israel and the Arabs would again run their bloody course. Yet, thanks largely to Anwar Sadat's legacy, there is hope that the tragic bloodstained relationship between the Israelis and the Arabs will come to an end. Such a development became practicable once the Soviet Union, with its backing for extreme Arab demands, collapsed and disappeared. After reviling Anwar Sadat for years, the Palestine Liberation Organisation leader Yasser Arafat, and Syrian President Hafez Assad are following in his footsteps – hesitatingly and suspiciously, but still acknowledging that there is no alternative to peace. Ironically, it is the Arabs who are using the famous Israeli motto: *Ein Breira*, no alternative. It is not inevitable that the Muslim fundamentalists should take over the Middle East. Anwar Sadat would have exploded in fury if such an idea had been presented to him. He would have insisted that each Arab country should make peace with Israel, be at peace with each other, and bring the benefits of modern science and invention to their peoples.

Anwar Sadat was not a saint. He had his faults. In his formative years he could be biased. He admired Hitler – not because the Nazi leader persecuted the Jews but because he brought success to Germany. He was prepared to work for the Germans during the Second World War and he would have welcomed them had they entered Cairo – as would many thousands if not millions of his fellow citizens. He could use bloodthirsty language against the Israelis and threaten them with constant wars. Yet once his army crossed the Suez Canal and breached the Israeli Bar Lev Line, regaining the honour the Egyptian Army lost in the Six-Day War, Anwar Sadat underwent an amazing personal, political and spiritual transformation. His style of addressing audiences became less bombastic, he gradually became more introspective, his faith in Islam deepened, his thoughts became imbued with mystical concepts of religious and human harmony and he perceived peace with Israel as an overwhelming necessity that he owed to the suffering Egyptian people.

As his wife, Jihan, remarked recently in London, no one in the Arab world, apart from the fanatical fundamentalists, now doubts that he was abundantly right, that his vision of peace and reconciliation was the only possible path for the present and the future. Golda Meir remarked that she did not know whether Sadat and Begin deserved the Nobel Peace Prize but she was certain that they deserved Oscars. It was a cruel, though witty, jibe. It revealed her disappointment that not she but Begin 'the extremist' obtained the long-sought peace with the largest Arab State. The truth is that Sadat, like Begin, deserved both prizes; they needed both states-manship and showmanship, qualities which both possessed in abundance, Sadat, perhaps more than anyone. Yet it was Golda Meir who stressed one quality which distinguished Sadat more than any other statesman and particularly and strikingly in the Arab world: daring.

He dared where others dithered. He dared to confound all his advisers and his closest friends to set out for Jerusalem. In his earlier years, he dared to defy the authorities, he dared to outsmart them in long years in prison. He dared to challenge the mighty Soviet Union. He dared to outwit the Israelis and launch an offensive across the Suez Canal. And while the whole Arab world stood up in consternation and disbelief, Anwar Sadat dared to make a lasting peace with the Jewish State of Israel.

Today Anwar Sadat is a hero in the Western world, among thoughtful Arabs and in Jerusalem. His stature is growing daily. His message of peace and reconciliation is perceived as particularly pertinent and relevant. Among the Jews his message of Shalom, the eternal prayer, strikes a particular chord, even though it comes from a man who years ago caused them much destruction and suffering. As the peace negotiations between Israel and the Arabs proceed, despite obstacles and tragedies, the name of Sadat is frequently mentioned, almost as a talisman. In October 1981 the Arab fundamentalist terrorists attempted to kill not only Sadat but his ideas and his vision for, above all, he was a visionary. Yet Anwar Sadat and all that he stood for is more alive today than ever he was in the last dramatic days in Cairo.

Epilogue

When Yitzhak Rabin, Israel's courageous and far-seeing Prime Minister, was shot dead at the end of a huge peace rally in Tel Aviv on the night of 4 November 1995, observers of the Middle East noted the striking similarity of his tragic death and the assassination of Egyptian President Anwar Sadat.

Both were the victims of ruthless and determined religious fanatics who wanted to destroy peace between Israelis and Arabs. Both came to the decision, after long and anguished deliberations, that concessions had to be made for the sake of peace – and both were gunned down at a moment when they were beginning to taste the fruits of their hard and painful endeavours. Both were warned that evil men were trying to kill them but did not take special precautions – Mr Rabin did not wear a bullet-proof vest at the great rally assembled to praise his peace policy; Anwar Sadat stood exposed at a parade held as much in tribute to the Egyptian people as to himself. In each tragic case horrendous lapses by the security services facilitated the murders.

A Jew killed a Jewish Prime Minister and an Egyptian shot an Egyptian President, but the assassins had the same kind of hatred in their hearts even though their aims, apart from the desire to kill peace, were totally different. It was this hatred that Anwar Sadat and Yitzhak Rabin fought to defeat, hoping to substitute instead an era of understanding and goodwill.

Several times Yitzhak Rabin spoke with admiration of the vision and the courage of Anwar Sadat in breaking taboos and paving the path for peace between Jew and Arab. Anwar Sadat was, for Yitzhak Rabin, the great visionary who opened new roads of understanding. Like Anwar Sadat, Yitzhak Rabin became a visionary, a creator and a victim.

The momentous changes brought about by these two men were demonstrated at the funeral of Yitzhak Rabin where among the chief mourners was Anwar Sadat's successor, President Hosni Mubarak, joining King Hussein of Jordan, President Bill Clinton, and other world leaders. This made it clear that the message of peace and reconciliation proclaimed by Anwar Sadat and Yitzhak Rabin will live on. The names of Sadat and Rabin are for ever intertwined as a new era opens in the Middle East and in Israeli–Arab relations. The bombers and gunmen, spurred on by religious fanaticism, will not be allowed to extinguish their message – but their threat will remain and will only be kept at bay by unremitting vigilance.

J.F.   *December 1995*

Index